WHAT DOES THE BIBLE SAY ABOUT THAT?

Carolyn Larsen,
Illustrated by Rick Incrocci

:: CROSSWAY®

WHEATON, ILLINOIS

What Does the Bible Say about That?
Copyright © 2009 Educational Publishing Concepts, Inc.

Published by Crossway
> 1300 Crescent Street
> Wheaton, Illinois 60187

Typesetting: Educational Publishing Concepts

Cover design: Jessica Dennis

Cover illustration: Dana Thompson

Illustrations: Rick Incrocci

First printing 2009

Printed in the United States of America

Scripture quotations are from the ESV® Bible (*The Holy Bible: English Standard Version®*), copyright © 2001 by Crossway. Used by permission. All rights reserved.

Trade paperback ISBN: 978-1-4335-0213-2

PDF ISBN: 978-1-4335-0571-3

Mobipocket ISBN: 978-1-4335-0572-0

Library of Congress Cataloging-in-Publication Data

Larsen, Carolyn, 1950-

  What does the Bible say about that? / Carolyn Larsen ; illustrated by Rick Incrocci.
    p. cm.
  ISBN 978-1-4335-0213-2 (tpb)
  1. Bible—Miscellanea—Juvenile literature. I. Incrocci, Rick. II. Title.

BS612.L34 2008
220—dc22   2008026908

Crossway is a publishing ministry of Good News Publishers.

VP   22   21   20   19   18   17
        11   10   9   8   7   6   5

Contents

W

Introduction

News flash! Learning to live for God doesn't happen overnight. Nope, it's a journey. Think about it—when you start out on a long road trip, more than likely your mom or dad has the trip mapped out. Well, your Christian life journey is mapped out, too—in the Bible. This amazing book is not just a bunch of "do this and don't do that" lists. It's the story of God's love for you and how his Spirit living in you will guide, protect, love, forgive, and love you again.

Newsflash Two: There will be times in your Christian life when you fall flat on your face. Yep, everyone does. That's because we're all fighting our sinful hearts that want to do things our own way, not to mention fighting Satan who wants to keep us from obeying God. But every time we disobey God or just totally mess up, he lovingly helps us stand up and try again. That's his grace in action—grace to forgive us over and over and help us learn from our failures and mistakes. Grace that teaches us. Grace that means he loves us.

What Does the Bible Say about That? will help you understand how God's love and grace is part of your everyday life. Yep, it is right there in the center of the thoughts, actions, and experiences you have every single day. God cares about every part of your life—the highs and the lows. And he wants you to know that he is not just "called into your life" when you are thinking about him or in church or praying. He's *always* with you. So, read what the Bible says about your thoughts, anger, family, friends, even homework (yes, God cares about homework). You'll see that you're not on this journey alone. God is right there with you, guiding, helping, and teaching—because *he loves you*!

ABANDONMENT

What Does the Bible Say about Abandonment?

Someone left. . . . A parent walked away from the family or your best friend turned his back on you. It hurts when that happens—a lot. Does God care that you feel betrayed and left alone? Of course he cares. He promises *never* to leave you alone.

What the Bible Says

No man shall be able to stand before you all the days of your life. Just as I was with Moses, so I will be with you. I will not leave you or forsake you.

JOSHUA 1:5

For the LORD will not forsake his people;
he will not abandon his heritage.

PSALM 94:14

And behold, I am with you always, to the end of the age.

MATTHEW 28:20

Time to Face the Facts

Humans—people—mess up. Some people get caught up in self-centered ideas and they hurt other people, even people they love. Sometimes they abandon people they love. If that has happened to you, remember that you will never be abandoned by God. He is with you always, and he cares about everything that happens to you.

Today I Will . . .

Thank God for being with me. Forgive anyone who has left. Read God's Word and start getting to know him better.

"Okay, you keep them."

What Does the Bible Say about Abilities?

Many people have a secret dream to do something amazing. They dream of being the best athlete ever; a researcher who discovers the cure to some terrible disease; author of a great novel; or maybe a world-class musician. Dreams keep us going sometimes. Does each person have any unique abilities, though? Yep, God gave each person what she needs to be the person he planned.

What the Bible Says

Each has his own gift from God, one of one kind and one of another.

1 CORINTHIANS 7:7

Having gifts that differ according to the grace given to us, let us use them: if prophecy, in proportion to our faith; if service, in our serving; the one who teaches, in his teaching; the one who exhorts, in his exhortation; the one who contributes, in generosity; the one who leads, with zeal; the one who does acts of mercy, with cheerfulness.

ROMANS 12:6–8

Well done, good and faithful servant. You have been faithful over a little; I will set you over much.

MATTHEW 25:21

Time to Face the Facts

You have what you need to serve God. He gave you the tools, but you must develop those abilities. Never fear, though—the seeds are there. Think about what you love to do . . . what brings you joy and what others say you are good at. That's a good tip as to what God has given you.

"I really want to be a great soccer player, but I'm just a straight 'A' student."

Today I Will . . .

Stop wishing I could do other things and start working at what I'm good at. Ask God to show me how I can use my abilities to serve him.

What Does the Bible Say about Abuse?

Abuse is no fun. It comes in different forms. It might be from someone constantly telling you that you're worthless. This constant assault of negative words tears down your self-image and confidence. Abuse can also be physical—being slapped around. Whatever it is, abuse is painful. God doesn't want you to suffer from abuse. He loves his children, and he tells his children to love one another. God's plan is love.

What the Bible Says

So whatever you wish that others would do to you, do also
to them, for this is the Law and the Prophets.

MATTHEW 7:12

Love does no wrong to a neighbor; therefore love is the fulfilling of the law.

ROMANS 13:10

Love is patient and kind; love does not envy or boast; it is not arrogant.

1 CORINTHIANS 13:4

Time to Face the Facts

Abuse of any kind is wrong. If you are the victim of abuse, it would be a good idea to tell someone you trust. Your teacher or pastor would be a good place to start. Also, learn from these verses that being the abuser is wrong. God's desire is for you to love people around you, not hurt them.

"You're such a numbskull!"

Today I Will . . .

Talk with someone about my situation if I am the victim of abuse. Think about how I treat others. If my behavior is abusive, I will change it . . . with God's help.

What Does the Bible Say about Addictions?

Imagine having a big, heavy chain wrapped around your ankle. The other end of the chain is attached to a tree. So, you're tied up, can't get away. That's what addiction is like. It controls your thoughts and actions. There are different kinds of addictions: drugs, alcohol, food, Internet, approval are a few. How does God feel about addictions? God wants to control your life. He doesn't want you to be controlled by whatever you are addicted to.

What the Bible Says

For the Lord your God is a consuming fire, a jealous God.

DEUTERONOMY 4:24

No one can serve two masters, for either he will hate the one and love the other, or he will be devoted to the one and despise the other.

MATTHEW 6:24

Do you not know that if you present yourselves to anyone as obedient slaves, you are slaves of the one whom you obey, either of sin, which leads to death, or of obedience, which leads to righteousness?

ROMANS 6:16

Time to Face the Facts

Honesty time: What's controlling your thoughts and actions? Is it God or something else? If there's one thing you plan your life around—one thing you *must* do every day—then you have an addiction. Bottom line is God wants to be *number one* in your life. He is jealous of anything else.

Today I Will . . .

Be honest. I will evaluate how I spend my time and admit if there is some-

"I'm not addicted—I've only been playing for six hours."

thing that has pushed God out of first place in my life. I can't change that by myself, but I will ask God to help me. His strength can beat anything!

AMBITION

What Does the Bible Say about Ambition?

You've got drive—you've set goals and you'll do just about anything to reach them. Is that wrong? Nope. Doesn't God want you to be the best you can be? Sure he does. However, his wish is two-pronged: Be the best you that you can be, but don't forget to love him and others along the way.

What the Bible Says

Do nothing from rivalry or conceit, but in humility count others more significant than yourselves.

PHILIPPIANS 2:3

But we urge you, brothers, to . . . aspire to live quietly, and to mind your own affairs, and to work with your hands, as we instructed you, so that you may walk properly before outsiders and be dependent on no one.

1 THESSALONIANS 4:10–12

Let us not become conceited, provoking one another, envying one another.

GALATIANS 5:26

Time to Face the Facts

Watch it: There's a fine line between having a lot of ambition and being filled with pride. It's okay to want to be the best at something, but don't push other people down in the process of lifting yourself up. Remember, God does want your excellent service but not at the expense of loving others. The greatest commandment is to love God, the second greatest is to love others. Don't lose sight of that.

Today I Will . . .

Think about how I am treating other people. I know what my ambitions are, and I don't want to hurt anyone as I try to reach them.

What Does the Bible Say about Angels?

Are angels really those white beings with big fluffy wings that you see in pictures? Do they just kind of float around and sing all the time? Are they more important to God than people are? Here's the scoop: angels are God's messengers and workmen. They follow God's commands in taking care of you. How cool is that?

What the Bible Says

For he will command his angels concerning you
to guard you in all your ways.

PSALM 91:11

And the angel said to her, "Do not be afraid, Mary, for you have found
favor with God. And behold, you will conceive in your womb
and bear a son, and you shall call his name Jesus.

LUKE 1:30–31

And behold, an angel of the Lord stood next to him, and a light shone
in the cell. He struck Peter on the side and woke him, saying,
"Get up quickly." And the chains fell off his hands.

ACTS 12:7

Time to Face the Facts

Wow! God loves you! He really loves you! He commands his angels to watch out for you; they are probably doing that even when you don't realize it. You see in Scripture how his angels bring messages to people and how they protect people. It only makes sense that God still uses angels to do those same jobs. Aren't you so glad God loves you that much?

Today I Will . . .

Thank God for the zillions of times he has sent his angels to protect me and watch out for me.

"I hope my angel doesn't see everything I do."

What Does the Bible Say about Anger?

It's no big deal if you blow your top once in a while, right? Everyone gets angry sometimes. God doesn't have rules about that, too, does he? Yep. God knows you're going to get upset sometimes, but he wants you to keep your cool and not say or do things you will be sorry about later.

What the Bible Says

Refrain from anger, and forsake wrath!
Fret not yourself; it tends only to evil.

PSALM 37:8

Whoever is slow to anger has great understanding,
but he who has a hasty temper exalts folly.

PROVERBS 14:29

Be angry and do not sin; do not let the sun go down on your anger.

EPHESIANS 4:26

Time to Face the Facts

Nothing good ever comes from losing your temper. You say things you shouldn't say and hurt people when there is no need to. When you're upset about things, don't lose your cool. Talk it over and state your feelings without saying mean things.

Today I Will . . .

Keep my anger in control. If I get upset with someone, I won't shoot my mouth off; instead I'll calmly explain my feelings. This way I won't lose a friend and will get a chance to hang out with this friend again.

"I'm really not happy about having to do my homework over again."

What Does the Bible Say about Animals?

From dogs and cats to elephants and lions, our world is filled with amazing animals. Some people take animals for granted, or at least they don't really think about them. Why did God make animals, anyway? Some kinds of animals are a food source, some are just very cute, and some are important to the environment. God made animals for different reasons, and he was happy with all he created.

What the Bible Says

God said, "Let the earth bring forth living creatures according to their kinds—livestock and creeping things and beasts of the earth according to their kinds." And it was so. And God made the beasts of the earth according to their kinds and the livestock according to their kinds, and everything that creeps on the ground according to its kind. And God saw that it was good.

GENESIS 1:24–25

By faith we understand that the universe was created by the word of God, so that what is seen was not made out of things that are visible.

HEBREWS 11:3

Time to Face the Facts

Think about all the different kinds of animals God made and what enjoyment they bring to people. From your pet cat, dog, or tarantula to the amazing big cats or tiny hummingbird, God's creativity is amazing. He wants you to respect and enjoy his creation. So . . . go ahead.

Today I Will . . .

Give my pet a hug and a treat. Thank God for every aspect of his creation. Appreciate the variety of that creation.

"I wonder why God made elephants big, frogs with long legs, bunnies cute, and dogs cuddly?"

What Does the Bible Say about Apostles?

What's an apostle? It's not a word you hear in normal life. You don't call your friends your apostles, do you? If you do, they probably aren't your friends anymore. The official definition of *apostle* is someone who saw Jesus in person . . . well, that's kind of official. So how does God feel about the apostles? He trusted them to learn firsthand from Jesus and then continue God's work on earth after Jesus went back to heaven.

What the Bible Says

Seeing the crowds, he went up on the mountain, and when he sat down, his disciples came to him. And he opened his mouth and taught them. . . .

MATTHEW 5:1–2

Then he said to his disciples, "The harvest is plentiful, but the laborers are few; therefore pray earnestly to the Lord of the harvest to send out laborers into his harvest."

MATTHEW 9:37–38

Go therefore and make disciples of all nations, baptizing them in the name of the Father and of the Son and of the Holy Spirit, teaching them to observe all that I have commanded you. And behold, I am with you always, to the end of the age.

MATTHEW 28:19–20

Time to Face the Facts

Jesus taught the apostles how to serve him and how to teach others about him. Since that teaching is recorded in the Bible you know that he wants you to learn from it as you learn to serve him and teach others, too. The apostles were men who walked with Jesus on the earth. You have the opportunity to learn the same things they learned by reading about them. Then, you can teach others about God and his love for them.

Today I Will . . .

Read some of the things Jesus taught the apostles. For example, I'll read the Sermon on the Mount in Matthew 5–7 and learn one lesson today from what Jesus taught the apostles.

What Does the Bible Say about Arguing?

When you're right, you're right. If people don't understand that you are right, then your only choice is to argue with them, right? After all, they have to be convinced. Does God have a problem with that? Well, can you love someone and still argue with them all the time? Remember that God thinks loving one another is pretty important.

What the Bible Says

> A fool's lips walk into a fight,
> and his mouth invites a beating.
>
> **PROVERB 18:6**

> But I say to you who hear, Love your enemies,
> do good to those who hate you.
>
> **LUKE 6:27**

> By this all people will know that you are my
> disciples, if you have love for one another.
>
> **JOHN 13:35**

Time to Face the Facts

Think about it . . . have you ever really changed another person's mind by arguing? Probably not. You may have scared someone into agreeing with you on the surface, but you probably didn't really change their mind. There's no love in arguing. It gets you nowhere.

Today I Will . . .

Not argue. If I have a difference of opinion with someone, I'll calmly explain how I feel and hope that we can have a peaceful and intelligent discussion.

"I thought we were
having a peaceful,
intelligent conversation."

What Does the Bible Say about Attitude?

"My attitude doesn't affect anyone but me." Yeah, right. Have you noticed how you feel when someone in your family or a good friend is in a stinky mood? One bad attitude can spoil the attitudes of everyone else. God has strong feelings about attitudes and how you treat those around you. Read on. . . .

What the Bible Says

Put on then, as God's chosen ones, holy and beloved, compassionate hearts, kindness, humility, meekness, and patience, bearing with one another and, if one has a complaint against another, forgiving each other; as the Lord has forgiven you, so you also must forgive.

COLOSSIANS 3:12–13

A new commandment I give to you, that you love one another: just as I have loved you, you also are to love one another.

JOHN 13:34

Love is patient and kind; love does not envy or boast; it is not arrogant or rude. It does not insist on its own way; it is not irritable or resentful.

1 CORINTHIANS 13:4–5

Time to Face the Facts

Apparently (actually, *for sure*), God cares about how you get along with other people. Your attitude is a big part of that because kindness, gentleness, and patience show that you love God and other people, which, by the way, he commanded you to do!

Today I Will . . .

Adjust my attitude to not think only about myself. I will think about others—how they're doing and what they're feeling.

"At least the dog isn't in a bad mood—I don't think."

AUTHORITY

What Does the Bible Say about Authority?

"Someone is always telling me what to do! It feels like I have a million bosses!" Have you ever felt that way? Maybe you get so frustrated with everyone else's authority over you that once in a while you just ignore it. Or maybe when you get together with your friends you make fun of those authority figures. So what, right? The *so what* is that God has pretty strong feelings about your respecting those in authority over you.

What the Bible Says

Remember your leaders, those who spoke to you the word of God.
Consider the outcome of their way of life and imitate their faith.

HEBREWS 13:7

Obey your leaders and submit to them, for they are keeping watch over your souls,
as those who will have to give an account. Let them do this with joy and
not with groaning, for that would be of no advantage to you.

HEBREWS 13:17

First of all, then, I urge that supplications, prayers, intercessions,
and thanksgivings be made for all people, for kings and
all who are in high positions, that we may lead a peaceful
and quiet life, godly and dignified in every way.

1 TIMOTHY 2:1–2

Time to Face the Facts

Yep, God has instructions for how you handle authority: respect it and learn from it. Even Jesus respected authority; read what he prayed in Matthew 26:39 when he was facing the cross. The people in authority over you know more than you do (even if you don't believe that sometimes) and can help you learn how to be a strong adult and caring Christian.

Today I Will . . .

Stop complaining about authority and listen to see what I can learn from those over me.

What Does the Bible Say about Beauty?

Beautiful people sure get a lot of attention in our world, don't they? Maybe you've heard the saying, "beauty is only skin deep." What does that mean? Is it saying that just having a pretty face or gorgeous hair isn't real beauty? Guess what? That's exactly what God says. He says that being beautiful from the inside out is what real beauty is all about.

What the Bible Says

> But the LORD said to Samuel, "Do not look on his appearance or on the height of his stature, because I have rejected him. For the LORD sees not as man sees: man looks on the outward appearance, but the LORD looks on the heart."
>
> **1 SAMUEL 16:7**

> Charm is deceitful, and beauty is vain,
> but a woman who fears the LORD is to be praised.
>
> **PROVERBS 31:30**

> Do not let your adorning be external—the braiding of hair and the putting on of gold jewelry, or the clothing you wear—but let your adorning be the hidden person of the heart with the imperishable beauty of a gentle and quiet spirit, which in God's sight is very precious.
>
> **1 PETER 3:3–4**

"I wonder if she looks good on the inside."

Time to Face the Facts

No matter how much time is spent on trying to "be beautiful" if you're not beautiful on the inside—loving God and others and trying to live in obedience to God—well, the outside stuff is a waste of time.

Today I Will . . .

Stop concentrating so much on how I look, instead concentrating on how I'm living.

What Does the Bible Say about Being Noticed?

So I like people to notice me. I like to be the center of attention. Why not? I'm cute and funny and fun to be around. What's the big deal? God made you just the way you are. He's impressed with you . . . but he doesn't want you to be impressed with yourself. Thinking about other people more than yourself is his preference.

What the Bible Says

But this is the one to whom I will look:
he who is humble and contrite in spirit
and trembles at my word.

ISAIAH 66:2

Whoever exalts himself will be humbled,
and whoever humbles himself will be exalted.

MATTHEW 23:12

For by the grace given to me I say to everyone among you not to think of himself
more highly than he ought to think, but to think with sober judgment,
each according to the measure of faith that God has assigned.

ROMANS 12:3

Time to Face the Facts

It's not all about you . . . don't think more of yourself or about yourself than you do about others. Give others a chance to shine while you take a backseat. Yeah, that's showing God's love to them. That's what it's all about.

Today I Will . . .

Be quiet more often. Let others tell jokes or stories. Give someone else a chance to shine.

"If it's not all about me what else could it be about?"

BELONGING

What Does the Bible Say about Belonging?

Everyone wants to belong somewhere. In your case, maybe you want to belong to a certain group at school. Maybe they are the "A" crowd. Or maybe you want to belong to a group that has the same interests you do—sports, music, theater . . . whatever. Is it wrong to want to belong? Of course not, as long as you remember that first and foremost you belong to God, and none of your efforts to belong to another group should compromise that.

What the Bible Says

The eternal God is your dwelling place,
and underneath are the everlasting arms.

DEUTERONOMY 33:27

Listen to my voice, and do all that I command you.
So shall you be my people, and I will be your God.

JEREMIAH 11:4

For as in one body we have many members, and the members
do not all have the same function, so we, though many,
are one body in Christ, and individually
members one of another.

ROMANS 12:4–5

Time to Face the Facts

Right, there's nothing wrong with wanting to belong to some group unless you try to hide your relationship with God in order to be accepted. You can't put the fact that you're a Christian in your back pocket and just pull it out when it's safe. Any group that doesn't accept your faith just isn't worth belonging to.

Today I Will . . .

Take an honest look at the groups I already belong to and the ones I want to belong to. Do they accept my relationship with God? I will not hide that in order to belong . . . so I've got some choices to make. Here we go. . . .

What Does the Bible Say about the Bible?

Is this a trick question? Does the Bible say something about itself? It's just words, right? You remember the parts you like and forget about the parts you don't like. Yeah . . . not so simple. God has definite ideas about his Word being honored and respected. Just read on. . . .

What the Bible Says

This Book of the Law shall not depart from your mouth, but you shall meditate on it day and night, so that you may be careful to do according to all that is written in it. For then you will make your way prosperous, and then you will have good success.

JOSHUA 1:8

Your word is a lamp to my feet
and a light to my path.

PSALM 119:105

All Scripture is breathed out by God and profitable for teaching,
for reproof, for correction, and for training in righteousness.

2 TIMOTHY 3:16

Time to Face the Facts

The fact is the Bible is God's instructions to you on how to live—how to obey him and how to treat others. Everything you need to know is in it. The only way you're going to get the info out is to read it, study it, and remember it.

Today I Will . . .

Find a version of the Bible that's readable and understandable to me. Then, start reading and learning!

"If everything I need to Know is in here I guess it is a pretty important book."

BITTERNESS

What Does the Bible Say about Bitterness?

"Come on," you say. "Don't preach to me about not being bitter. If you knew what so-and-so did to me, you'd want them to fall into a cactus patch, too!" Okay, so you understand that bitterness means you're so angry and resentful that you *will not* consider forgiveness. God's Word shows that bitterness is not acceptable—you can't love and be bitter at the same time!

What the Bible Says

You have heard that it was said, "You shall love your neighbor and hate your enemy." But I say to you, Love your enemies and pray for those who persecute you, so that you may be sons of your Father who is in heaven. For he makes his sun rise on the evil and on the good, and sends rain on the just and on the unjust.

MATTHEW 5:43-45

Let all bitterness and wrath and anger and clamor and slander be put away from you, along with all malice. Be kind to one another, tenderhearted, forgiving one another, as God in Christ forgave you.

EPHESIANS 4:31-32

See to it that no one fails to obtain the grace of God; that no "root of bitterness" springs up and causes trouble, and by it many become defiled.

HEBREWS 12:15

"I can see how this can solve a lot of problems."

Time to Face the Facts

You can try a million ways to justify your bitterness toward someone else, but it will never be the right way to live. God says bitterness is wrong. He says to love your enemies and pray for them. Bitterness only causes more problems in the long run.

Today I Will . . .

Sigh . . . ask God to help me get over being bitter. Ask his help in forgiving the person I've been so angry at. I can't do this without God's help.

What Does the Bible Say about Blasphemy?

Right, you're a kid—what do you know about blasphemy? Do you even know what it is? Here's a simple definition: blasphemy is insulting or showing contempt for God. Truthfully, it is "dissing" God by ignoring who he is or not giving him credit for what he does. Blasphemy does not please God. He wants your worship and respect. He wants to be the only God in your life.

What the Bible Says

You shall worship no other god, for the LORD,
whose name is Jealous, is a jealous God.

EXODUS 34:14

The reward for humility and fear of the LORD
is riches and honor and life.

PROVERBS 22:4

Truly, I say to you, all sins will be forgiven the children of man,
and whatever blasphemies they utter, but whoever blasphemes
against the Holy Spirit never has forgiveness,
but is guilty of an eternal sin.

MARK 3:28–29

Time to Face the Facts

Whoa . . . blasphemy is serious. God commands respect and honor. He demands to be the only One you worship. Do you give him that honor and respect? Do you give him the credit for all he does, for his power, his love? Maybe you'd better reevaluate your thoughts.

Today I Will . . .

Do some serious thinking on what my true, heart opinion of God is. If it doesn't seem to be respect and honor, I'll get busy changing that by reading my Bible and learning all I can about him.

What Does the Bible Say about Books?

Do you love to read? It's fun to pick up a book and get lost in the story as you let your imagination visualize the characters and setting. Books are also a great way to learn new things and explore new ideas that make you think and cement your beliefs in your mind. Is it weird to think that God has an opinion about books? He must because he encourages you to grow and think and enjoy the blessings he provides for you.

What the Bible Says

Wisdom gives strength to the wise man
more than ten rulers who are in a city.

ECCLESIASTES 7:19

Every good gift and every perfect gift is from above, coming down from the Father of lights with whom there is no variation or shadow due to change.

JAMES 1:17

Time to Face the Facts

Books and the wisdom they give and the entertainment they give are gifts from God. They are a means of learning and exploring as well as exercising your mind. Enjoy them, celebrate them, and turn off the TV and computer so you can enjoy them. *However*, be careful that the books you choose to read have topics and content that honor God and the way he wants you to live.

Today I Will . . .

Turn off the TV and computer and sit down with a good book. I'll exercise my brain and imagination as I read, and yes, I will be careful about my choices of topics.

"I'd always rather be lost in a book than lost on the Internet."

What Does the Bible Say about Boredom?

Nothing exciting going on? Every day is a ho-hum copy of the one before it? You can't find anything that grabs your attention and where you'd like to put your energy? Does Almighty God really care whether or not you're bored? Think about this: he went to a lot of creative work to give you things to look at and stuff to do.

What the Bible Says

In the beginning, God created the heavens and the earth.

GENESIS 1:1

For by him all things were created, in heaven and on earth, visible and invisible, whether thrones or dominions or rulers or authorities—all things were created through him and for him.

COLOSSIANS 1:16

Now there are varieties of gifts, but the same Spirit; and there are varieties of service, but the same LORD; and there are varieties of activities, but it is the same God who empowers them all in everyone.

1 CORINTHIANS 12:4–6

Time to Face the Facts

There is really no reason to be bored. God made an amazing world filled with creative creations for you to enjoy. He gave you abilities and talents to share with the world. He placed people around you whom you can enjoy or help as situations arise. Being bored is a waste of time!

Today I Will . . .

Look around and see things I may have missed before. Enjoy creation; help someone; work on developing a talent . . . just do something!

"How can you be bored? School's out and it's a great day for a game?"

What Does the Bible Say about Boys?

This one is for *girls only*. Maybe you've started noticing these interesting creations of God and caring what boys think of you. Even if you're not there yet, there may be some of your friends who talk about boys all the time. Does God have an opinion on the whole boy/girl thing? Yep, he does, and while he wants you to enjoy each other, he's big into keeping things pure.

What the Bible Says

> The body is not meant for sexual immorality,
> but for the Lord, and the LORD for the body.
>
> **1 CORINTHIANS 6:13**

> No temptation has overtaken you that is not common to man.
> God is faithful, and he will not let you be tempted beyond your
> ability, but with the temptation he will also provide the way of
> escape, that you may be able to endure it.
>
> **1 CORINTHIANS 10:13**

> For this is the will of God, your sanctification:
> that you abstain from sexual immorality;
> that each one of you know how to control
> his own body in holiness and honor.
>
> **1 THESSALONIANS 4:3–4**

Time to Face the Facts

Maybe sex is the farthest thing from your mind right now. Good. You're just trying to figure out how to talk to a boy and not sound like a babbling fool. Yeah, that's the process. You'll learn it and maybe even enjoy the process. But here's a thought—make some firm choices right now that you will remain pure in your relationships with boys. Decide that now and never waver from it.

Today I Will . . .

Thank God for boys. Make a commitment to God that I will remain pure in my relationships.

What Does the Bible Say about Brothers and Sisters?

Brothers and sisters get on your nerves and can be *so* annoying, right? Does God care if you fight with them or even pick on them once in a while? Isn't that just what brothers and sisters do? You need to know that God does care. Not only are families a gift from him, he wants you to show his love to everyone!

What the Bible Says

Whoever restrains his words has knowledge,
and he who has a cool spirit is a man of understanding.

PROVERBS 17:27

See that no one repays anyone evil for evil, but always
seek to do good to one another and to everyone.

1 THESSALONIANS 5:15

Beloved, let us love one another, for love is from God,
and whoever loves has been born of God and knows God.

1 JOHN 4:7

Time to Face the Facts

You don't get a pass on treating your brothers and sisters with love. God wants you to control your temper and show love to your family. Even though that may be harder than showing love to your friends, when you do it, you're showing that you know God.

Today I Will . . .

Control my temper when one of my siblings annoys me. Just once . . . it's a start!

"I love people—it's my family I can't stand."

What Does the Bible Say about Careers?

Have you started thinking about what you want to be when you grow up? If you don't know yet, don't worry, some grown-ups don't know yet either. Does God care about what career you choose? Actually, he does. He has given you intelligence, talents, and abilities, and he has a definite plan for your life.

What the Bible Says

For I know the plans I have for you,
declares the Lord, plans for welfare
and not for evil, to give you a future and a hope.

JEREMIAH 29:11

Each has his own gift from God,
one of one kind and one of another.

1 CORINTHIANS 7:7

He gave the apostles, the prophets,
the evangelists, the shepherds and teachers,
to equip the saints for the work of ministry,
for building up the body of Christ.

EPHESIANS 4:11–12

Time to Face the Facts

How cool is it that God has a plan for you? He has already given you the tools you need for the career ahead of you. All you have to do is develop those tools. You can be sure you already have an interest and maybe even a passion for whatever it is. Ask him to open your eyes to it and to help you learn more and more so you're ready to jump right in some day.

"God has wired me the way I am to serve Him."

Today I Will . . .

Think about where my passions lie. What do I get excited about? How can that passion grow into a career where I can serve God by honoring him and others?

What Does the Bible Say about Celebration?

Who doesn't like a party? Especially if it is for you, right? Birthday parties or celebrations of accomplishments honor someone, and usually food and gifts are involved. Cool. How does God feel about celebrations? He likes them when they celebrate the right things. He encourages his people to take time out from ordinary life to celebrate things.

What the Bible Says

For the LORD your God has blessed you in all the work of your hands. He knows your going through this great wilderness. These forty years the LORD your God has been with you. You have lacked nothing.

DEUTERONOMY 2:7

Go your way. Eat the fat and drink sweet wine and send portions to anyone who has nothing ready, for this day is holy to our Lord.

NEHEMIAH 8:10

Clap your hands, all peoples! Shout to God with loud songs of joy!

PSALM 47:1

Time to Face the Facts

The best things to celebrate are God's gifts, love, and protection. Celebrate God! That includes celebrating life (birthdays) and accomplishments, which are possible because of the wisdom, skill, and talents he has given you. So, go ahead and celebrate . . . but don't forget to include God in the celebrations and to thank him for making it all possible!

Today I Will . . .

Enjoy all God has given me and make every day a mini-celebration of thanks to him.

What Does the Bible Say about Change?

Change . . . stinks. At least sometimes it does. Change means loved ones moving away. Change happens when a parent loses a job, which means financial changes for the family. Changing schools is tough. The bottom line is change is seldom easy, even if it's a change for good. God knows that change is hard for you. That's why he encourages you to hang on to him and let him be your anchor in whatever changes life brings.

What the Bible Says

The LORD is a stronghold for the oppressed,
a stronghold in times of trouble.

PSALM 9:9

Jesus Christ is the same yesterday and today and forever.

HEBREWS 13:8

Casting all your anxieties on him,
because he cares for you.

1 PETER 5:7

Time to Face the Facts

It's comforting to know that God cares about the struggles of life. He cares about how hard change is for you. He is the one thing in this whole world that never changes. He is always the same. So, when you turn to him for comfort and help, he is always there and he will always comfort you. When the changes of life start knocking you down . . . let him pick you up.

Today I Will . . .

Tell God about the changes that are up-setting me. Ask him to help me see be-

"I'm all for change—as long as it doesn't affect me!"

yond what's changing to what the future holds and how exciting that will be.

What Does the Bible Say about Character?

What do people say about you? Are you honest? Are you kind? Are you dependable? What people say about you reflects what your character is. Character is who you are—the *real* you. God has pretty strong opinions about character. He wants his children to have character that reflects who he is.

What the Bible Says

For you are a people holy to the LORD your God.
The LORD your God has chosen you to be a
people for his treasured possession, out of
all the peoples who are on the face of the earth.

DEUTERONOMY 7:6

And we all, with unveiled face, beholding the
glory of the Lord, are being transformed
into the same image from one degree
of glory to another. For this comes from
the Lord who is the Spirit.

2 CORINTHIANS 3:18

More than that, we rejoice in our sufferings,
knowing that suffering produces endurance,
and endurance produces character, and character
produces hope, and hope does not put us
to shame, because God's love has been poured
into our hearts through the Holy Spirit
who has been given to us.

ROMANS 5:3–5

Time to Face the Facts

You belong to God's family, and the family likeness should show in your character. Kindness, generosity, love, honesty, courage . . . and on and on are characteristics of God. So, being unkind and dishonest and just plain mean are not things you want in your character.

Today I Will . . .

Take an honest look at myself and see whether there are things in my character that should be changed. That's not going to be easy, but I'll ask God to help me.

What Does the Bible Say about Cheating?

You "accidentally" notice someone else's answer on a test question. Or a store clerk gives you too much change, and you just slip it in your pocket. You pad your score in a game so you win . . . these are all examples of cheating. Some cheats are so small—no big deal, right? Wrong. Honesty in all things is what God desires from you.

What the Bible Says

You shall do what is right and good in the sight of the LORD, that it may go well with you.

DEUTERONOMY 6:18

A false balance is an abomination to the LORD,
but a just weight is his delight.

PROVERBS 11:1

One who is faithful in a very little is also faithful in much, and one
who is dishonest in a very little is also dishonest in much.

LUKE 16:10

Time to Face the Facts

No one likes to be the victim of cheating. Remember that when you're tempted to cheat. Someone is always the victim. A person who is obeying God and living for him will try her best to be honest in all things, even when it's hard. Honesty is really the best policy.

Today I Will . . .

Not cheat. Yeah, even when it's hard because it means I come in second in a game or don't do well on a test or don't have much money. I want to obey God and live the way he wants.

"If you don't get caught, it's not cheating."

What Does the Bible Say about Children?

You probably feel that there are times when your opinions don't count because, after all, you are just a kid. Adults have more power, so they are more important, right? Well, that is true in some ways, but children do matter to God. He planned childhood as a time to learn and grow and as a more carefree time to have fun and enjoy life before taking on lots of responsibilities.

What the Bible Says

And [Jesus] said, "Truly, I say to you, unless you turn and become like children, you will never enter the kingdom of heaven. Whoever humbles himself like this child is the greatest in the kingdom of heaven."

MATTHEW 18:3–4

And he took a child and put him in the midst of them, and taking him in his arms, he said to them, "Whoever receives one such child in my name receives me, and whoever receives me, receives not me but him who sent me."

MARK 9:36–37

Time to Face the Facts

Children were important to Jesus. He encouraged grown-ups to have a simple faith like children do. So, that means, as a kid, your faith is important. Remember that God made this beautiful world for you to enjoy. Enjoy all of God's creations.

Today I Will . . .

Understand that I am important to God. I will enjoy this time of life when I don't have a lot of heavy responsibilities but will watch and learn so I can be a responsible adult.

"I don't want to grow up."

What Does the Bible Say about Choices?

Life is filled with choices. Every day you face little ones such as what to wear or what to eat. Some things you do are choices you don't even think about such as what tone of voice you use to answer your mom or dad or how kind you are to people around you. Does God really care about those little every-day choices? Yep. God wants all of your choices to be to show love to those around you and to him.

What the Bible Says

Make me to know your ways,
O Lord; teach me your paths.

PSALM 25:4

If any of you lacks wisdom, let him ask God,
who gives generously to all without reproach,
and it will be given him.

JAMES 1:5

But solid food is for the mature,
for those who have their powers of
discernment trained by constant
practice to distinguish
good from evil.

HEBREWS 5:14

Time to Face the Facts

God will help you make choices . . . even the little ones. Just ask him. Remember that the choices you make show how you feel about obeying God deep inside. They also show how much you respect other people.

Today I Will . . .

Admit that even my little choices reflect my opinion of God and how important he is in my life. I'll think about that.

What Does the Bible Say about Church?

Okay, be honest—how do you feel about church? Is it boring to you? Does it have no connection to your everyday life? Do you spend service times writing notes to your friends or daydreaming? Here's the scoop on what God thinks: he instructs his children to get together to worship him and to pray. He believes that being together with others who believe will be an encouragement.

What the Bible Says

And let us consider how to stir up one another to love and good works, not neglecting to meet together, as is the habit of some, but encouraging one another, and all the more as you see the Day drawing near.

HEBREWS 10:24-25

Two are better than one, because they have a good reward for their toil. For if they fall, one will lift up his fellow. But woe to him who is alone when he falls and has not another to lift him up!

ECCLESIASTES 4:9-10

Therefore, confess your sins to one another and pray for one another, that you may be healed. The prayer of a righteous person has great power as it is working.

JAMES 5:16

Time to Face the Facts

Church is important. It's a good thing to meet with others to study God's Word and to be encouraged in your Christian life. Yeah, sometimes some things may be boring to you, but that's okay. If you're bored, read your Bible or pray. But also realize that the boredom might be your fault—your mind and heart need to be open to learning about God.

"The family that prays together stays together."

Today I Will . . .

Admit it . . . sometimes I don't pay attention in church. I'll give it a try and see if I learn anything. I'll thank God for my church and for our pastor. I'll be thankful for my Sunday school teacher, too, and that all of them care about me.

What Does the Bible Say about Classmates?

"Some of my classmates are a pain in the neck because they brag about their good grades or how good they are at sports. I don't have to like *all* of them, do I?" Are those things you might have said? Does God really want you to like *everyone*? God wants you to love everyone. That doesn't mean you're going to be best friends with everyone, but that you will treat them with love and respect.

What the Bible Says

Hatred stirs up strife,
but love covers all offenses.

PROVERBS 10:12

A new commandment I give to you,
that you love one another:
just as I have loved you, you also
are to love one another.

JOHN 13:34

Above all, keep loving one another earnestly,
since love covers a multitude of sins.

1 PETER 4:8

Time to Face the Facts

Not everyone is easy to love, and people whom you just know at school can easily fall into that category. But guess what? Your classmates are a great mission field, and the way you treat them may be the first impression of God and his children that some of them ever have.

Today I Will . . .

Show love to my classmates. That doesn't mean I'm going to be best friends with all of them, but I can be kind, honest, and fair. I don't want to do or say anything that will give them a bad impression of who God is.

What Does the Bible Say about Clothes?

Fancy designer duds or baggy hole-filled jeans . . . what's your style? Does it bug you that some kids have tons of the exact clothes you want? Do you spend lots of time thinking about clothes, shopping for them, or begging your parents for more? Does God care what you wear? Yes, God does care about things you care about. He promises to take care of your daily needs.

What the Bible Says

Do not be anxious about your life, what you will eat or what you will drink, nor about your body, what you will put on. Is not life more than food, and the body more than clothing? Look at the birds of the air: they neither sow nor reap nor gather into barns, and yet your heavenly Father feeds them. Are you not of more value than they?

MATTHEW 6:25–26

Consider the lilies of the field, how they grow: they neither toil nor spin, yet I tell you, even Solomon in all his glory was not arrayed like one of these. But if God so clothes the grass of the field, which today is alive and tomorrow is thrown into the oven, will he not much more clothe you? . . .

MATTHEW 6:28–30

Time to Face the Facts

It's okay to want to look good. It's okay to have "a style." What isn't okay is to be so focused on what you wear that you get jealous of others or spend tons of time thinking about clothes. Face it . . . there are more important things than what you wear. Just be glad you have any clothes at all.

Today I Will . . .

Try to stop focusing on getting the clothes I want. Yes, I will be thankful that I have clothes to wear.

"Clothes make the man!"

What Does the Bible Say about Clubs?

There are generally two views about clubs—if you're in one, you love being a part of it. If you're not, then you may think clubs are kind of snooty. Clubs can easily become cliques. It's nice to be part of a group of people who have the same interests you do. But there is the real danger of excluding other people. How does God feel about this? Clubs are fine . . . but nothing should be more important to you than God is, and you should always show love to other people.

What the Bible Says

May the Lord make you increase and abound in love for one another and for all, as we do for you.

1 THESSALONIANS 3:12

Humble yourselves before the Lord, and he will exalt you.

JAMES 4:10

No one has ever seen God; if we love one another, God abides in us and his love is perfected in us.

1 JOHN 4:12

Time to Face the Facts

If you're kind of proud of the fact that you belong to a club and you feel a little better than anyone who isn't a member . . . stop it. There's no love in feeling that way. Belonging to a club is fine. But don't forget the most important thing—loving others.

Today I Will . . .

Spend some time with friends who are not part of any club I'm in. I'll look for someone who has completely different interests than I do. Maybe I'll learn something new!

"Wish I was part of the in crowd."

What Does the Bible Say about Community?

Friends make life a lot more fun, don't they? Why is that? It's fun to hang out with people who have the same interests. Friends are encouragers in hard times and celebrators in good times. Friends are a community—a group of people around you who care about you. God knows you need the strength that a community brings. So he encourages you to belong to a community and to enjoy the give and take, encouragement, laughter, help, and care.

What the Bible Says

A friend loves at all times, and a brother is born for adversity.

PROVERBS 17:17

Two are better than one, because they have a good reward for their toil. For if they fall, one will lift up his fellow. But woe to him who is alone when he falls and has not another to lift him up!

ECCLESIASTES 4:9–10

And though a man might prevail against one who is alone, two will withstand him—a threefold cord is not quickly broken.

ECCLESIASTES 4:12

Time to Face the Facts

Having people around you who care about you is a good thing—whether it's family or friends. Enjoy them. Celebrate them. Care about them and allow them to care about you. Remember that they can help you become a better person who lives the way God wants you to live.

Today I Will . . .

Thank God for my friends and family. He knew just the right people to put in my life. They are awesome! Each of them helps me in a different way. I am

"Life sure is a lot better when we're all together."

so glad they are here to help me become a better person. I'll help them, too. We're a team!

What Does the Bible Say about Compassion?

Compassion? That's probably not a word you use every day, is it? It's kind of a grown-up word that means caring for others. Being the one who gets cared for is always nice. Sometimes being the one who gives the compassion is not so much fun. It can take a lot of energy, and sometimes it seems to go on for a long time. Does God have an opinion about compassion? Oh yeah, he offers it to you because he loves you. He wants you to offer it to others because you love him.

What the Bible Says

The steadfast love of the LORD never ceases;
his mercies never come to an end;
they are new every morning;
great is your faithfulness.

LAMENTATIONS 3:22–23

Religion that is pure and undefiled before God, the Father,
is this: to visit orphans and widows in their affliction,
and to keep oneself unstained from the world.

JAMES 1:27

Casting all your anxieties on him, because he cares for you.

1 PETER 5:7

Time to Face the Facts

Compassion means feeling another person's pain. It means sharing that pain and caring about how that person feels. God does that for you. He cares. One way of showing love to other people is to have compassion when they are hurting. God has compassion for you. Other people have compassion for you. You have compassion for them. It's a way to help each other.

Today I Will . . .

Be compassionate. Sometimes I'm not because it takes a lot of time or whatever. But now I see that other people need compassion as much as I do, and I know how good I feel when someone cares about me. So, today I will care about others.

COMPETITION

What Does the Bible Say about Competition?

Do you love to win? Yeah, who doesn't? Success is usually measured by who wins and the losers are . . . well . . . losers. Winning is awesome! Healthy competition makes you work harder, study more, train better. Doesn't God like winners, too? Sure, he loves for you to win—fair and square. Competition is a good thing as long as it's healthy and fair.

What the Bible Says

Do you not know that in a race
all the runners run, but only one
receives the prize? So run that
you may obtain it.

1 CORINTHIANS 9:24

I press on toward the goal for the prize of the
upward call of God in Christ Jesus.

PHILIPPIANS 3:14

Whatever you do, work heartily, as for the Lord
and not for men, knowing that from the Lord
you will receive the inheritance as your reward.
You are serving the Lord Christ.

COLOSSIANS 3:23–24

Time to Face the Facts

Competition is a good thing because it makes you work harder. But remember to have a healthy view of competition—winning is *not* everything (though it is cool). Working hard and doing the best that you can is pretty cool, too. Don't push other people down in order to make yourself a winner. Just do your best.

Today I Will . . .

Play fair. Work hard. Do my best. If I win, I win. If I don't, well, I'll celebrate that I did my best.

What Does the Bible Say about Complaining?

Whine, whine, whine. Do you know someone who complains all the time? Someone who always sees the bad side of things? Couldn't be you, could it? A complainer is no fun to be around. People who complain about everything are really only thinking about themselves. God reminds you to celebrate the good things and think of other people's feelings. Don't complain all the time!

What the Bible Says

Do nothing from rivalry or conceit, but in humility count others more significant than yourselves. Let each of you look not only to his own interests, but also to the interests of others.

PHILIPPIANS 2:3–4

Do all things without grumbling or questioning, that you may be blameless and innocent, children of God without blemish in the midst of a crooked and twisted generation, among whom you shine as lights in the world.

PHILIPPIANS 2:14–15

Giving thanks always and for everything to God the Father in the name of our Lord Jesus Christ.

EPHESIANS 5:20

Time to Face the Facts

Constant complaining is a sin—plain and simple. You can't be complaining all the time and also have a thankful heart. And complaining means you're thinking about how everything affects you—not about other people's feelings. God's command to love others gets lost in all the complaining.

Today I Will . . .

Listen to myself. If I'm guilty of constant complaining, I'll stop it. I'll ask God to help me focus on the positives and not the negatives of things that happen.

"If nobody heard her, would she still complain?"

What Does the Bible Say about Compromise?

Compromise? *No way* . . . it's my way or the highway! Is that your feeling? If it is, you probably have a little trouble getting along with other people. You wouldn't be considered a team player. So what? God likes strong people, right? Yes, being strong and knowing your own mind is good, especially when it keeps you from being influenced to do wrong things. But remember, remember, remember—loving others is God's way.

What the Bible Says

Whoever restrains his words has knowledge,
and he who has a cool spirit is a man of understanding.

PROVERBS 17:27

I appeal to you, brothers, to watch out for those
who cause divisions and create obstacles contrary
to the doctrine that you have been taught; avoid them.

ROMANS 16:17

Do not be unequally yoked with unbelievers.
For what partnership has righteousness
with lawlessness? Or what fellowship
has light with darkness?

2 CORINTHIANS 6:14

Time to Face the Facts

Holding firm to your Christian values is a good thing—no compromising there. But being a stubborn person on other points, just for the sake of being stubborn, is not good. Think about how you are making others feel. Everyone likes to get his own way once in a while.

Today I Will . . .

Two things: I'll stand firm on the right and wrong I know from the Bible. But on other things, I'll let others get their way once in a while. That's the fair thing to do.

What Does the Bible Say about Confession?

Do you think that if you do something wrong but don't get caught then you've gotten away with it? Yeah, and then if you've gotten away with it, there is *no reason* to confess to it, right? *Wrong*. No matter if your parents, teachers, or friends don't know what you've done, God does. Confessing is a necessary part of knowing God, and not confessing will block your relationship with him.

What the Bible Says

> I acknowledged my sin to you,
> and I did not cover my iniquity;
> I said, "I will confess my transgressions to the LORD,"
> and you forgave the iniquity of my sin.
> Selah
>
> **PSALM 32:5**

> If we confess our sins, he is faithful and just to forgive us our sins and to cleanse us from all unrighteousness.
>
> **1 JOHN 1:9**

Time to Face the Facts

Confession is good for you—cleanses all the guilt out of your heart. Be honest now, you know that you don't "get away" with things because God always knows what you've done. When you've got unconfessed sin in your heart, it's like a wall that keeps you and God apart. That's no fun. So, what are you going to do about it?

"Lord, please heal that window."

Today I Will . . .

Be honest with myself and others about what I need to confess. I won't make excuses about my behavior. I will confess and ask God to help me do better in the future.

What Does the Bible Say about Confidence?

"I can't." Have you ever whined that you can't do something or that some task is too hard? Is your self-confidence about as big as a pinpoint? Well, you don't want to be filled with pride, that's for sure, but should you have confidence in yourself? *Yes* . . . God gave you abilities and he will help you do the things he wants you to do.

What the Bible Says

It is better to take refuge in the LORD
than to trust in man.

PSALM 118:8

Having gifts that differ according to the grace given to us,
let us use them: if prophecy, in proportion to our faith.

ROMANS 12:6

That Christ may dwell in your hearts through faith—that you,
being rooted and grounded in love, may have strength to
comprehend with all the saints what is the breadth
and length and height and depth, and to know the love of
Christ that surpasses knowledge, that you may be
filled with all the fullness of God.

EPHESIANS 3:17–20

Time to Face the Facts

You can do some things well . . . okay, not everything. But that's not the point. Understanding that God gave you abilities does not mean you are proud. It will give you confidence to do the jobs God puts in front of you—whether it's as simple as being a friend to someone or being a concert pianist or a foreign missionary. God has something just for you.

Today I Will . . .

Think about the things I enjoy doing . . . could my gifts and abilities from God be in those things? Cool. Then I will do them and serve him with confidence!

What Does the Bible Say about Conflict?

"I'm right! "No, you're not, I am!" Conflict—it's really not possible to be around other people without some conflict some of the time. How you handle the conflict is the key. Does God have opinions on that? Of course he does; God encourages his children to settle conflicts. He instructs his children to act in love. Conflict can actually help you understand others better.

What the Bible Says

Hatred stirs up strife, but love covers all offenses.

PROVERBS 10:12

Whoever restrains his words has knowledge,
and he who has a cool spirit is a man of understanding.

PROVERBS 17:27

So if you are offering your gift at the altar and there remember that your brother
has something against you, leave your gift there before the altar and go.
First be reconciled to your brother, and then come and offer your gift.

MATTHEW 5:23–24

Time to Face the Facts

Do you sometimes lose your temper and say things that are mean? That's not good. Disagreeing with others is okay, but realize that you aren't always right—sometimes the other person is right. Losing your temper and saying mean things will only hurt others and maybe even end friendships. When you have a conflict, how will you handle it? With kindness and love or with anger and mean words?

"Let's all just get along."

Today I Will . . .

Control my temper and think before I speak. I don't want to hurt others—even when I'm angry. I'll try to listen to the other person's opinions and see what I can learn. Then, I'll try to settle any conflict in a peaceful, kind way.

What Does the Bible Say about Conscience?

You find five dollars on the ground and you pick it up and stick it in your pocket. Yahoo! You want to celebrate your find, but that nagging voice in your head says, "Uh uh. That money isn't yours. You know that lady who just walked by dropped it." Bummer. Conscience is that voice you hear inside that tries to stop you when you're doing something wrong. It gently (or not so gently) points out right and wrong. What does conscience have to do with God? Well, sometimes that voice you hear may be his voice encouraging you to do what's right!

What the Bible Says

For you are a people holy to the LORD your God. The LORD your God has chosen you to be a people for his treasured possession, out of all the peoples who are on the face of the earth.

DEUTERONOMY 7:6

Blessed are the pure in heart, for they shall see God.

MATTHEW 5:8

I always take pains to have a clear conscience toward both God and man.

ACTS 24:16

Time to Face the Facts

Your conscience tries to remind you to obey God. It slows you down when you're flying into something that would be disobedient or dishonoring to God. Yeah, sometimes that little voice seems to be nagging. But when you think about it, isn't it really trying to protect you?

Today I Will . . .

Sigh . . . stop complaining about my conscience and actually listen to it. In the long run that will save me lots of trouble. Plus, I'll know I'm pleasing God and being thoughtful of other people!

What Does the Bible Say about Consequences?

"Grounded? Why are you grounding me? So I told a little lie. Big deal!" Here's the big deal . . . actions have consequences. Yep. That should make you stop and think before you do something: *Will the consequences of this action be good or bad?* God gives you the freedom to choose your actions, but he wants you to remember that there are consequences for your choices.

What the Bible Says

Whoever brings blessing will be enriched,
and one who waters will himself be watered.

PROVERBS 11:25

Give, and it will be given to you. Good measure, pressed down, shaken together, running over, will be put into your lap. For with the measure you use it will be measured back to you.

LUKE 6:38

Do not be deceived: God is not mocked,
for whatever one sows, that will he also reap.

GALATIANS 6:7

Time to Face the Facts

The bottom line is you will reap what you sow. What does that mean? Here's a couple of examples: If you're dishonest, people won't trust you. If you are mean and spiteful, you won't have friends. Get the idea? On the flip side, if you're kind and loving, you'll have tons of friends. If you're honest and truthful, people will trust you. How you live is up to you. What consequences will come to you?

"It was just a 'little' lie."

Today I Will . . .

Accept the fact that many things that happen to me are a result of the way I live or treat others. I'm going to clean up my act . . . with God's help!

What Does the Bible Say about Contentment?

More! More! More! Are you always wanting more? Are you never satisfied? Well then, you aren't content. Contentment is peace and satisfaction with the stuff you have, the relationships you have, and the life you have. It doesn't mean you don't keep growing. It means that you're not consumed with "getting." God wants you to keep learning and growing and becoming more mature. But he also instructs you to have peace in your life.

What the Bible Says

You keep him in perfect peace whose mind is stayed on you, because he trusts in you.

ISAIAH 26:3

Not that I am speaking of being in need, for I have learned in whatever situation I am to be content.

PHILIPPIANS 4:11

Now there is great gain in godliness with contentment, for we brought nothing into the world, and we cannot take anything out of the world.

1 TIMOTHY 6:6–7

Time to Face the Facts

Wanting to know God better and serve him more obediently . . . that kind of discontent is okay because it helps you grow. Wanting more stuff or more popularity is just going to make you crazy. There's no contentment in that. Give up the quest for that kind of stuff. Be content with what you have; don't be content with who you are. Keep growing and learning how to be more like Jesus.

"Just one more trip to the store and I think I will have enough."

Today I Will . . .

Think about that one thing I've been obsessing about. I'll ask God to help me stop wanting it so much. I'll ask him to help me focus on being more like Jesus!

What Does the Bible Say about Control?

Is this true of your world: things are just fine as long as everyone plays by your rules. Do you like to call the shots? For example, what games are played; who is "in" or "out" of your friends group; just generally be in control of everything? And why not, you may ask . . . after all, don't you have the best ideas? Yeah, well, maybe not everyone agrees. So, who is more qualified to be in control than you? Try this on for size—God should be in control of everything in your life.

What the Bible Says

Trust in the LORD with all your heart,
and do not lean on your own understanding.
In all your ways acknowledge him,
and he will make straight your paths.

PROVERBS 3:5–6

By him all things were created, in heaven and on earth, visible and invisible, whether thrones or dominions or rulers or authorities—all things were created through him and for him. And he is before all things, and in him all things hold together.

COLOSSIANS 1:16–17

He put all things under his feet and gave him as head over all things to the church, which is his body, the fullness of him who fills all in all.

EPHESIANS 1:22–23

Time to Face the Facts

Always being the one in control is a lot of work. Trying to control all the people around you is just going to frustrate you and make your friends not want to be around you. So, lighten up. Enjoy other people's ideas and let them choose activities once in a while. Let God be in control of you—your attitudes, your habits, your actions. He loves you. He'll guide you. He'll take care of you. Believe it.

Today I Will . . .

Oh, wow, it's so hard. I like to be in control. But, okay, I'll try to lighten up and let others make decisions. But I'm going to need God's help to do this.

What Does the Bible Say about Conversion?

Conversion? What's that? It sounds like something to do with math and *I don't do math well*. Actually, conversion doesn't have to do with math. It has to do with change. Converting or changing from one way of life to another. And . . . it's a good thing when it is conversion from being a person who pays no attention to God to a person who tries to obey and honor him. Get the idea? God thinks conversion is very important. He sent his only Son to earth to make it possible.

What the Bible Says

For God so loved the world,
that he gave his only Son,
that whoever believes in him should
not perish but have eternal life.

JOHN 3:16

Repent therefore, and turn again,
that your sins may be blotted out.

ACTS 3:19

Therefore, if anyone is in Christ,
he is a new creation. The old has
passed away; behold, the new has come.

2 CORINTHIANS 5:17

Time to Face the Facts

Conversion is a good thing—turning away from an old way of life where you focused on yourself and doing what you wanted and turning to God where you focus on knowing him and obeying him. Conversion means entering a new way of life. It's a way of life that promises being with God forever!

Today I Will . . .

Think seriously about conversion. If I haven't made the choice to turn away from my old way of life and follow God, well, maybe it's time I did that.

What Does the Bible Say about Coolness?

Doesn't everyone want to be cool? The cool kids wear the right clothes. They like the same things—music, movies, even food. Everyone wants to be like them. Being cool is . . . cool! What's God's opinion of coolness? Well, it's probably different than yours because he wants to be the most important thing in your life. He also wants you to treat other people with love and kindness. Living for God . . . now that's cool!

What the Bible Says

I the LORD your God am a jealous God.

EXODUS 20:5

Love the LORD your God, and walk in all his ways and keep his commandments and cling to him and serve him with all your heart and with all your soul.

JOSHUA 22:5

Now concerning brotherly love you have no need for anyone to write to you, for you yourselves have been taught by God to love one another.

1 THESSALONIANS 4:9

Time to Face the Facts

Putting a lot of energy and thought into being cool is not cool. Especially if it takes away from your time with God. He made you just the way he wants you to be and that means you are the very best you possible. So, enjoy who you are and celebrate how God made you. Thank him for who you are . . . that's cool!

Today I Will . . .

Try to accept myself just the way I am. It's hard because I do want to be cool. But maybe I'll make a whole new definition of coolness by just being me!

"If you have to try that hard to be 'cool,' it's really not very 'cool.'"

What Does the Bible Say about Cooperation?

You think you can get a lot of stuff done by yourself? So much more can be accomplished when a group is working together. However, in order for that to be successful there must be cooperation. You have to work as a team. Think of a crew rowing a boat: if the crew members don't all row in the same direction, they will go nowhere. God knows you need the people around you and that if all his children work together, his work will get done on this earth.

What the Bible Says

Two are better than one, because they have a good reward for their toil. For if they fall, one will lift up his fellow. But woe to him who is alone when he falls and has not another to lift him up. . . . And though a man might prevail against one who is alone, two will withstand him—a threefold cord is not quickly broken.

ECCLESIASTES 4:9–10, 12

For just as the body is one and has many members, and all the members of the body, though many, are one body, so it is with Christ.

1 CORINTHIANS 12:12

But God has so composed the body, giving greater honor to the part that lacked it, that there may be no division in the body, but that the members may have the same care for one another. If one member suffers, all suffer together; if one member is honored, all rejoice together.

1 CORINTHIANS 12:24–26

Time to Face the Facts

Yep, there's strength in numbers. So get together with people who share your values and faith. Work together. Cooperate. Help each other. Good things will come from that . . . for you, them, and God's kingdom.

Today I Will . . .

Stop resisting working together with others. See how I can be more cooperative and more of a team player. Find strength in my team!

What Does the Bible Say about Courage?

No one wants to be called a chicken, but let's face it, some things are scary. Right? What kinds of things scare you? Public speaking? Spiders? Changes like moving to a new town? Taking a stand for your beliefs? Where do you get courage when you need it? God's strength is available to you and he wants you to call on him for strength. In fact, he offers his strength.

What the Bible Says

Be strong and courageous. Do not be frightened, and do not be dismayed, for the Lord your God is with you wherever you go.

JOSHUA 1:9

Fear not, for I am with you; be not dismayed, for I am your God;
I will strengthen you, I will help you, I will uphold you
with my righteous right hand.

ISAIAH 41:10

I have said these things to you, that in me you may have peace. In the world you will have tribulation. But take heart; I have overcome the world.

JOHN 16:33

Time to Face the Facts

Some things in life are scary, there's no getting away from that. But you don't have to go through anything alone. God is with you always. His strength is available if you just call on him and ask him for it. So, live with courage since you have the God of creation behind you!

"My hero."

Today I Will . . .

Face my fears. I'm going to be honest with myself and God about what scares me. Then I'm going to ask him to give me courage to move forward. Even if I'm scared (which is okay), I know I can trust him to help me.

What Does the Bible Say about Creativity?

You can't write a best-selling book or paint a picture. Maybe you can't act in a play, sing, or play an instrument. If you can't do any of those things, does that mean you aren't creative at all? Nope. Creativity comes in many different forms (some you might not recognize) because God gave everyone different gifts. He's the master of creativity—look at the world around you that he made from scratch. God gave you creativity and desires that you give it right back to him as your form of worship.

What the Bible Says

> My heart overflows with a pleasing theme;
> I address my verses to the king;
> my tongue is like the pen of a ready scribe.

PSALM 45:1

> I will also praise you with the harp
> for your faithfulness, O my God;
> I will sing praises to you with the lyre,
> O Holy One of Israel.

PSALM 71:22

> By faith we understand that the universe was created by the word of God,
> so that what is seen was not made out of things that are visible.

HEBREWS 11:3

Time to Face the Facts

Here's an interesting thought: God has already placed in your hand whatever you need to do the work he wants you to do and to praise him creatively. Yep, it's there. You just have to look around and see what he has given you and think about how to creatively use it for his glory!

Today I Will . . .

Have the courage to start thinking that I might be creative. I'll think about what I most love to do and understand that it might be a gift from God. So, I'll see how I can use it to praise and honor him.

What Does the Bible Say about Crime?

Crime stinks. People get hurt or killed. Stuff gets destroyed or stolen. Lives are wrecked. Why does there have to be crime anyway? Crime exists because people make bad choices about how they are going to live. It isn't God's desire for people to hurt each other through crime, but he gives people the freedom to make choices. You even have choices to make . . . obey God and be honest and fair or disobey God and be dishonest and unfair.

What the Bible Says

The integrity of the upright guides them,
but the crookedness of the treacherous destroys them.

PROVERBS 11:3

So whatever you wish that others would do to you, do also to them,
for this is the Law and the Prophets.

MATTHEW 7:12

Time to Face the Facts

The best way to live is to treat others the way you'd like to be treated—honestly and fairly. No crime there. But the truth is that crime is going to happen because not everyone will make good choices. So, what do you do? Trust God to protect you. Make wise choices in where you go and what you do. And, if something bad happens to you, ask God to help you forgive and love the person who did it.

"And stay out!"

Today I Will . . .

Make sure my choices are good. Examine my attitude toward those who may have committed crimes. Begin to sincerely pray for those people to come to know Christ.

What Does the Bible Say about Criticism?

Criticism is mean. When you criticize people you're cutting down their own opinion of themselves so you're attacking their self-image. Critical words are hard to take back. You can apologize or blow it off by declaring that you were just joking, but the damage is done. People don't easily forget critical things said to them. How does God feel about criticism? Well, he said that the second most important command (after loving him) is to love others, so he's probably not crazy about criticism.

What the Bible Says

You shall love the Lord your God with all your heart and with all your
soul and with all your mind and with all your strength. The second
is this: You shall love your neighbor as yourself. There is no
other commandment greater than these.

MARK 12:30-31

Love is patient and kind; love does not envy or boast; it is not arrogant or rude.
It does not insist on its own way; it is not irritable or resentful.

1 CORINTHIANS 13:4-5

May the Lord make you increase and abound in love
for one another and for all, as we do for you.

1 THESSALONIANS 3:12

Time to Face the Facts

Honesty time . . . are you critical of others? Look deep in your own heart: do you criticize others to make you feel better about yourself? If you answer yes to these questions, you've got some work to do. Loving others is God's command. Criticism and love don't go together.

Today I Will . . .

Do an honest evaluation of whether or not I'm critical of others. If I am, well, I obviously need to stop it. I'm going to need God's help for that. I don't like to be criticized, and when I think about it, I guess others don't either.

What Does the Bible Say about Crying?

What makes you cry? Hurt feelings? Bad things happening? Fear? Physical pain? Yes, all of those are good reasons for tears. Crying is a good emotional release for the pain in your life. But how does God feel about it? That's not hard to figure out . . . God loves you. He doesn't want you to hurt, but he also knows that life has pain in it. God promises that even through your tears you can know that he is with you all the time. You won't go through any painful times alone.

What the Bible Says

He will swallow up death forever;
and the Lord GOD will wipe away tears from all faces,
and the reproach of his people he will take away from all the earth,
for the LORD has spoken.

ISAIAH 25:8

Blessed be the God and Father of our Lord Jesus Christ, the Father of mercies and God of all comfort, who comforts us in all our affliction, so that we may be able to comfort those who are in any affliction, with the comfort with which we ourselves are comforted by God.

2 CORINTHIANS 1:3–4

Humble yourselves, therefore, under the mighty hand of God so that at the proper time he may exalt you, casting all your anxieties on him, because he cares for you.

1 PETER 5:6–7

Time to Face the Facts

It's okay to cry. Honest. Sometimes you just have to. But remember through your tears that God loves you very, very much. He is there wanting to be your comfort. So, lean on him, trust him, let him surround you with his love.

Today I Will . . .

Turn to God with my hurts. I'll be quiet and concentrate on him so that his love and comfort can surround me.

"oh no! I got a new pimple."

What Does the Bible Say about Dancing?

Some people think dancing is wrong—not an activity that honors God. Some don't have a problem with it. What does God think about dancing? Maybe it depends on how it's done. Suggestive dancing that has sexual overtones does not bring honor to him. But perhaps dancing that comes from a heart overflowing with praise brings him joy. God wants your praise and worship; if that comes with joyful dancing . . . then dance away!

What the Bible Says

You have turned for me my mourning into dancing;
you have loosed my sackcloth and clothed me with gladness.

PSALM 30:11

Praise him with tambourine and dance;
praise him with strings and pipe!

PSALM 150:4

Then shall the young women rejoice in the dance,
and the young men and the old shall be merry.
I will turn their mourning into joy;
I will comfort them, and give them gladness for sorrow.

JEREMIAH 31:13

Time to Face the Facts

Sometimes the joy spills out and the music in your heart just makes you move. You can give that praise dance to God in worship. Other kinds of dancing can be a hot button. Search your own heart and be sure that your actions and desires are pure before God. Don't let anything, even dancing, come between you and him.

Today I Will . . .

Let go of my inhibitions and do a dance of praise and love for God. I'll also be sure that any other dancing I do is done with a pure heart before God.

"Dancing to the tune in my head."

What Does the Bible Say about Dating?

Are you dreaming about going out on dates? Does it look like so much fun? Maybe even group dates where a whole bunch of friends go to the mall or a movie? Sure, dating can be fun, and maybe it seems pretty innocent to you. So, does God really have an opinion about it? God's opinion is that you keep yourself pure, sexually and morally. Remember that your body is his temple!

What the Bible Says

Blessed are the pure in heart, for they shall see God.

MATTHEW 5:8

You have heard that it was said, "You shall not commit adultery." But I say to you that everyone who looks at a woman with lustful intent has already committed adultery with her in his heart.

MATTHEW 5:27

You may be sure of this, that everyone who is sexually immoral or impure, or who is covetous (that is, an idolater), has no inheritance in the kingdom of Christ and God.

EPHESIANS 5:5

Time to Face the Facts

Wow, fooling around with sex is pretty serious. God wants you to keep yourself pure—and that starts in your mind. So, think pure thoughts, and when impure ones sneak in, chase them out. Prepare yourself for dating by how you think. Dating can be a lot of fun, but keep it pure.

Today I Will . . .

Not mess around with impure thoughts. It's easy to get lazy about letting them roll around in my mind, but I'm going to stop that (with God's help) and concentrate on healthier things to think about.

"Gee thanks. Wow, it looks just like one of the tulips from my mother's garden."

What Does the Bible Say about Death?

Death is scary from a lot of different angles. It might hurt. It's so final. And what really happens to you after you die? Maybe you don't think about death much since you're young. But aren't you just a little bit curious as to what God says about death? Everyone is going to die, that's why God wants you to know him. Then, leaving this planet just means you are with him forever.

What the Bible Says

> In my Father's house are many rooms. If it were not so,
> would I have told you that I go to prepare a place for you?
>
> **JOHN 14:2**

> For I am sure that neither death nor life, nor angels nor rulers, nor things present nor
> things to come, nor powers, nor height nor depth, nor anything else in all creation,
> will be able to separate us from the love of God in Christ Jesus our Lord.
>
> **ROMANS 8:38-39**

> O death, where is your victory? O death, where is your sting? The sting of
> death is sin, and the power of sin is the law. But thanks be to God,
> who gives us the victory through our Lord Jesus Christ.
>
> **1 CORINTHIANS 15:55-57**

Time to Face the Facts

Death isn't really as much of an unknown as you might think. God has it all planned out. If you know him—have asked Jesus into your heart—then death just means you go to heaven to be with him. What could be cooler?

Today I Will . . .

Ask Jesus into my heart, if I haven't already done that. Begin learning to know God better and better because, after all, we're going to be together for a long time!

"Heaven is on the other side."

What Does the Bible Say about Deceit?

Cover up the truth or twist the facts just enough that you always come out smelling like a rose . . . that's deceit. If you can do that, no one will ever know, right? The bad thing about deceit is that you have to plan to do it. So, it's a calculated effort to lie to someone else. How does God feel about deceit? He stands for truth, honesty, and purity, so deceit is not in his plan for your life!

What the Bible Says

Let no one deceive himself. If anyone among you thinks that he is wise in this age, let him become a fool that he may become wise.

1 CORINTHIANS 3:18

Do not be deceived: God is not mocked, for whatever one sows, that will he also reap.

GALATIANS 6:7

Therefore, having put away falsehood, let each one of you speak the truth with his neighbor, for we are members one of another.

EPHESIANS 4:25

Time to Face the Facts

You might fool other people when you twist the truth, but you're not fooling God. You're not fooling yourself, either. You know what you're doing. When other people find out about your deceit (and they will), it breaks their trust with you. Nothing good can come from it. Honesty is always the best policy.

Today I Will . . .

Okay, so I need to just be honest . . . even if it means I get in trouble. It's better than trying to deceive others or even deceive God. Honesty is the best policy . . . even when it's hard.

What Does the Bible Say about Decisions?

Decisions are sometimes so hard! Do you do this or that? What will be the long-term effects of this decision? What will others think of me for this decision? Argh! It's sometimes so hard to know what decisions to make. Does God care about the decisions you have to make? Sure he does. He wants you to make good choices, and he promises to help you with those choices.

What the Bible Says

> Make me to know your ways, O Lord;
> teach me your paths.
>
> **PSALM 25:4**

> Ask, and it will be given to you; seek, and you will find;
> knock, and it will be opened to you.
>
> **MATTHEW 7:7**

> If any of you lacks wisdom, let him ask God,
> who gives generously to all without reproach,
> and it will be given him.
>
> **JAMES 1:5**

Time to Face the Facts

Isn't it cool to know that you aren't on your own to make hard decisions? God wants to help you. All you have to do is ask him for help, then put yourself in position to hear his answer. Read his Word, pray, and just be quiet enough to let him guide you.

Today I Will . . .

Be quiet. Yeah, that isn't easy in my noisy world. But if I want to hear God's direction, I think I need to be quiet for a while. So, I'll ask him for help, I'll read the Bible and pray, and then I'll be still so I can hear his direction . . . and I'll stop stressing about decisions.

What Does the Bible Say about Depression?

Ever have one of those times when it feels like the sun doesn't shine on you? Like it's always cloudy and rainy? Like nothing goes right for you? Your friends don't like you . . . you can't do well at anything . . . you just kind of feel like pond scum? Yeah, that's depression. A great thing to remember when you feel depressed is that God loves you . . . a lot!

What the Bible Says

How precious to me are your thoughts, O God!
How vast is the sum of them!
If I would count them, they are more than the sand.
I awake, and I am still with you.

PSALM 139:17–18

Neither death nor life, nor angels nor rulers, nor things present nor things to come, nor powers, nor height nor depth, nor anything else in all creation, will be able to separate us from the love of God in Christ Jesus our Lord.

ROMANS 8:38–39

Time to Face the Facts

Sometimes depression comes because a lot of bad things happen. Then it's a real comfort to remember that God is right there with you and that he loves you. Sometimes depression comes because you focus too much on yourself. Then, it's helpful to get your mind off yourself and see how you can help someone else. God loves you, so pass that love along to others.

Today I will . . .

Remember that God loves me very much. The super heavy things I'm dealing with in life are a little easier to bear when I remember that he's willing to help me with them.

"Why is it just raining on me?"

What Does the Bible Say about Diaries?

Seriously . . . diaries and the Bible? Diaries are where you keep a record of what you've been doing and who you have spent time with. Your diary usually has your private thoughts, hopes, and dreams. What does God care about that? He cares about your thoughts, dreams, and ideas because he loves you and wants to be a major part of those thoughts, dreams, and ideas.

What the Bible Says

The LORD your God is in your midst,
a mighty one who will save;
he will rejoice over you with gladness;
he will quiet you by his love;
he will exult over you with loud singing.

ZEPHANIAH 3:17

Let the words of my mouth and
the meditation of my heart
be acceptable in your sight,
O LORD, my rock and my redeemer.

PSALM 19:14

On God rests my salvation and my glory;
my mighty rock, my refuge is God.

PSALM 62:7

Time to Face the Facts

Keeping a diary is a good idea. Writing down your thoughts and dreams gives you a place to look back to see how God has guided your life. Also, sometimes writing down the things that are bothering you helps you see that they really aren't so terrible. Your diary will show you how much of a priority you make God in your life.

Today I Will . . .

Look back through my diary (if I keep one) and see how often I mentioned God and living for him. As I write in my diary from now on, I'll include my thoughts of God and maybe even write down some of the things I'm praying about.

What Does the Bible Say about Diets?

"You're *not* going to tell me that dieting is a sin, are you?" Okay, if that thought ran through your mind, maybe your outside looks are a bit too important to you. Some people are totally consumed with how they look, and they freak out if they gain a half a pound. So . . . does God care about whether or not you're on a diet? Yeah, he kind of does because he wants you to take care of this body he gave you. But he also wants you to care about the inside you (your heart and soul). You need to take care of both of them.

What the Bible Says

I appeal to you therefore, brothers, by the mercies of God, to present your bodies as a living sacrifice, holy and acceptable to God, which is your spiritual worship.

ROMANS 12:1

While bodily training is of some value, godliness is of value in every way, as it holds promise for the present life and also for the life to come.

1 TIMOTHY 4:8

Time to Face the Facts

God gave you one body, and he does want you to take care of it. So, concentrating on a healthy diet is good. But depriving your body of the nutrients it needs is not a good idea. Starving your body so you can be Hollywood-thin is not good. The key is to take care of yourself. Enjoy the blessings of food God provides. But if you're going to focus your time and attention on one particular part of life—make it the inside you. Concentrate on having a heart filled with God's love and a soul that knows and loves him.

Today I Will . . .

Stop obsessing about weight. I'll take care of my body but focus my energy on knowing God better instead of worrying about every morsel that goes into my mouth.

"I'll start my diet tomorrow."

What Does the Bible Say about Difficulties?

Sometimes life stinks. Maybe your friends are being mean to you or you're having a hard time in school. Maybe you're dealing with something worse, like parents getting a divorce or someone you love being really sick. Difficulties come into all lives at one time or another. Does God care about your difficulties? Yes, he does. He cares very much. He stays right beside you during hard times. He'll help you and strengthen you and be your comforter.

What the Bible Says

The LORD is good,
a stronghold in the day of trouble;
he knows those who take refuge in him.

NAHUM 1:7

Cast your burden on the LORD,
and he will sustain you;
he will never permit
the righteous to be moved.

PSALM 55:22

Time to Face the Facts

When you were a child, did you have a special blanket or stuffed animal that was your comfort when you were upset? Kind of hard to have a blankie when you grow up though, right? Isn't it nice to know that God cares about the hard times in your life? He has given many promises about being your strength and comfort. He wants you to turn to him and trust him to be your strength as you go through difficult times.

"What will my folks say about this?"

Today I Will . . .

Read over the verses about God being my strength and comfort. I want to learn how to trust him so that I can experience his strength and comfort. I'm glad to be reminded that God cares for me so much.

What Does the Bible Say about Disappointments?

When you hang your hopes on something that's important to you and it doesn't happen, disappointment is what you feel. It hurts, and it sometimes takes a while to get over. Maybe you look around at other kids and think they never have disappointment. It may seem that way, but it's not true. Everyone has disappointments. Honest—everyone. When you are disappointed, how do you recover? What do you do? God can help you get through whatever you have to face. He is an expert at encouragement!

What the Bible Says

When in their distress they turned to the Lord, the God of Israel,
and sought him, he was found by them.

2 CHRONICLES 15:4

For you, O Lord, are my hope,
my trust, O Lord, from my youth.

PSALM 71:5

I am sure of this, that he who began a good work in you
will bring it to completion at the day of Jesus Christ.

PHILIPPIANS 1:6

Time to Face the Facts

Part of growing into a mature adult is learning how to handle disappointment. It's okay to be sad and disappointed sometimes, but it's important to learn how to get past the disappointment. Learning from disappointment and getting on with life shows maturity in your faith. The cool thing is that God will help you through this process; after all, there is absolutely no one who loves you more than he does!

Today I Will . . .

Look back over some of my big disappointments and see what lessons I can learn from those. I'll do my best to learn instead of complain when I'm disappointed. I know that God loves me and will help me, so I'll read his Word and ask him to teach me from it. I'll thank him every day for his love and care.

What Does the Bible Say about Discipleship?

Are you thinking, *what does discipleship have to do with anything else?* It is the kind of word that you hear more in relation to the Bible and Christian things than pretty much anything else. Discipleship really means being a student—learning from a teacher you trust and want to be like. So, yes, discipleship has a big place in learning to follow Christ. Of course, God wants you to learn to live like Christ, so he thinks discipleship is pretty important.

What the Bible Says

As for me and my house, we will serve the LORD.

JOSHUA 24:15

We all, with unveiled face, beholding the glory of the Lord, are being transformed into the same image from one degree of glory to another. For this comes from the Lord who is the Spirit.

2 CORINTHIANS 3:18

Have this mind among yourselves, which is yours in Christ Jesus, who, though he was in the form of God, did not count equality with God a thing to be grasped, but made himself nothing, taking the form of a servant, being born in the likeness of men.

PHILIPPIANS 2:5–7

Time to Face the Facts

A good student does the homework assigned and listens to the lessons the teacher explains. Often times a student will begin to think like a favorite teacher, speaking the same ideas and values. The student learns everything the teacher can teach. That's the goal of discipleship. Jesus is the best teacher and the best example of living for God and being a loving, obedient person. So, when you are his disciple, you learn to be more like Jesus!

Today I Will . . .

Become a disciple of Jesus. I'll study his messages in the Gospels, and I'll study his life to see how he lived and how he treated people. I want to be like him.

What Does the Bible Say about Discipline?

Are you looking forward to the day when you're a grown-up because you think grown-ups don't have to deal with discipline? Well, guess what—they do! Everyone is disciplined once in a while. Discipline is what happens when you've done something wrong or been disobedient. It's a corrective reminder to straighten up and fly right. God encourages you to accept his discipline with the right attitude, which is that discipline helps you learn to be more obedient to him.

What the Bible Says

Whoever loves discipline loves knowledge, but he who hates reproof is stupid.

PROVERBS 12:1

For the moment all discipline seems painful rather than pleasant, but later it yields the peaceful fruit of righteousness to those who have been trained by it.

HEBREWS 12:11

Time to Face the Facts

Okay, you don't like to be disciplined. No one does. But try this—think about discipline as a lesson in how to become a better person and a better God-follower. It's all about learning. If you were never disciplined, you would probably just keep on doing what you do and never learn. So, now that you know that . . . how do you feel about being disciplined?

"It's your turn to be in the doghouse."

Today I Will . . .

I think I get it. Discipline from God and even from my parents is a good thing because it's teaching me things. If I accept it and learn from it, I'll be a better person and a stronger Christian. In the scheme of my whole life, that's the goal, so now I understand that discipline is a good thing, and I won't fight it anymore.

What Does the Bible Say about Disease?

Being sick is no fun. Being really sick for a long time is even less fun. Why does there have to be sickness and disease anyway? Couldn't God just stop all the health problems and make everyone well? He does have that power, right? Yes, he does. This is always a tough thing to understand. God does have the power to heal all disease. He doesn't do it, though, because he doesn't usually go against the way things happen naturally. We live in a world where people get sick and die. What God does do is stay close beside you when you're sick or when someone you love is sick. He comforts and loves and strengthens you. And sometimes . . . he does heal diseases.

What the Bible Says

He gives power to the faint, and to him who has no might he increases strength.

ISAIAH 40:29

The prayer of faith will save the one who is sick, and the Lord will raise him up.

JAMES 5:15

Time to Face the Facts

God's plan was never for people to be sick. When he made the world and the first people, everything was perfect and there was no illness or disease. When sin came into the world, that changed everything. It must make God as sad as it does you when someone is sick. He doesn't stop sickness because it was man's choice to choose his own way over God's way. But God does care, and he will comfort and strengthen you. Just lean on him.

"I look so much better when I'm well!"

Today I Will . . .

Trust God. I never thought about him being sad about sickness, too. If he's sad, then I know he wants to comfort me and take care of me through sickness because he loves me.

DIVORCE

What Does the Bible Say about Divorce?

Divorce can tear up a family and rip out your heart. It's usually not a pretty situation, and the kids can be caught right in the middle of it. Does God care how painful this is for you? Yeah, he does care, and he will be your strength and foundation during the whole process.

What the Bible Says

The LORD is my strength and my shield;
in him my heart trusts, and I am helped;
my heart exults,
and with my song I give thanks to him.

PSALM 28:7

My flesh and my heart may fail,
but God is the strength of my heart
and my portion forever.

PSALM 73:26

He gives power to the faint,
and to him who has no might he increases strength.

ISAIAH 40:29

Time to Face the Facts

No one gets married with the plan to be divorced. It isn't God's plan either. However, it happens and it hurts. Sometimes it hurts the children most. God doesn't leave you alone to deal with that pain. He walks beside you and will be your strength if you will lean on him.

Today I Will . . .

Tell God how I feel about what's happening in our family. I'll ask him for strength and do my best to lean on him.

DOUBT

What Does the Bible Say about Doubt?

Do you ever doubt whether God exists? Do you doubt whether you are truly important to him? That's not a very secure way to live, is it? Doubt can creep into your thoughts so quietly. Sometimes it's just plain old doubt. Sometimes it's Satan planting doubt thoughts in your mind. What does God think about doubts? Bottom line is that he doesn't want you to have doubts. He says over and over in his Word that he loves and cares for you—you matter to him.

What the Bible Says

> For our heart is glad in him,
> because we trust in his holy name.

PSALM 33:21

> Trust in the LORD with all your heart,
> and do not lean on your own understanding.
> In all your ways acknowledge him,
> and he will make straight your paths.

PROVERBS 3:5–6

> Let us hold fast the confession of our hope without wavering,
> for he who promised is faithful.

HEBREWS 10:23

Time to Face the Facts

It all comes down to faith—believing that what God says is true. He does say over and over that he loves you. You are his child. He has a plan for your life. He cares for you and blesses you. It must make him sad when he has done so much for you but you still doubt whether he loves you. However, he probably understands how questions creep in when life gets hard, but all you have to do in times like that is read his Word and remember how he has taken care of you in the past.

Today I Will . . .

Ask God to help me trust. I know that his Word says he loves me. I want to believe it—even in the hard times. Doubting his care makes me feel sad and alone. It must make him sad, too. I want to trust his care.

What Does the Bible Say about Drama?

If you've been bitten by the acting bug, then drama—theater—may be your passion. The energy you get from an audience, the fun of playing another character, the message that can be taught from a play . . . it's all fun. But drama is really pretending, so how does God feel about that? Simple answer: he gave you the talents and abilities you have, so it brings him joy when you use them, especially if you use them to share the message of his love.

What the Bible Says

Go therefore and make disciples of all nations, baptizing them in the name of the Father and of the Son and of the Holy Spirit, teaching them to observe all that I have commanded you.

MATTHEW 28:19–20

Having gifts that differ according to the grace given to us, let us use them. . . .

ROMANS 12:6

He gave the apostles, the prophets, the evangelists, the shepherds and teachers, to equip the saints for the work of ministry, for building up the body of Christ.

EPHESIANS 4:11–12

Time to Face the Facts

Isn't that cool? God planted a passion in your heart and gave you the ability to do it. He also gives you opportunities to do the work he wants you to do. Be careful to choose ways to use drama that are pure and that either bring joy to people or teach them about God's love. He gave you drama and creativity, so use it with joy!

"Break a leg."

Today I Will . . .

Examine the choices of how I use my drama passion. Whether my passion is performing drama, writing it, or simply enjoying watching what others do, I will make sure that the plays or programs I see or participate in have a wholesome message or teach truths of God's love.

What Does the Bible Say about Dreams?

A giant blue tomato rolls down the street toward you. Just as it reaches you it stops and speaks to you, saying, "You always hurt the ones you love." Then it turns and rolls away. Weird? Yes? Dream? Yes. What's the purpose of dreams? You'll find that oftentimes in the Bible, God used dreams to speak to people. Okay, maybe not with giant blue tomatoes, but he did send special messages through dreams.

What the Bible Says

I will instruct you and teach you in the way you should go;
I will counsel you with my eye upon you.

PSALM 32:8

Hope deferred makes the heart sick, but a desire fulfilled is a tree of life.

PROVERBS 13:12

An angel of the Lord appeared to him in a dream. "Joseph, son of David, do not fear to take Mary as your wife. For that which is conceived in her is from the Holy Spirit."

MATTHEW 1:20

Time to Face the Facts

Some dreams are probably just dreams that mean your subconscious mind is working overtime. Sometimes those dreams are kind of fun. Other dreams could actually be God speaking to your subconscious mind as you sleep to give you directions and guidance. When you're so busy and your world is so noisy, God may be able to get your attention only in the stillness and silence of sleep. So, pay attention to your dreams.

"Attack of the giant tomato."

Today I Will . . .

Think about my dreams and see if there are any lessons I can draw from them. If I have one dream over and over, maybe I can ask someone older about it. Maybe talking about it will help me understand.

What Does the Bible Say about Drinking?

First of all, let's set the record straight: drinking does not refer to water . . . it refers to alcohol. Some kids think it makes them look cool to drink; after all, some teenagers and adults do it. What's the big deal? Does God really care what you do on a Friday night at a friend's house? Well, duh. Of course he cares, and yes, he cares about what you put into your body. He also knows what you do—even if you think you're hiding your drinking from your parents . . . God knows.

What the Bible Says

But the Lord is in his holy Temple; the Lord's throne is in heaven. His eyes see, his eyelids test the children of man.

PSALM 11:4

O Lord, you have searched me and known me! You know when I sit down and when I rise up; you discern my thoughts from afar.

PSALM 139:1-2

Do you not know that your body is a temple of the Holy Spirit within you, whom you have from God? You are not your own.

1 CORINTHIANS 6:19

Time to Face the Facts

Alcohol impairs your judgment; it's hard to think straight and make wise decisions when your brain is in an alcohol fog. That means you can be tempted to do things you wouldn't do if you were thinking straight. You may think that drinking makes you look cool—but it doesn't to the people who really matter. God's opinion should be most important to you. He knows that you're not old enough or mature enough to handle the effects of alcohol and what it does to your brain and that you might make unwise choices because of the alcohol fogging over your thought process. He also knows alcohol isn't good for your growing body. Take care of the one body and one brain he gave you.

Today I Will . . .

Make a choice, and it may be hard. I want to care more about God's opinion than what the cool kids think of me. I don't think it's a good idea for a kid my age to drink. Nothing good will come of it. I want to take care of my body and keep it healthy and strong so I can enjoy a long life and do good work for God.

What Does the Bible Say about Drug Abuse?

No doubt you know that drugs are available around you. Maybe you even know people who take drugs and talk about how good they make you feel or how they relax you or give you courage or whatever. So, if drugs do all those good things, then what's wrong with them? God says that your body is a temple where he lives. He says to take care of your body. Drugs change the way your mind works, making it work in a different way than God planned. The effects of the drugs can make you make unwise choices, even dangerous ones. There's another little issue, too . . . drugs are illegal.

What the Bible Says

Do not enter the path of the wicked, and do not walk in the way of the evil.
Avoid it; do not go on it; turn away from it and pass on.

PROVERBS 4:14–15

In everything the prudent acts with knowledge, but a fool flaunts his folly.

PROVERBS 13:16

Fix your thoughts on what is true, and honorable, and right, and pure, and lovely, and admirable. Think about things that are excellent and worthy of praise.

PHILIPPIANS 4:8

Time to Face the Facts

Just like drinking, drug abuse is very serious. Both drinking and drugs hurt your body, causing poor judgment and bad health. Both drinking and drugs can be addicting so that you never get enough, and finding ways to get money for more and more alcohol or drugs becomes all your focus. That leads to stealing things to sell or stealing money—even from your family and friends. Schoolwork is lost, friends are lost, everything is focused on how to get more. God is lost and health is lost. No good comes from getting hooked on drugs.

Today I Will . . .

Refuse to get involved in drugs. I know that drugs are available around me. I know kids who are already hooked on them. I understand that getting hooked on drugs sacrifices my life because it just takes over. I won't do that.

What Does the Bible Say about Eating?

Food . . . glorious food! Do you love to eat? Pizza, chips, ice cream! Yum! There's nothing wrong with eating is there? Of course, not, food is a gift from God. He made food! However, God encourages you to eat wisely—eat healthy food and don't get caught up in gluttony (eating like a pig). No good will come from that.

What the Bible Says

Be not among drunkards
or among gluttonous eaters of meat,
for the drunkard and the glutton will come to poverty,
and slumber will clothe them with rags.

PROVERBS 23:20–21

Therefore I tell you, do not be anxious about your life, what you will eat or what you will drink, nor about your body, what you will put on. Is not life more than food, and the body more than clothing? Look at the birds of the air: they neither sow nor reap nor gather into barns, and yet your heavenly Father feeds them. Are you not of more value than they?

MATTHEW 6:25–26

Time to Face the Facts

Food is good. Thank God for it. The danger where eating is concerned is that of overdoing it and gaining too much weight, which makes your body unhealthy. Moderation is the key. God has provided all food that is available. Eating is a social event. People often go to lunch or dinner together just for fun. So enjoy eating and thank God for food. But be wise about what you eat and how much you eat. And don't forget to share what you have with those who may not have enough to eat.

"So much to eat—so little time."

Today I Will . . .

Thank God for food.

What Does the Bible Say about Ecology?

You throw candy wrappers on the ground or plastic water bottles in the trash, so what? Maybe your dad dumps old paint or gasoline down the sewer, too. What's the big deal? The big deal is that God gave us this planet that was once filled with healthy water and air. He wants us to take care of the earth.

What the Bible Says

Let us make man in our image, after our likeness. And let them have dominion over the fish of the sea and over the birds of the heavens and over the livestock and over all the earth and over every creeping thing that creeps on the earth.

GENESIS 1:26

By the word of the LORD the heavens were made, and by the breath of his mouth all their host.

PSALM 33:6

All things were made through him, and without him was not any thing made that was made.

JOHN 1:3

Time to Face the Facts

God made the earth and everything in it. He gave people the job of taking care of it. Littering and polluting mess it up. It's his world—mess it up and it's like turning your back on him.

Today I Will . . .

Pick up garbage I see on the ground. Recycle and encourage others to do the same.

Reuse
Renew
Recycle

What Does the Bible Say about Education?

School, yippee! Do you enjoy school? Classes, homework, tests? Well some parts of school are more fun than others. Do you ever wonder if the stuff you're learning at school is really important? Will you use history or science or math in real life? Maybe you've even made the argument that you could be out working for God if you didn't have to go to school and do homework. Well . . . God isn't on your side with that argument. He wants you to learn everything you can—use that brain he gave you!

What the Bible Says

For the LORD gives wisdom;
from his mouth come knowledge and understanding.

PROVERBS 2:6

If any of you lacks wisdom, let him ask God, who gives generously
to all without reproach, and it will be given him.

JAMES 1:5

Time to Face the Facts

Someday you might have a high-powered, big money job; but for now, your job is to go to school. Actually, if you don't go to school that high-powered, big money job is a lot less likely to happen. Seriously, your job right now is to be the best student you can be. That's honoring to God because he gave you a brain to use and the chance to go to school. Of course, while you're going to school, you can treat others with love and respect, which is pleasing to him!

"I'm a smart cookie."

Today I Will . . .

Have a good attitude about going to school. I will listen to my teacher, do my homework, and learn everything I can. Sometimes it isn't fun, but I know it's building my future. So . . . I'll use the brain God gave me!

What Does the Bible Say about Embarrassment?

Being embarrassed is no fun. It means you've done something dumb in front of other people. They have probably laughed at you. Or maybe no one knows about your dumb move, but every time you think about it, you're embarrassed. It's no fun to feel like you're a goof-up. Does God care when you're embarrassed? Sure he does. God loves you and wants to be your strength and confidence.

What the Bible Says

The LORD is my light and my salvation; whom shall I fear?
The LORD is the stronghold of my life; of whom shall I be afraid?

PSALM 27:1

They who wait for the LORD shall renew their strength;
they shall mount up with wings like eagles;
they shall run and not be weary;
they shall walk and not faint.

ISAIAH 40:31

I do not cease to give thanks for you, remembering you in my prayers, that the God of our Lord Jesus Christ, the Father of glory, may give you a spirit of wisdom and of revelation in the knowledge of him, having the eyes of your hearts enlightened, that you may know what is the hope to which he has called you, what are the riches of his glorious inheritance in the saints, and what is the immeasurable greatness of his power toward us who believe. . . .

EPHESIANS 1:16–19

Time to Face the Facts

Everyone is embarrassed at some time, whether they admit it or not. You get embarrassed because you care what other people think. That's not a bad thing unless their opinion of you becomes more important than God's opinion. His opinion of you isn't based on one event or choice. He loves you and thinks you are very cool. So, find your strength in his opinion. He values you as a person.

Today I Will . . .

Try not to care so much what other people think of me. I want to care more about what God thinks. I understand that doing something dumb once in a while does not mean I'm a dumb person. When I feel that way though, I'll remember how special I am to God.

What Does the Bible Say about Emotions?

Do you sometimes feel like your emotions are riding on a roller coaster? One minute you're happily bouncing around and the next minute you're in a gray funk. What is that all about? Emotions do hop around based on circumstances and even your mood. That's why you shouldn't make important decisions based only on emotions. God knows your emotions change often, and he will help you handle them. Just tell him how you're feeling.

What the Bible Says

Be angry and do not sin; do not let the sun go down on your anger, and give no opportunity to the devil.

EPHESIANS 4:26–27

Casting all your anxieties on him, because he cares for you.

1 PETER 5:7

Time to Face the Facts

Emotions actually are a roller coaster, and you are about at the age where they start flying at high speed. Believe it or not, that's part of the process of growing up. God will help you control your emotions so that the words you speak and your actions do not just reflect what's happening in your emotions at the moment. Ask God to help you keep from spouting your emotions and hurting other people by your words.

"Lows & highs & everything in between."

Today I Will . . .

Ask God to help me. Sometimes my emotions surprise me. They seem to jump up and then take a dive. I don't want to hurt others by the words I speak when I'm angry or hurt. I'll ask God to help me control my responses and even to help my emotions to stay more even. I'm glad he cares. I'm glad he understands.

What Does the Bible Say about Empathy?

Empathy means caring about what other people are feeling and what they are going through. Well, it's more than just caring, it's more like sharing the pain or joy that they are experiencing. Empathy is part of loving others. God instructed his children to love other people as much as you love yourself. He loves you and has empathy for you. He wants you to do the same for others.

What the Bible Says

A new commandment I give to you, that you love one another: just as I have loved you, you also are to love one another.

JOHN 13:34

May the Lord make you increase and abound in love for one another and for all, as we do for you.

1 THESSALONIANS 3:12

Religion that is pure and undefiled before God, the Father, is this: to visit orphans and widows in their affliction, and to keep oneself unstained from the world.

JAMES 1:27

Time to Face the Facts

It's easy to say you love others and maybe even to mean it. But feeling empathy for what people around you are going through is love in action. When you care that much for them, you will be more likely to pray for them and to do what you can to help them. Empathy is the first step to putting feet on your faith. If you don't feel empathy, you may want to examine your love-o-meter and see if you need to work on that.

Today I Will . . .

Think about this. Do I love others enough to share their pain or joy? If I don't, then maybe I'm too self-focused. I'll ask God to help my love for others grow deeper . . . to the point that my prayers are focused on them and my actions show I care.

ENCOURAGEMENT

What Does the Bible Say about Encouragement?

Do you like to be encouraged? Sure you do. It's nice to know someone believes in you and wants you to succeed. Should you be encouraging other people? What do you think? God says to love other people as much as you can and, yes, to encourage them.

What the Bible Says

Therefore encourage one another and build one another up, just as you are doing.

1 THESSALONIANS 5:11

But exhort one another every day, as long as it is called "today," that none of you may be hardened by the deceitfulness of sin.

HEBREWS 3:13

And let us consider how to stir up one another to love and good works.

HEBREWS 10:24

Time to Face the Facts

All people on this planet are part of a team. That includes you. Helping your team members be the best they can be means they need encouragement, and that encouragement can come from you. Take the time to notice what people are good at and what they enjoy doing.

"You can do it. I'm here for you."

Today I Will . . .

Say something encouraging to a friend or family member. Encourage another person to keep working hard and learning more.

What Does the Bible Say about Enemies?

Is this how you pray sometimes: "Get 'em God. Take 'em down. Make 'em pay!" Of course, that would be your enemies you're talking about, not your friends. Do you want God to blast someone just because he or she is not your favorite person? Hmm, the thing is, God said you should love your enemies.

What the Bible Says

When a man's ways please the LORD,
he makes even his enemies to be at peace with him.

PROVERBS 16:7

You have heard that it was said, "You shall love your neighbor and hate your enemy."
But I say to you, Love your enemies and pray for those who persecute you.

MATTHEW 5:43–44

But love your enemies, and do good, and lend, expecting nothing in return,
and your reward will be great, and you will be sons of the Most High,
for he is kind to the ungrateful and the evil.

LUKE 6:35

Time to Face the Facts

Anyone can love his friends. It takes a person who is letting God love through her to love her enemies. That's what God said to do, though. Show his love to the world by loving even the people who are hard to love.

Today I Will . . .

Say or do something kind to someone I'm mad at a lot. I'll take the first step to making this person a friend. I'm going to need God's help for this.

"It's really going to be hard to dislike him after this."

What Does the Bible Say about the Environment?

Seems like someone is always talking about the environment. You're told to recycle, reuse, and conserve. Does God really care whether or not you do those things? Well, think about it . . . God made the world. He made the environment. He made clean air and clean water. He made trees and plants. He made the glaciers and the ozone layer. He made it all. So, of course he cares whether or not you take care of it.

What the Bible Says

Then God said, "Let us make man in our image, after our likeness. And let them have dominion over the fish of the sea and over the birds of the heavens and over the livestock and over all the earth and over every creeping thing that creeps on the earth."

GENESIS 1:26

By faith we understand that the universe was created by the word of God, so that what is seen was not made out of things that are visible.

HEBREWS 11:3

Time to Face the Facts

Have you ever created something? Maybe you wrote a story or drew a picture— whatever it was you were very proud of it. So, if anyone says anything negative about your work, it kind of hurts, right? Well, God made the world and everything in it. The world is really a gift for you to enjoy and appreciate. So, when you litter or waste energy, you aren't taking care of what God made. There is only one environment—take care of it.

"Aha! . . . Air you can see!"

Today I Will . . .

Think of things I can do to take care of the environment. I can start a campaign in my neighborhood encouraging everyone to recycle, reuse, and conserve energy. I want to take care of God's world!

What Does the Bible Say about Eternal Life?

Eternal? That means . . . um . . . forever, right? Why should you care about that? You're just a kid. Maybe it is even hard to think about next week for you, but eternal life is a really big topic in the Bible. God says that every single person is going to live forever. Where each person spends forever, well, that's up to each person. Forever can be spent with God in heaven, if you have accepted Jesus as your Savior. However, if you have not, then forever will be spent in hell where Satan reigns. God cares a lot about eternal life. He wants every person to be with him in heaven because he loves each person a lot!

What the Bible Says

For God so loved the world, that he gave his only Son, that whoever believes in him should not perish but have eternal life.

JOHN 3:16

In this the love of God was made manifest among us, that God sent his only Son into the world, so that we might live through him.

1 JOHN 4:9

For the wages of sin is death, but the free gift of God is eternal life in Christ Jesus our Lord.

ROMANS 6:23

Time to Face the Facts

God cares so much about your eternal life that he gave his own Son, Jesus, to die for you. He really wants you to accept Jesus as your Savior so you can be with him in heaven forever. He loves you a lot. It's your choice, though. You must understand that you are a sinner, ask forgiveness for those sins, and invite Jesus into your heart. When you do that, your eternal life in heaven is for sure.

Today I Will . . .

Ask Jesus to be my Savior, if I haven't already done that. If I have done that, then I'll keep reading my Bible and learning about God, Jesus, and heaven, my future home!

What Does the Bible Say about Evil?

Satan is not a nice guy. He is determined to do whatever he can to mess up your relationship with God. Evil is his tool, and it is all around you. Some people do terrible things to other people—that's evil. Not everything bad that happens in our world is caused by Satan, some things just happen. But Satan will always do his best to surround you with evil and tempt you to join in the evil. How does God feel about evil? He doesn't like it, and he does all he can to protect you from it.

What the Bible Says

He will deliver you from six troubles;
in seven no evil shall touch you.

JOB 5:19

A perverse heart shall be far from me;
I will know nothing of evil.

PSALM 101:4

The LORD will keep you from all evil;
he will keep your life.

PSALM 121:7

Time to Face the Facts

Evil is real, and it's pretty scary. Satan will stop at nothing to keep your faith in God from growing strong. You cannot fight evil on your own. Only God can defeat Satan. So, when you sense evil around you or when you are tempted to do evil things, turn to God for strength. He will help you, and he will protect you.

"The devil made me do it."

Today I Will . . .

Ask God to protect me from evil. The Psalms are full of prayers asking God for protection, so I know he will protect me. I'll also ask God to keep me from doing evil things. I want to live the way God wants, not the way Satan wants.

What Does the Bible Say about Excellence?

Do you think that the definition of excellence is different to different people? Excellence is not just better than average. It's not just pretty good. Excellence is amazing, wonderful, incredible. It is . . . excellent. Something to remember, though, is that true excellence is not possible apart from God. He is the creator of everything excellent, and everything he does is excellent. God cares about excellence in you, too. He encourages you to strive to be excellent . . . with his help.

What the Bible Says

And he gave the apostles, the prophets, the evangelists, the shepherds and teachers, to equip the saints for the work of ministry, for building up the body of Christ.

EPHESIANS 4:11–12

Earnestly desire the higher gifts. . . .

1 CORINTHIANS 12:31

As each has received a gift, use it to serve one another, as good stewards of God's varied grace: whoever speaks, as one who speaks oracles of God; whoever serves, as one who serves by the strength that God supplies—in order that in everything God may be glorified through Jesus Christ. To him belong glory and dominion forever and ever.

1 PETER 4:10–11

Time to Face the Facts

Pretty good just isn't good enough when it comes to serving God and living for him. Your goal is to become more and more like Christ—that's excellence! God will help you; in fact, he has already given you the gifts and abilities you need to serve him. You can ask him to help you develop them and use them with excellence.

Today I Will . . .

Strive for excellence. I know I can't achieve excellence by myself. I need God's help, and I must be serious about learning how to use the gifts and abilities he has given me. So, I will ask him to help me. I will not be willing to settle for pretty good when I know excellence is possible.

What Does the Bible Say about Excuses?

Okay, honesty time—how much time do you spend thinking up excuses for things you've messed up or not done? Some excuses are honest explanations, such as, "I couldn't do my homework because I was sick." Some excuses are not good, such as, "I cheated because someone dared me." How does God feel about excuses? He wants you to be honest and not blame others for your failures or mistakes.

What the Bible Says

Who shall ascend the hill of the LORD?
And who shall stand in his holy place?
He who has clean hands and a pure heart,
who does not lift up his soul to what is false
and does not swear deceitfully.

PSALM 24:3–4

Either make the tree good and its fruit good, or make the tree bad and its fruit bad, for the tree is known by its fruit.

MATTHEW 12:33

Time to Face the Facts

When you fail, you can make excuses til you're blue in the face. You may fool people around you. But you'll never fool God. All you'll do is disappoint him. He doesn't want excuses for why you disobey him or are unkind to others or fail in other ways. It's better to be honest and ask his forgiveness and strength to try again. Don't make excuses, make goals to do better.

"Really, I'd be home on time but there was this flying saucer . . ."

Today I Will . . .

Stop spouting excuses and just be honest with myself, others, and God. Everyone makes mistakes or fails sometimes. So, rather than deny it or blame someone else, I understand that it's better to admit my failures and strive to do better.

What Does the Bible Say about Failure?

Some people are so afraid of failing that they won't try anything new. These people have to be sure they can succeed before they will put forth any effort. Are you afraid of failing? Well, failure is no fun, that's for sure. But anyone courageous enough to try new things fails once in a while. How does God feel about failure? He appreciates the courage it takes to try new things. He wants you to learn from failure. He wants you not to be afraid of failure.

What the Bible Says

Be strong and courageous and do it. Do not be afraid and do not be dismayed, for the LORD God, even my God, is with you. He will not leave you or forsake you, until all the work for the service of the house of the LORD is finished.

1 CHRONICLES 28:20

The steadfast love of the LORD never ceases;
his mercies never come to an end;
they are new every morning;
great is your faithfulness.

LAMENTATIONS 3:22–23

My grace is sufficient for you, for my power is made perfect in weakness.

2 CORINTHIANS 12:9

Time to Face the Facts

Failure is not the end of the road. When you fail, you can at least be happy that you tried and you can learn from your failures and do better the next time you try. God doesn't want you to give up when you fail. He wants you to try again, with the knowledge you gained from trying the first time. He will help you with his incredible power and strength.

"If at first you don't succeed—stop trying???"

Today I Will . . .

Not be afraid to fail. If I don't ever try anything new, I'll spend the rest of my life just doing what I'm doing.

What Does the Bible Say about Fairness?

Life is not fair. That's the bottom line. You can complain all you want about that truth, but it won't change anything. Every person has unique circumstances to deal with and certain ways of dealing with them. So, don't waste time looking around at others and complaining that they have more than you do or have an easier life. Does God care that you think life isn't fair? He sees a bigger picture than you do. He knows that in the end the only fairness that matters is that he loves you and will help you with whatever you need.

What the Bible Says

God is a righteous judge,
and a God who feels indignation every day.

PSALM 7:11

The LORD works righteousness
and justice for all who are oppressed.

PSALM 103:6

So whatever you wish that others would do to you, do also to them,
for this is the Law and the Prophets.

MATTHEW 7:12

Time to Face the Facts

Yep, life isn't fair. Things happen to some people and not to others. But one thing you can depend on is that God is always fair. He loves you and will take care of you always. Remember to treat others fairly and with respect . . . just as God treats you.

Today I Will . . .

Stop complaining about what's fair and what isn't. I'll just deal with the stuff life gives me and trust God to help me through it all.

"At least I didn't drop the winning pass in the big game. That woudl REALLY stink."

What Does the Bible Say about Faith?

What *doesn't* the Bible say about faith? That's about all you hear talked about at church, isn't it? What does "faith" mean, though? When you have faith in something, you believe in it . . . but you don't just believe in it a little; it's like you trust your very life to this thing. You believe it so much, so completely that you can trust your life to it. God wants your faith in him to be that deep and strong.

What the Bible Says

And whatever you ask in prayer,
you will receive, if you have faith.

MATTHEW 21:22

Truly, truly, I say to you, whoever hears my
word and believes him who sent me has
eternal life. He does not come into judgment,
but has passed from death to life.

JOHN 5:24

Now faith is the assurance of things hoped for,
the conviction of things not seen.

HEBREWS 11:1

Time to Face the Facts

It's impossible to please God unless you have faith in him. Trusting him shows that you believe he is in control of all things and that he loves you more than anything. It's not always easy, but it's the basis of the Christian life. One important way to grow your faith is to know God better. Read your Bible and get to know him, his character, and how he has worked in the lives of his people. As you get to know him better, you will trust him more.

Today I Will . . .

Start reading my Bible every day. I want to know God more and more so that my faith in him will grow stronger. I know there are times when faith is hard, but I want those to become less and less and my faith to be the most important thing in my life.

What Does the Bible Say about Fame?

Who wouldn't want to be famous . . . at least for good reasons? Being famous means people know who you are and they usually clamor to be around you and get your attention. It usually means you're rich, too. How cool is that? People seem to care a lot about the opinions of famous musicians or actors or politicians. But the Bible says that fame should not be your goal in life. Humble people have a great place in God's world. If you do become famous, use that responsibility well.

What the Bible Says

Beware of practicing your righteousness before other people in order to be seen by them, for then you will have no reward from your Father who is in heaven.

MATTHEW 6:1

Whoever humbles himself like this child is the greatest in the kingdom of heaven.

MATTHEW 18:4

Clothe yourselves, all of you, with humility toward one another, for God opposes the proud but gives grace to the humble.

1 PETER 5:5–6

Time to Face the Facts

If God directs your life to the place where you become famous, use your fame to direct people's attention to God, not yourself. Fame has a responsibility that goes with it. Be careful how you view famous people, too. Don't adopt their views on life simply because they are famous. No one and nothing should be more important than God.

"Can we have your autograph?"

Today I Will . . .

Change my opinion of famous people. I mean, I shouldn't have to do what they do or think what they think just because they are famous. God is most important in my heart, and he is the one I want to be like.

What Does the Bible Say about Family?

Families were God's idea from the very beginning when he created Eve to be with Adam. Families are a great place to learn about God as parents teach children about their faith. Families are also places where you know you're loved unconditionally, no matter what. Oh sure, families can make you crazy sometimes, but when push comes to shove, they should be the ones you can count on. God gave instructions to love and respect family members and to pass along faith through the family. He even calls all Christians his family.

What the Bible Says

These words that I command you today shall be on your heart. You shall teach them diligently to your children, and shall talk of them when you sit in your house, and when you walk by the way, and when you lie down, and when you rise.

DEUTERONOMY 6:6–7

My son, keep your father's commandment,
and forsake not your mother's teaching.
Bind them on your heart always;
tie them around your neck.
When you walk, they will lead you;
when you lie down, they will watch over you;
and when you awake, they will talk with you.

PROVERBS 6:20–22

Finally, all of you, have unity of mind, sympathy, brotherly love,
a tender heart, and a humble mind.

1 PETER 3:8

Time to Face the Facts

Even if your family sometimes makes you crazy, you know they all truly love you and you love them. Family should be a safe place where you can be yourself and you can love and encourage one another. You have a responsibility there, too, to be encouraging and loving and helpful. Be a good child and a good sibling.

Today I Will . . .

Thank God for my family. Love them with all my heart and try to get along with each family member.

What Does the Bible Say about Fasting?

So . . . you love your cheeseburgers and fries. You couldn't make it through a weekend without ice cream, and pizza is a life need. That means fasting is pretty much not a valid consideration, right? Do you have trouble understanding why anyone would want to go days without eating? Well, fasting is not skipping meals just for the sake of skipping meals. It's a way to focus your attention on God. Instead of eating, you pray and think about him. So, yeah, fasting has a lot to do with the Bible.

What the Bible Says

> You will seek me and find me, when you seek me with all your heart.
>
> **JEREMIAH 29:13**

> When you fast, do not look gloomy like the hypocrites, for they disfigure their faces that their fasting may be seen by others. Truly, I say to you, they have received their reward. But when you fast, anoint your head and wash your face, that your fasting may not be seen by others but by your Father who is in secret. And your Father who sees in secret will reward you.
>
> **MATTHEW 6:16–18**

Time to Face the Facts

You have to figure that fasting is pretty important if Jesus did it. He did—for forty days! Okay, that may be a little extreme for you. But it was what Jesus needed to do to focus his attention on God and find strength in God's power. There are several examples in Scripture of people fasting in order to find God's direction and to be dependent on him. So, would you be willing to fast, say for a day, in order to grow closer to God and seek his direction in your life?

"Looks good but God is more important"

Today I Will . . .

I want to have the right attitude of seeking to grow closer to God. I'm going to pray about that before I commit to fasting.

What Does the Bible Say about Fear?

No one wants to be considered a fraidycat, so some people put on a big show of being super-brave when inside they are one big quivering ball of fear. What scares you? Really, what scares you enough to keep you awake at night? Why are you so afraid of it? Where does fear play into the whole "trust God and he will take care of you thing?" Yeah, that is key because God wants you to trust him and believe that he will take care of you. He promises to do that.

What the Bible Says

God is our refuge and strength,
a very present help in trouble.
Therefore we will not fear though the earth gives way,
though the mountains be moved into the heart of the sea.

PSALM 46:1–2

For he will command his angels concerning you to guard you in all your ways.

PSALM 91:11

Time to Face the Facts

Some things in this crazy world are scary—there's no getting away from that. Sometimes it's even smart to be afraid because it keeps you from doing something dangerous or dumb. But generally speaking, trusting God is the antidote to fear. He has power and authority over everything in the world, and he promised to take care of you. So, when you think about it there is really no reason to be afraid of anything . . . if you trust him.

"I really want to trust God. It is just a little easier with this on."

Today I Will . . .

Tell God what scares me. Then I will ask him to help me trust him more and more. My head knows there is no reason to be afraid but my heart sometimes gets scared anyway. I want to learn how to trust God more.

FIGHTING

What Does the Bible Say about Fighting?

Sisters, brothers, friends . . . who do you most often fight with? Some people are just easy to fight with, aren't they? They just seem to ask for it by being pushy or bossy or selfish or whatever. But do you ever wonder how God feels about your fighting? Well, that's an easy answer because God said the second greatest commandment is for people to love each other. How do you fight with someone all the time and still love him?

What the Bible Says

Whoever restrains his words has knowledge,
and he who has a cool spirit is a man of understanding.

PROVERBS 17:27

You have heard that it was said, "You shall love your neighbor and hate your enemy."
But I say to you, "Love your enemies and pray for those who persecute you, so that you
may be sons of your Father who is in heaven. For he makes his sun rise on the
evil and on the good, and sends rain on the just and on the unjust.

MATTHEW 5:43–45

Every kingdom divided against itself is laid waste,
and no city or house divided against itself will stand.

MATTHEW 12:25

Time to Face the Facts

Okay, it only makes sense that sometimes you get angry at your friends or family members. But what you do with that anger is important. Punching someone or calling them names is not the way to handle anger. If you have a problem with someone, talk with them about it and try to settle things peaceably. Want to know a secret for getting along with others? Pray for them. It's hard to fight with someone you are praying for. So, pray and love—much better than fighting.

Today I Will . . .

Stop fighting all the time. The suggestion to pray for people I'm mad at just might work. I'll try that and see if I can have more peaceful relationships with those around me.

FORGIVENESS

What Does the Bible Say about Forgiveness?

The truth is that some things are hard to forgive, like when a friend tells lies about you or doesn't stand up for you or something like that. Do you ever get so mad that there is no way you can forgive? What does God think about that? He understands, right? Sorry, Charlie. God forgives you for a bunch of stuff all the time, and he wants you to pass that forgiveness along to others.

What the Bible Says

If my people who are called by my name humble themselves, and pray and seek my face and turn from their wicked ways, then I will hear from heaven and will forgive their sin and heal their land.

2 CHRONICLES 7:14

If your brother sins, rebuke him, and if he repents, forgive him, and if he sins against you seven times in the day, and turns to you seven times, saying, "I repent," you must forgive him.

LUKE 17:3–4

If we confess our sins, he is faithful and just to forgive us our sins and to cleanse us from all unrighteousness.

1 JOHN 1:9

Time to Face the Facts

Be honest now, God forgives you for *a lot*, right? Even when you keep doing the same dumb thing over and over, he keeps forgiving. He loves you, that's why. He tells you in the verse in Luke to forgive, forgive, forgive when other people hurt you. Let love rule your heart, not anger.

Today I Will . . .

Forgive someone whom I've been holding a grudge against. I'll just let it go.

What Does the Bible Say about Fortune-Telling?

Wouldn't you like to know what the future holds? Do you wonder if you'll be rich or famous when you grow up? Will you be a successful surgeon or a teacher? Will you live in a city or out in the country? Yeah, it would be nice to know the future. Some people think fortune-tellers or horoscopes can accurately predict the future. Not so. God is the only one who really and truly knows what your future holds. He has had a plan for you since before you were born. If you want to know your future . . . turn to God. He wrote the book on it.

What the Bible Says

Trust in the LORD with all your heart,
and do not lean on your own understanding.
In all your ways acknowledge him,
and he will make straight your paths.

PROVERBS 3:5–6

For I know the plans I have for you, declares the LORD, plans for welfare and not for evil, to give you a future and a hope.

JEREMIAH 29:11

Time to Face the Facts

It's normal to be curious about the future. But rather than putting stock in fortune cookies or fortune-tellers or horoscopes, turn to God. He's the one with the answers. He planned out your life even before you were born. So, read his Word and spend time praying to him. Ask him to direct your life and guide your steps. He does have a plan for you, and he will gladly reveal it to you if you seek that answer with your whole heart and mind.

Today I Will . . .

Read my Bible and pray every day. I will get to know God better and better so that I will know when it is him directing my steps and guiding me. I know he has a plan for my life, and I want to follow his plan.

"I see that you owe me $20."

What Does the Bible Say about Free Time?

Free time—no homework, no chores, nothing to do but hang out. What's your favorite thing to do with your free time? Read; play sports; hang out with friends; play video games; sleep . . . there's a bunch of things to choose from. Does God care what you do with free time? Well, yeah, he actually does. While God knows that you need down time and some fun in your life, he warns against wasting your time doing foolish things. Spend your time in ways that connect you with others or with God.

What the Bible Says

And now, Israel, what does the Lord your God require of you, but to fear the Lord your God, to walk in all his ways, to love him, to serve the Lord your God with all your heart and with all your soul, and to keep the commandments and statutes of the Lord, which I am commanding you today for your good?

DEUTERONOMY 10:12–13

And if it is evil in your eyes to serve the Lord, choose this day whom you will serve, whether the gods your fathers served in the region beyond the River, or the gods of the Amorites in whose land you dwell. But as for me and my house, we will serve the Lord.

JOSHUA 24:15

You shall love the Lord your God with all your heart and with all your soul and with all your mind. This is the great and first commandment. And a second is like it: You shall love your neighbor as yourself.

MATTHEW 6:37–39

Time to Face the Facts

There's nothing wrong with reading, playing sports, hanging out with friends, or even playing video games. The thing to be careful about is whether the things you do in your free time hurt anyone else. Also, if your free time activity is messing up someone else's property . . . not good. Use free time to relax and to connect with other people and even to worship and learn about God. Free time doesn't mean wasting time.

Today I Will . . .

Use my free time to do something nice for someone else or to memorize a Bible verse or do a job for my mom or dad—without being asked!

FREEDOM

What Does the Bible Say about Freedom?

The thing about freedom is that if you have it—if you live in a free country where you can go where you want or attend the church you want—then you probably don't think about freedom very much. You take freedom for granted. Those who have served in the military will tell you that freedom is not free. It cost something, usually the lives of soldiers. What is freedom anyway? Where does it come from? Here's a different take on freedom: true freedom comes only from knowing God.

What the Bible Says

Now the Lord is the Spirit, and where the Spirit of the Lord is, there is freedom.

2 CORINTHIANS 3:17

For you were called to freedom, brothers. Only do not use your freedom as an opportunity for the flesh, but through love serve one another.

GALATIANS 5:13

Live as people who are free, not using your freedom as a cover-up for evil, but living as servants of God.

1 PETER 2:16

Time to Face the Facts

Real freedom comes from knowing and serving God. It may sound like knowing God's Word and obeying him is the exact opposite of freedom, but that's not true. God loves you and knows what's best for your life and for getting along with others. That's freedom. So, thank God for the freedom you have to worship him and to live in freedom. Then understand that real freedom in life is found only in obeying God.

"It costs a lot to be free!"

Today I Will . . .

Appreciate the freedom I have because of where I live. Understand that living the Christian life is not living by a bunch of rules that keep me tied up.

What Does the Bible Say about Friends?

Come on, everyone has friends. Seriously, does God care whether or not you have friends? Does the Bible say anything about how you should treat your friends? Well, yeah. God cares. He knows that friends are a blessing who make life more enjoyable.

What the Bible Says

A friend loves at all times,
and a brother is born for adversity.

PROVERBS 17:17

Oil and perfume make the heart glad,
and the sweetness of a friend comes from his earnest counsel.

PROVERBS 27:9

Greater love has no one than this,
that someone lay down his life for his friends.

JOHN 15:13

Time to Face the Facts

Don't take your friends for granted. Enjoy them, love them, help them, and be kind to them. Let them be a friend to you, too, by allowing them to do those same things for you. Bottom line—don't be selfish or crabby to your friends. Be kind and loving instead.

Today I Will . . .

Tell my friends that I appreciate them. Thank God for them. Be nice.

BFF!

FRUSTRATION

What Does the Bible Say about Frustration?

Frustration is so . . . frustrating. It's not really anger. It's not really giving up. It's definitely not success. Disappointment, loss, and defeat can make you feel frustrated. Sometimes when you're frustrated, you can feel as though things will never get better and you'll always be stuck in the mud of frustration. How does God feel about frustration? He would want you to remember that whatever caused your frustration is just temporary. It won't last forever. He encourages you to "keep on keeping on." Work through the problem or disappointment and when you get to the other side of it you will be a lot stronger.

What the Bible Says

Have I not commanded you? Be strong and courageous. Do not be frightened, and do not be dismayed, for the LORD your God is with you wherever you go.

JOSHUA 1:9

You ask and do not receive, because you ask wrongly, to spend it on your passions.

JAMES 4:3

Time to Face the Facts

Frustration is tiring. It wears you out emotionally, and the situation that causes frustration takes a lot of mental energy because it's hard to think about anything else. You probably get frustrated because things don't go your way. So, working through frustration means giving up your own will and submitting to what God wants. God is your strength and power. When you "keep on keeping on," you trust God's strength and guidance and you just keep going through the problem instead of giving in to the frustration.

Today I Will . . .

Not give up. I believe God is the strength I need to keep going. Just because I'm frustrated doesn't mean I should give up. I'll trust God and his guidance to get me through this situation.

"My brain is on vacation."

What Does the Bible Say about Gangs?

Gangs are scary. Gang members have the reputation of bullying kids who are not part of their particular gang. Different gangs fight each other, and someone always gets hurt or even killed in that battle for power. It might feel good, in one way, to belong to a gang because it feels good to belong to something. But if you care about obeying God, the whole gang mentality will not be comfortable for you. Why? Because God says the most important thing (after loving and obeying him) is how you treat other people. Humility and love are important in relationships.

What the Bible Says

Hatred stirs up strife, but love covers all offenses.

PROVERBS 10:12

By this all people will know that you are my disciples, if you have love for one another.

JOHN 13:35

Love is patient and kind; love does not envy or boast; it is not arrogant or rude. It does not insist on its own way; it is not irritable or resentful; it does not rejoice at wrongdoing, but rejoices with the truth. Love bears all things, believes all things, hopes all things, endures all things.

1 CORINTHIANS 13:4–7

Time to Face the Facts

Sure it feels good to belong to a group. There is security in that. But belonging to a group that pushes other kids around or even hurts others in a battle for power and control is not a godly thing at all. From God's viewpoint, power and control are nothing, because his power and control are all that matter. God says to love one another and to encourage others to be all that they can be. If your gang doesn't do that . . . get out of it.

Today I Will . . .

Think about whether my group of friends might be considered a gang. I'll think about how we treat other people or other groups of people. If we have a gang mentality, I'll try to change it. If I can't change it, I'll drop out of it. I want to obey God and love others.

GENEROSITY

What Does the Bible Say about Generosity?

Are you pretty good at sharing? For example, if you have ten cookies, you might give one to a friend, right? Or, if you have several dollars in your pocket, you would gladly buy a soft drink for yourself and a friend. But what if you only have one cookie or only enough money for one soft drink? Are you generous when you just have a little bit of something or are you generous only out of your extra stuff? True generosity gives even when it hurts. That's what God said: help one another anytime you can and share what you have.

What the Bible Says

Both riches and honor come from you, and you rule over all. . . .
1 CHRONICLES 29:12

You will be enriched in every way to be generous in every way, which through us will produce thanksgiving to God.
2 CORINTHIANS 9:11

Time to Face the Facts

Trying to accumulate more and more stuff while other people don't have what they need to live is just wrong. God said that people of faith show their faith by helping others. He said to take care of widows and orphans. It's putting your faith in action to be generous to others—generous, even when it hurts. So, give, share, and help anytime you can. Even if it takes time out of your busy schedule or takes money or "stuff" that means a lot to you.

"If I have two cookies, then you've got one."

Today I Will . . .

Stop holding on to stuff. I will look around me and notice people who need help. I will be generous with my time and with my stuff. It's a cool way to show that I love God and that God loves everyone.

GENTLENESS

What Does the Bible Say about Gentleness?

There isn't much gentleness in our world. Need proof? Watch the evening news or even a prime time show. Play a video game. Drive down the highway and notice how drivers treat one another. There is not much gentleness. Why is gentleness important? Because it is kind and is the right thing to do. Jesus was gentle. He modeled gentleness for all mankind. Gentleness doesn't mean weakness; in fact, it's power under control.

What the Bible Says

The LORD passed by, and a great and strong wind tore the mountains and broke in pieces the rocks before the LORD, but the LORD was not in the wind. And after the wind an earthquake, but the LORD was not in the earthquake. And after the earthquake a fire, but the LORD was not in the fire. And after the fire the sound of a low whisper.

1 KINGS 19:11–12

A soft answer turns away wrath,
but a harsh word stirs up anger.

PROVERBS 15:1

Put on then, as God's chosen ones, holy and beloved, compassionate hearts, kindness, humility, meekness, and patience, bearing with one another and, if one has a complaint against another, forgiving each other; as the Lord has forgiven you, so you also must forgive.

COLOSSIANS 3:12–13

Time to Face the Facts

Gentleness does not mean wimpiness. Power and strength out of control is what the world already has. Power and strength under control is gentleness—power that considers the feelings of others and tries to interact with others in a way that shows respect. That's gentleness. This kind of behavior brings peace to the hearts of others. God deals gently with his children and calls his children to deal with others in the same way.

Today I Will . . .

Think about how I treat others. I know I'm not always gentle and respectful with others. Usually getting my own way is more important than being gentle. But I want to learn to treat others the way God wants me to . . . gently. It will be a nice change from other stuff going on in our world.

What Does the Bible Say about Gifts and Talents?

Does it bug you that some people seem to be able to do amazing things? Do you sometimes wish that you could do the things other people do so easily? Playing the piano, sports, getting good grades, singing . . . whatever it is. How does God feel about your wishing dreams? He may be smiling at you because he knows he has given you specific gifts and talents. It's true. God says that every person has gifts and talents to do exactly what he wants them to do.

What the Bible Says

Having gifts that differ according to the grace given to us, let us use them: if prophecy, in proportion to our faith; if service, in our serving; the one who teaches, in his teaching; the one who exhorts, in his exhortation; the one who contributes, in generosity; the one who leads, with zeal; the one who does acts of mercy, with cheerfulness.

ROMANS 12:6–8

Time to Face the Facts

God put you on this planet to do specific work for him. He gave you the talents and gifts you need to do those jobs. He promised that. Now, you may need to explore those talents and develop them, but they are there inside you already. Don't waste time wishing you had someone else's abilities or talents. Work on your own talents and seek God's guidance as to what he wants you to do.

Today I Will . . .

Stop wishing that I could have different gifts or talents. I'll stop and think about the things I love to do because my gifts and talents are probably connected to those things I love. So, I'll work on those things and get better and better and watch to see how God will use them.

"How did she learn that?"

What Does the Bible Say about Giving?

Giving is not just about giving money in an offering. A bigger way of giving is giving your time to others when they need help. Giving your sympathy and kindness. Yeah, that kind of giving is sometimes harder because it takes more time and emotional investment. It sure is nice though when you're the one who needs help and someone gives to you, isn't it? How does God feel about giving to others? Wow, he likes it because it shows love to others and that's what he wants from people.

What the Bible Says

For I was hungry and you gave me food, I was thirsty and you gave me drink,
I was a stranger and you welcomed me, I was naked and you clothed me,
I was sick and you visited me, I was in prison and you came to me.

MATTHEW 25:35–36

Religion that is pure and undefiled before God, the Father, is this:
to visit orphans and widows in their affliction, and to keep
oneself unstained from the world.

JAMES 1:27

Beloved, let us love one another, for love is from God,
and whoever loves has been born of God and knows God.

1 JOHN 4:7

Time to Face the Facts

The Bible says that the more you give, the more you receive. What does that mean? If you give some money, you'll get more back? No, that's not what the Scripture means. It means that if you give of yourself (your time and emotions) you'll be blessed by the appreciation of others. You'll see how you matter in other people's lives and how God uses you to help and encourage others.

Today I Will . . .

Be willing to give of my time and emotions to help and connect with others. I see how I can be God's hands and heart in the lives of those around me if I'm just willing to do it.

GOALS

What Does the Bible Say about Goals?

There's a saying that if you want to make God smile, tell him your plans. Why is that true? Because you aren't really in control of your life, he is. You can set goals and make plans, but God's plans and goals are the only ones that truly matter. It's better to seek God's guidance and direction in your life and make your only goal to get to know him better and be more obedient to him.

What the Bible Says

Do not boast about tomorrow, for you do not know what a day may bring.

PROVERBS 27:1

Come now, you who say, "Today or tomorrow we will go into such and such a town and spend a year there and trade and make a profit"—yet you do not know what tomorrow will bring. What is your life? For you are a mist that appears for a little time and then vanishes. Instead you ought to say, "If the Lord wills, we will live and do this or that."

JAMES 4:13–15

Time to Face the Facts

People may constantly ask you what you want to be when you grow up or what your plans are. Those are normal questions, and it's okay to think about those things. But before you make certain plans to move toward certain goals, be sure you pray about your plans and seek God's direction and guidance. Let him set your goals and plans and let them develop as you get to know him better.

"I have it all planned out. Now I just need to check with God."

Today I Will . . .

Begin asking God what his plans are for my life. Commit to spend time reading the Bible every day and praying for God's direction and guidance. I want his goals and plans to be my goals and plans.

GOD'S GLORY

What Does the Bible Say about God's Glory?

Well, that's a silly question. God's glory has everything to do with the Bible, doesn't it? Yes, throughout the Bible God is honored and glorified. His power is told, his love is shown, his strength is evident. The Bible speaks about God's glory on every page. What do you do with that information?

What the Bible Says

O LORD, our Lord,
how majestic is your name in all the earth!
You have set your glory above the heavens.

PSALM 8:1

Who is this King of glory?
The LORD, strong and mighty,
the LORD, mighty in battle!

PSALM 24:8

And the Word became flesh and dwelt among us,
and we have seen his glory, glory as of the only
Son from the Father, full of grace and truth.

JOHN 1:14

Time to Face the Facts

When you read about God's glory and power, it can just make you want to drop to your knees and worship him. Recognizing his glory puts all things into perspective. Little things don't really matter that much and any problems you have can be trusted to this magnificent God. He is glorious and more powerful than anything or anyone else. You can trust him.

Today I Will . . .

It's hard to imagine God's glory. I can see some of it in the nature around me. But I only really know it by reading my Bible and seeing his glory. I know that the more I understand his glory, the more I will trust him with my life.

GOD'S LOVE

What Does the Bible Say about God's Love?

Duh . . . there wouldn't be a Bible if it weren't for God's love. Do you ever doubt that God truly loves *you* . . . not just mankind, but *you*? Do you need some convincing? Well, all you have to do is look around you for plenty of evidences: the beautiful world he created; the freedom you have to worship him; your family; your friends; his guidance and direction; and the greatest gift of all . . . his Son, Jesus.

What the Bible Says

> For God so loved the world, that he gave his only Son, that whoever believes in him should not perish but have eternal life.
>
> **JOHN 3:16**

> In this is love, not that we have loved God but that he loved us and sent his Son to be the propitiation for our sins.
>
> **1 JOHN 4:10**

Time to Face the Facts

Sometimes it is hard to "feel" God's love because life can be a little painful and difficult at times. But at those times, there are two things you need to do. The first one is remember. Remember what he has done for you in the past. Remember the ways he has shown his love to you. The second is to read his Word. Let him tell you how much he loves you. As you read about his care and the sacrifice of Jesus' life, you'll be reminded how very, very much he loves *you*!

Today I Will . . .

Remember. God has shown his love for me in many ways. The truth of that gets lost in my problems sometimes and I forget his love. So, I'll remember, and I'll read his Word and be convinced again of his incredible love for me.

"I can just feel God's love. I hope everybody can."

What Does the Bible Say about God's Protection?

The world can be a scary place—some people are mean and want to do bad things to others. Accidents happen, tragedy strikes. But you can't live your life in a bubble to protect you from any of that. So, what do you do? Scripture is full of God's promises of protection. He loves you and will take care of you.

What the Bible Says

The LORD is a stronghold for the oppressed,
a stronghold in times of trouble.

PSALM 9:9

Oh, how abundant is your goodness,
which you have stored up for those who fear you
and worked for those who take refuge in you,
in the sight of the children of mankind!
In the cover of your presence you hide them
from the plots of men;
you store them in your shelter
from the strife of tongues.

PSALM 31:19–20

But the Lord is faithful. He will establish you and guard you against the evil one.

2 THESSALONIANS 3:3

Time to Face the Facts

Okay, God loves you and will take care of you. Does that mean you will never have problems, illnesses, or accidents? Not necessarily. Sure, sometimes God does physically protect you. Sometimes he does that when you don't even know it. But God will take care of the most important part of you—your heart. He will protect your heart from the evil of Satan and the temptations that cross your path every day. God cares a lot about your heart.

Today I Will . . .

Seek God's protection. It's okay to ask him to physically protect me and my loved ones. I'll also ask him to protect my heart from the temptations that I so easily give in to.

What Does the Bible Say about Goodness?

Goodness? What does that mean? What it does not mean is being good at something such as sports or music or math. A person whose goodness shows through is a person who looks like God. A "good person" is one who shows God's love, fairness, kindness, compassion, and goodness by how he or she treats other people. A person filled with goodness is one who is becoming more and more like God.

What the Bible Says

Behold, I long for your precepts; in your righteousness give me life!

PSALM 119:40

The good person out of his good treasure brings forth good, and the evil person out of his evil treasure brings forth evil.

MATTHEW 12:35

Time to Face the Facts

Goodness like this doesn't just happen . . . it takes an effort. A person desiring to become more like God must get to know him better and better. That happens by reading his Word and talking with him. It also helps to spend time with other Christians who already know him well. Goodness like this cannot be faked because it shows in the way you treat other people . . . all people, not just your friends.

Today I Will . . .

Take an honest look at myself. Sure, I'm kind, fair, and loving to my friends, but what about to others? I never thought about the fact that my actions show my heart's true opinion of God. I want to respect and love him. I want to honor him with my actions toward others. So, I'm going to need to spend more time reading his Word and just being still before him so he can grow my heart to be good.

"Grandpa, you're so good to me."

What Does the Bible Say about Gossip?

The Bible says something about gossip? Well, that stinks. God really cares about something like that? Of course he cares. Think about it . . . does gossip do any good for anyone? Nope. It only hurts. Gossip hurts reputations and breaks up friendships. The bottom line is that it hurts people. That is directly opposite of what God wants.

What the Bible Says

Whoever goes about slandering reveals secrets,
but he who is trustworthy in spirit keeps a thing covered.

PROVERBS 11:13

Let no corrupting talk come out of your mouths, but only such as is good for building up, as fits the occasion, that it may give grace to those who hear.

EPHESIANS 4:29

Time to Face the Facts

Maybe you're thinking, *But gossip is so easy, and my friends and I don't mean to hurt anyone. We make each other laugh with silly comments. It's all in fun.* Yeah, well, it's not so much fun for the person who is the topic of your silly comments. Put yourself in that person's shoes for a while and you'll probably want to go barefoot. God's commands are for you to love others. There is no way gossip is showing love to anyone.

"I wouldn't think of gossiping, but did you hear . . . ?"

Today I Will . . .

Think about the things my friends and I talk about. When we're gossiping about someone—even if it's comments that are just to get a laugh—I'll think about how our comments are hurting another person. I wouldn't want to be the topic of anyone else's gossip, so in the whole "do unto others as you want them to do unto you" theme, I'll stop gossiping.

GRACE

What Does the Bible Say about Grace?

When your teacher says an assignment is due on Monday but you don't get it finished so she gives you until Wednesday to turn it in . . . that's grace. It's called a grace period. Cool, huh? God is the major grace-giver. In church terms, grace is defined as undeserved favor or mercy when you don't expect it. God offers you salvation and eternity with him for nothing! It's free; all you have to do is accept it.

What the Bible Says

For the law was given through Moses; grace and truth came through Jesus Christ.

JOHN 1:17

All have sinned and fall short of the glory of God, and are justified by his grace as a gift, through the redemption that is in Christ Jesus, whom God put forward as a propitiation by his blood, to be received by faith. This was to show God's righteousness, because in his divine forbearance he had passed over former sins.

ROMANS 3:23–25

Now the law came in to increase the trespass, but where sin increased, grace abounded all the more.

ROMANS 5:20

Time to Face the Facts

Imagine that; salvation is free because of God's grace. There's no way you can earn your way into heaven. There is nothing you can do to deserve it. Just thank him for his mercy and grace in loving you and planning eternity for you. He loves you . . . simply loves you and wants you with him forever. Sometimes grace is defined as *God's riches at Christ's expense*. Your eternity in heaven is secured because Christ died for your sins. All you need to do is believe and accept. That's grace.

Today I Will . . .

Thank God for his amazing love. That love is why he shows grace to me. I know I don't deserve it, but I'm really thankful for it. Because of his grace, I will show grace to others through kindness and forgiveness. I hope God's grace will flow through me.

What Does the Bible Say about Grandparents?

Grandparents can be cool. Sometimes they like to buy you things, right? They usually don't have as many rules as parents do. But how does God feel about grandparents? Oh, he thinks they're cool, too. Know why? Because grandparents raised your parents, and they can pass down values, love, and the truth of God's love.

What the Bible Says

And these words that I command you today shall be on your heart. You shall teach them diligently to your children, and shall talk of them when you sit in your house, and when you walk by the way, and when you lie down, and when you rise.

DEUTERONOMY 6:6–7

As for me and my house, we will serve the LORD.

JOSHUA 24:15

I am reminded of your sincere faith, a faith that dwelt first in your grandmother Lois and your mother Eunice and now, I am sure, dwells in you as well.

2 TIMOTHY 1:5

Time to Face the Facts

Yeah, grandparents have even more value than just the fun stuff. For one thing, grandparents are more people who love you—you can never have too much love. They have lived a longer time in this world so they have had more experiences and learned more lessons. You can learn a lot from them about life and about walking with God.

"Did my grandparents ever have kids?"

Today I Will . . .

Sit down and talk with my grandparents or call them on the phone or email them. I want to learn all I can from them about their experiences in life. I want to know how they met each other; what my parents were like when they were my age; and what they've learned about God since they've probably known him a lot longer than I have.

What Does the Bible Say about Gratitude?

Do your parents make you write thank-you notes for gifts you receive? Why do you think they do that? It's nice to be thanked for gifts you've given or nice things you've done, right? It's nice to know your efforts are appreciated. That's gratitude. It's a good thing to show gratitude and appreciation when people do nice things for you. What about God? Does he want your gratitude, too? It's a good thing to thank him for all he does and show your gratitude to him for the gift of Jesus, for salvation, for eternal life, and for help in day-to-day living.

What the Bible Says

Oh give thanks to the Lord; call upon his name;
make known his deeds among the peoples!

1 CHRONICLES 16:8

Praise the Lord!
I will give thanks to the Lord with my whole heart,
in the company of the upright, in the congregation.
Great are the works of the Lord,
studied by all who delight in them.

PSALM 111:1–2

Let the word of Christ dwell in you richly, teaching and admonishing one another in all wisdom, singing psalms and hymns and spiritual songs, with thankfulness in your hearts to God.

COLOSSIANS 3:16

Time to Face the Facts

Showing gratitude takes a little bit of effort, but it is well worth it! Gratitude show others that you have noticed what they've done for you and how they've cared for you. It's a gift back to them to show gratitude. As for God, there may be times when you want to shout your thanks from the rooftops . . . praise him and thank him for all he does, from a heart filled with gratitude.

Today I Will . . .

Make a conscious effort to show gratitude to anyone who does something kind for me. I'll write thank-you notes for gifts and extra special kindnesses. But, even more importantly, I'll not take for granted all that God does for me. I will show my gratitude to God with a thankful heart of praise.

What Does the Bible Say about Greed?

Get an image in your mind of a person sweeping her arms around piles of money, scooping more and more into her own possession. While she sits hoarding her big pile of money, another person stands across the room who doesn't have money to even buy food and clothing to survive. That's greed—wanting more than your fair share, more than you need. Greed is not a popular topic with God. His Word instructs you to help others by sharing what you have.

What the Bible Says

One gives freely, yet grows all the richer;
another withholds what he should give, and only suffers want.

PROVERBS 11:24

The desire of the sluggard kills him,
for his hands refuse to labor.
All day long he craves and craves,
but the righteous gives and does not hold back.

PROVERBS 21:25–26

Give, and it will be given to you. Good measure, pressed down, shaken together, running over, will be put into your lap. For with the measure you use it will be measured back to you.

LUKE 6:38

Time to Face the Facts

If you have more than you need, share it. Giving to others is a way of showing God's love. Greed is selfish and self-indulgent. Greed is caring only about yourself, and there is no love in that. God's love motivates you to care about others and help in any way you can.

"I've got the 'gimmies.'"

Today I Will . . .

Look around my church, school, and town. I'll look at the news at how some people around the world must live. I'll compare that with what I have and share in any way I can.

What Does the Bible Say about Grief?

Losing someone you love hurts. If you've been praying for this loved one to be healed, when he or she dies it's hard to understand where God is. Grief colors everything else that happens. Joyous times are a little less joyous. Hard times are even harder. Does God understand how grief feels? He does understand, and God wants to be your comforter through the grief.

What the Bible Says

The LORD is near to the brokenhearted
and saves the crushed in spirit.

PSALM 34:18

He heals the brokenhearted
and binds up their wounds.

PSALM 147:3

Humble yourselves, therefore, under the mighty hand of
God so that at the proper time he may exalt you,
casting all your anxieties on him, because he cares for you.

1 PETER 5:6–7

Time to Face the Facts

God loves you. That means that when your heart is breaking, he wants to comfort you. Even if you don't understand why he didn't heal your loved one or why he didn't answer your prayers in the way you wanted, he wants to comfort you.

Today I Will . . .

Let God comfort me. Stop resisting and just rest in the truth that he loves me.

"I know my grandpa is with Jesus. I just miss him."

What Does the Bible Say about Guidance?

"Should I do this or that? Should I study to be a doctor when I grow up? Or maybe I should be a teacher. Should I cheat on a test, just this once? Should I try to be friends with the new kid in school when no one else likes her?" Sometimes it's hard to know the right thing to do. Sometimes it isn't. Maybe you need special guidance about some big decisions regarding your future. Where do you get that guidance? Does God have a plan for you? Yes, he does have a plan, and he promises to give you guidance, if you will ask him for it.

What the Bible Says

I will instruct you and teach you in the way you should go;
I will counsel you with my eye upon you.

PSALM 32:8

Trust in the Lord with all your heart,
and do not lean on your own understanding.
In all your ways acknowledge him,
and he will make straight your paths.

PROVERBS 3:5–6

For I know the plans I have for you, declares the Lord, plans for welfare and not for evil, to give you a future and a hope.

JEREMIAH 29:11

Time to Face the Facts

There are some things you don't have to ask guidance for because God has already given it . . . things like cheating and being a good friend. But some decisions can be more confusing. In those cases, ask God to guide you. He knows you better than anyone, and he wants you to be fulfilled in your life. He has a plan, so ask him to make it clear to you. Then follow it.

Today I Will . . .

Seek God's guidance. I want my life to count for something so I'll learn what God's plan is for me and I will follow his will.

What Does the Bible Say about Guilt?

You tell a little white lie, no big deal, right? Or maybe you spread a little gossip about someone, even though you knew it wasn't true. It could be because you cheated on a test or stole something from a store. Whatever it is, the guilt that lies on your heart after that is no fun. What do you do about that guilt? Does God have a remedy for it? Yes, he does. He instructs his children to confess their sins and ask for forgiveness. He is ready to forgive.

What the Bible Says

All have sinned and fall short of the glory of God.

ROMANS 3:23

If we confess our sins, he is faithful and just to forgive us
our sins and to cleanse us from all unrighteousness.

1 JOHN 1:9

Time to Face the Facts

Guilt is no fun. It's a hard emotion to shake. Once you start feeling guilty, that feeling doesn't go away until you do the right thing. Confessing your sin to God and asking his forgiveness assures that he will forgive you; then there may be two more steps. One is that if your sin has been against another person, you may need to ask that person's forgiveness, too. The second step is to forgive yourself. Confession and forgiveness lead to a fresh start—and not making the same mistake again.

"OK, OK! I did it."

Today I Will . . .

Honestly confess my sins to God and ask forgiveness. I want to make a fresh start with him with no guilt lying on my heart. Then I will ask forgiveness from any person I may have hurt. Lastly, I will ask God to help me forgive myself for the things I did.

What Does the Bible Say about Habits?

There are good habits, and there are bad habits. A certain behavior becomes a habit when you do it over and over until you finally do it without even thinking. God has a lot to say about habits that are good and teach you to be more and more like Christ.

What the Bible Says

For those who live according to the flesh set their minds on the things of the flesh, but those who live according to the Spirit set their minds on the things of the Spirit.

ROMANS 8:5

Set your minds on things that are above, not on things that are on earth.

COLOSSIANS 3:2

Do not love the world or the things in the world. If anyone loves the world, the love of the Father is not in him.

1 JOHN 2:15

Time to Face the Facts

Good habits are things like brushing your teeth each night, reading your Bible daily, and keeping your room clean. Bad habits are things like eating tons of junk food, staying up too late, or leaving your homework till the last minute. Habits that make you a healthier, better person who is learning to be more and more like Jesus are good habits. Those habits play into developing your character to help you become a godly person.

Today I Will . . .

Think about what some of my habits are and whether they are good or bad. I will be honest about which ones are bad. I will begin right away to work on stopping one bad habit and developing another good one.

HAIRSTYLES

What Does the Bible Say about Hairstyles?

A really cool hairstyle is important because then other kids will think you're cool, right? Girls and boys both sometimes try to copy the styles of the most popular kids. Everyone ends up looking the same because no one wants to be different. But seriously, does God care about your hairstyle? What he cares about is that you have confidence in yourself and that you don't feel that you have to go along with the crowd just to be popular.

What the Bible Says

> Even a child makes himself known by his acts,
> by whether his conduct is pure and upright.

PROVERBS 20:11

> Do not let your adorning be external—the braiding of hair and the putting on of gold jewelry, or the clothing you wear—but let your adorning be the hidden person of the heart with the imperishable beauty of a gentle and quiet spirit, which in God's sight is very precious.

1 PETER 3:3–4

Time to Face the Facts

Cool hairstyles are okay. But remember that going along with the crowd and looking like everyone else just to be accepted isn't really necessary. It's okay to be different . . . unique even. It's good to take care of yourself—wash your hair, keep it combed—but don't base all your self-esteem on how you look. Remember that outer looks are only one part of who you are; your character is most important.

"Dude, did you hit the space bar when you were gelling?"

Today I Will . . .

Okay, I'll take care of myself and make sure I look good. But I won't make that the most important thing. I know that what's going on in my heart as I learn to be more and more like Jesus is the most important thing.

What Does the Bible Say about Happiness?

Everybody wants to be happy. There's nothing wrong with that, is there? Well, of course it feels good to be happy. But did you ever notice that happiness comes and goes and can be upset by the simplest thing? Happiness is based on circumstances. What you really need is joy, and true joy comes only from God.

What the Bible Says

Praise the LORD!
Blessed is the man who fears the LORD,
who greatly delights in his commandments!

PSALM 112:1

Blessed are those who keep his testimonies,
who seek him with their whole heart.

PSALM 119:2

Not that I am speaking of being in need, for I have learned
in whatever situation I am to be content.

PHILIPPIANS 4:11

Time to Face the Facts

Some days you will be happy, happy, happy. Then some little thing will wreck your happiness, and you'll be crabby or sad. Happiness is dependent on outside circumstances, and those are sometimes completely out of your control or dependent on other people. Joy that is deep in your heart because of God's love and care is not dependent on circumstances or other people. So, even when things aren't going well, you can be joyous . . . which certainly feels like happiness!

"Doing the Happy Dance."

Today I Will . . .

Ask God to put joy in my heart. I know he loves me very much and will take care of me, and that knowledge makes me happy.

What Does the Bible Say about Hatred?

Hatred is anger gone crazy. You get really, really mad at someone, and you want bad things to happen to them. You refuse to be their friend, talk to them, or be friends with anyone who does. If you feel you have valid reasons for your feelings, then God will understand that, right? That might be a stretch since God's instructions to his children are to love one another . . . love others the way you love yourself.

What the Bible Says

You shall love the Lord your God with all your heart and with all your soul and with all your mind. This is the great and first commandment. And a second is like it: You shall love your neighbor as yourself.

MATTHEW 22:37–39

Let all bitterness and wrath and anger and clamor and slander be put away from you, along with all malice. Be kind to one another, tenderhearted, forgiving one another, as God in Christ forgave you.

EPHESIANS 4:31–32

Everyone who hates his brother is a murderer, and you know that no murderer has eternal life abiding in him.

1 JOHN 3:15

Time to Face the Facts

Hatred is a very strong emotion. In fact, the truth is that it's so strong that you probably don't ever really feel it. What you feel is anger, hurt, and frustration. So, how do you handle whatever the emotion is you are feeling? Cool down, then talk to the person you're upset with. Realize that loving others is more important than getting your own way. Work through the problem and save the relationship.

Today I Will . . .

Concentrate on the relationships I have. I know that loving others is the most important. When I get really angry with someone, I'll try to talk with the person calmly and work through the problem. I don't want to feel that I hate some-one. I want to love others.

Healing

What Does the Bible Say about Healing?

Many of the prayers prayed throughout history have been concerned with healing. When someone you love is sick, it's only natural to ask God to heal them. When you're the one who is sick—physically or emotionally—it's hard to think about anything except being healed. Does God care when you are sick and need healing? Yes, he cares. You can know that because he loves you, and when you love someone you don't want them to hurt.

What the Bible Says

But for you who fear my name, the sun of righteousness shall rise with healing in its wings. You shall go out leaping like calves from the stall.

MALACHI 4:2

Is anyone among you sick? Let him call for the elders of the church, and let them pray over him, anointing him with oil in the name of the Lord. And the prayer of faith will save the one who is sick, and the Lord will raise him up. . . .

JAMES 5:14–15

Time to Face the Facts

One of God's names is the Great Physician. He has the power to heal sickness, and sometimes he does. Sometimes he doesn't heal a person, but sticks really close to them throughout the illness, comforting and guiding. Sometimes he heals people through the miracle of medicine. Sometimes God loves you through an illness or problem with the love and support of the people around you. The bottom line is that you're never alone, no matter what you're going through.

"Does the big boy have a boo boo?"

Today I Will . . .

Pray for anyone I know who needs healing. Then, I'll watch to see how God answers that prayer, because I know he will in one way or another.

What Does the Bible Say about Health?

Does it sometimes seem to you that God has an opinion on just about everything? Well, yes, he probably does. What you need to remember is that his opinions are to help you be a better and healthier person. God wants you to enjoy good health by taking care of yourself, eating right, exercising regularly, and getting enough sleep.

What the Bible Says

> Bless the LORD, O my soul,
> and forget not all his benefits,
> who forgives all your iniquity,
> who heals all your diseases.

PSALM 103:2–3

> Do you not know that your body is a temple of the
> Holy Spirit within you, whom you have from God?
> You are not your own, for you were bought with a price.
> So glorify God in your body.

1 CORINTHIANS 6:19–20

> While bodily training is of some value, godliness is
> of value in every way, as it holds promise for the
> present life and also for the life to come.

1 TIMOTHY 4:8

Time to Face the Facts

Kids don't usually think about things like good health and what contributes to that. God does because he knows you have only one life to live on this earth and one body to live it in. So, you need to take care of that body. Keep it healthy so you can effectively do the work that God placed you in this life to accomplish.

Today I Will . . .

Cut back on sugar. Sleep more. Get enough exercise. Take care of my body.

What Does the Bible Say about Heaven?

Heaven is a mystery, isn't it? Do you sometimes wonder if heaven is real or if it's just a made-up place? And, if it is real, how can you know that you're going to have a place there? Well, God says it is real and that he's preparing a place just for you in heaven.

What the Bible Says

Do not lay up for yourselves treasures on earth, where moth and rust destroy and where thieves break in and steal, but lay up for yourselves treasures in heaven, where neither moth nor rust destroys and where thieves do not break in and steal.

MATTHEW 6:19–20

In my Father's house are many rooms. If it were not so, would I have told you that I go to prepare a place for you? And if I go and prepare a place for you, I will come again and will take you to myself, that where I am you may be also.

JOHN 14:2–3

But our citizenship is in heaven, and from it we await a Savior, the Lord Jesus Christ, who will transform our lowly body to be like his glorious body, by the power that enables him even to subject all things to himself.

PHILIPPIANS 3:20–21

Time to Face the Facts

Heaven is real, and God promises that I can come there because I am his child. He's been preparing a place for me. It's going to be wonderful, and it's going to be forever!

Today I Will . . .

Start living like I believe in heaven. I'll start laying treasures up there by serving and loving God with all my heart.

What Does the Bible Say about Hell?

Do you believe hell is a real place? Some people don't, you know. The truth is there are two choices for where each person spends eternity—in heaven with God or in hell with Satan. That's it. Two choices. God wants you to spend eternity with him. But he also makes no secret that hell is a real place, too.

What the Bible Says

> But I say to you that everyone who is angry with his brother will be liable to judgment; whoever insults his brother will be liable to the council; and whoever says, 'You fool!' will be liable to the hell of fire.
>
> **MATTHEW 5:22**

> But as for the cowardly, the faithless, the detestable, as for murderers, the sexually immoral, sorcerers, idolaters, and all liars, their portion will be in the lake that burns with fire and sulfur, which is the second death.
>
> **REVELATION 21:8**

Time to Face the Facts

Jesus left this earth and went to prepare heaven for you to come to. He's getting it ready for you, and he promised you could be with him forever there.

The Bible also talks about a real place where those who don't know God will spend eternity. It's sometimes called the lake of fire. It's a real place where Satan will spend forever. Hell is not a pleasant place. There's no joy, honesty, fairness, or safety. There is no good in hell. Two choices . . . the better one is heaven.

Today I Will . . .

Thank God that I don't have to worry about hell . . . if I've asked Jesus to be my Savior. If I haven't done that yet, I'm going to think very seriously about it right now. Hell doesn't sound like a place where I want to spend forever.

"Whew! It's hotter than I expected."

HELP

What Does the Bible Say about Help?

What pictures does the word "help" conjure up in your mind? Maybe it's helping with housework . . . the dreaded chores. Maybe it's helping someone cross the street like a good Boy Scout. Have you ever needed help? Everyone needs help sometimes. Maybe it's help to do a job, fix a damaged friendship, or learn something new. Does the Bible say anything about help? Of course, God promises to help you when you ask him . . . and when you are willing to do what he directs you to do.

What the Bible Says

When in their distress they turned to the Lord, the God of Israel, and sought him, he was found by them.

2 CHRONICLES 15:4

As each has received a gift, use it to serve one another, as good stewards of God's varied grace: whoever speaks, as one who speaks oracles of God; whoever serves, as one who serves by the strength that God supplies—in order that in everything God may be glorified through Jesus Christ. To him belong glory and dominion forever and ever. Amen.

1 PETER 4:10–11

"Try standing up."

Time to Face the Facts

God's promise is true—he will help you. But his help may not come in the way you expect or think. Sometimes he helps by making you strong enough to get through a problem instead of taking the problem away. Sometimes he helps you learn things. Sometimes he will change a situation in order to help you. The key is to seek him with your whole heart, mind, and soul . . . truly want his help, however it may come.

Today I Will . . .

Think about what it means to seek God's help with my whole heart, mind, and soul.

HISTORY

What Does the Bible Say about History?

"History? Are you kidding me? History is just a bunch of stories about old stuff and dead people. It's boring!" Is that what you think? And do you wonder how history could have any place in the Bible? Think about history this way . . . HIStory. The Bible is God's story. Reading the Bible lets you get to know God, how he works in people's lives, and how much he loves mankind. His story is important.

What the Bible Says

In the beginning, God created the heavens and the earth.

GENESIS 1:1

In the beginning was the Word, and the Word was with God, and the Word was God. He was in the beginning with God.

JOHN 1:1–2

All Scripture is breathed out by God and profitable for teaching, for reproof, for correction, and for training in righteousness.

2 TIMOTHY 3:16

Time to Face the Facts

The benefit of history is that it lets you look back to where a people or a nation has been and how it got to where it is today. You learn the struggles and the victories that have gone into making your nation, your world, your church, and your faith what it is today. Don't think of history as boring old stuff; think of it as what has given you the life you have today.

"Learn from the past."

Today I Will . . .

Read one story about the history of mankind and one story from Genesis about the history of God and his people. I want to learn what it has taken to form my life today.

What Does the Bible Say about Holiness?

In church or Sunday school is about the only time you hear the word "holiness," right? It's not the kind of word you use about normal everyday life. Holiness is purity by the absence of sin and doing wrong things. It matters to God because holiness means being completely dedicated to him—caring about him more than anything else in the world.

What the Bible Says

> The LORD will establish you as a people holy to himself,
> as he has sworn to you, if you keep the commandments
> of the LORD your God and walk in his ways.
>
> **DEUTERONOMY 28:9**

> Blessed be the God and Father of our Lord Jesus Christ,
> who has blessed us in Christ with every spiritual blessing in
> the heavenly places, even as he chose us in him before the
> foundation of the world, that we should be holy
> and blameless before him. . . .
>
> **EPHESIANS 1:3–4**

> Put on then, as God's chosen ones, holy and beloved,
> compassionate hearts, kindness, humility,
> meekness, and patience.
>
> **COLOSSIANS 3:12**

Time to Face the Facts

Holiness is not something you can achieve on your own. It just isn't possible. Holiness is available because God forgives your sin. The sin in your heart is replaced with his righteousness and purity. Your sin is completely forgiven . . . cool, huh? Being dedicated and devoted to God means that you care about what he thinks and what he wants more than anything else.

Today I Will . . .

Honestly evaluate how important God is in my life. Maybe I need to make some adjustments so that he has first place in my heart. The possibility of little old me being holy in his sight is awesome. I want to move in that direction.

What Does the Bible Say about the Holy Spirit?

Everything! Jesus promised when he left this earth to return to heaven that God would send a Comforter . . . a Guide . . . God's presence to be with God's children until the day that each of us goes to heaven. That Comforter is the Holy Spirit—God's presence in your heart.

What the Bible Says

But the Helper, the Holy Spirit, whom the Father will send in my name, he will teach you all things and bring to your remembrance all that I have said to you.

JOHN 14:26

But you will receive power when the Holy Spirit has come upon you, and you will be my witnesses in Jerusalem and in all Judea and Samaria, and to the end of the earth.

ACTS 1:8

Repent and be baptized every one of you in the name of Jesus Christ for the forgiveness of your sins, and you will receive the gift of the Holy Spirit.

ACTS 2:38

Time to Face the Facts

God lives in you. Think about that. His Spirit lives in your heart. You are never, ever alone in the struggles of life. The Holy Spirit lives in you, and through your thoughts and convictions he guides your life and directs your actions. He doesn't live in your heart because God wants to "keep an eye on you." No, he lives in your heart because God *loves* you that much. He wants to always be close to you. He wants to help you. He wants to teach and guide you. He wants you to love him.

"The Holy Spirit is always with me."

Today I Will . . .

Thank God for the Holy Spirit in me. I never thought about his presence being with me because God loves me that much. I'm so thankful for his presence in my life!

What Does the Bible Say about Homework?

Maybe you think God doesn't care how you feel about doing homework. *Wrong*! It's true that you're a kid so you don't have to work at a job to earn a living. However, that means homework is your job right now. God cares a lot about how you do your job.

What the Bible Says

Whatever you do, work heartily, as for the Lord and not for men.

COLOSSIANS 3:23

Whoever works his land will have plenty of bread, but he who follows worthless pursuits lacks sense.

PROVERBS 12:11

The sluggard does not plow in the autumn; he will seek at harvest and have nothing.

PROVERBS 20:4

Time to Face the Facts

It's pretty clear that the Bible (that means God) wants you to work hard at whatever work you have to do. Since right now you are a homework doer—be the very best homework doer you can be! Watching TV, playing a video game, listening to your tunes, and doing homework? Come on, get honest. If your brain needs to be thinking about math or history or science, give it a break and let it focus on just that.

"I can't figure out why I can't get my homework done."

Today I Will . . .

Finish my homework, then turn on the TV, video game, or tunes. I will work first—play later!

What Does the Bible Say about Honesty?

So . . . do you think that if you do something dishonest and no one finds out about it, then you've gotten away with it? You're safe? Sorry, Charlie . . . there is always one Person who knows what you've done . . . God. Honesty is important to him. It shows a respect and concern for other people (because you're not cheating them) and a respect and honor for him.

What the Bible Says

Who shall ascend the hill of the LORD?
And who shall stand in his holy place?
He who has clean hands and a pure heart,
who does not lift up his soul to what is false
and does not swear deceitfully.
He will receive blessing from the LORD
and righteousness from the God of his salvation.

PSALM 24:3–5

A just balance and scales are the LORD's;
all the weights in the bag are his work.

PROVERBS 16:11

One who is faithful in a very little is also faithful in much, and one who is dishonest in a very little is also dishonest in much.

LUKE 16:10

Time to Face the Facts

Honesty is a character trait. That means that at the core of your being you are committed to obeying God and treating others in a way that shows you respect them. Dishonesty is selfish; it shows that you believe life is all about you and how things affect you. God's instructions to love others even more than you love yourself means that honesty in how you treat others, how you play games with them, what you say about them . . . it's all important.

Today I Will . . .

Take a long, hard look at my life. Is honesty key in how I treat others? If I'm dishonest (even secretly) it shows that I'm more important to me than God or others.

What Does the Bible Say about Hope?

Hope is absolutely necessary to life. Whether it's hope of a better life, forgiveness, healing, love, friendship . . . whatever it may be. If there is no hope of things changing or improving, it's very hard to keep on going. God knows that. Perhaps that's why he has already given so many promises. He promised his presence, his help, his love. He promised eternity with him. What better hope could there be than that?

What the Bible Says

> The hope of the righteous brings joy, but the expectation of the wicked will perish.
> **PROVERBS 10:28**

> Now faith is the assurance of things hoped for, the conviction of things not seen.
> **HEBREWS 11:1**

Time to Face the Facts

Hope is what gives the energy and spunk to keep moving forward in life. It's hard to "keep on keeping on" if you feel there is no hope for things changing or being better. The hope of God's presence and help is actually a promise of those things. Does it give you hope to know that God's with you and has promised to always be with you? There's only one requirement for you to receive that hope: trust him. Just trust him to keep his promises.

"It would be pretty hard to go on if I didn't know God was with me."

Today I Will . . .

Trust. Okay, that's not easy sometimes. But I know I can never truly have hope in my heart if I don't trust God to keep his promises. I'll read his Word and learn all about him and his promises so I can learn to trust.

HOSPITALITY

What Does the Bible Say about Hospitality?

How good does it feel to be welcomed into someone's home, served a good meal, and enjoy laughter and conversation? Maybe you even stay overnight in that home in a comfortable room with a nice soft bed. That's hospitality. Hospitality is a way of showing love to others. That's what God said people should do for one another.

What the Bible Says

I was hungry and you gave me food, I was thirsty and you gave me drink, I was a stranger and you welcomed me, I was naked and you clothed me, I was sick and you visited me, I was in prison and you came to me.

MATTHEW 25:35–36

Contribute to the needs of the saints and seek to show hospitality.

ROMANS 12:13

Show hospitality to one another without grumbling.

1 PETER 4:9

Time to Face the Facts

Some people are really good at hospitality. But it's something everyone can work at. It doesn't take much to be kind and to invite others into our homes. You don't have to serve a gourmet meal or have a fancy home. Just good conversation with milk and cookies works just fine. Hospitality is caring about others' needs and sharing your own stuff and your time with them.

Today I Will . . .

Appreciate the hospitality that is shown to me . . . and say thank you to those who show it. I'll think about what I can do, at my age, to show hospitality to others.

What Does the Bible Say about Humility?

Do you know what humility is *not*? It's not thinking that you are worthless and can't do anything. It's also not being so proud of yourself that you brag about what you can do or how good-looking you are or how smart you are. Ugh. Humility is an honest understanding of who you are because of God's work in you. Seeing yourself as God sees you—nothing less and nothing more.

What the Bible Says

Whoever exalts himself will be humbled,
and whoever humbles himself will be exalted.

MATTHEW 23:12

I, therefore, a prisoner for the Lord, urge you to walk in a manner worthy
of the calling to which you have been called, with all humility and
gentleness, with patience, bearing with one another in love.

EPHESIANS 4:1–2

God opposes the proud, but gives grace to the humble.

JAMES 4:6

Time to Face the Facts

People who brag about themselves all the time are no fun to be around, are they? It gets old listening to them sing their own praises. It's also not much fun to be around people who constantly tear themselves down. There is a place right in the middle, though. A humble person knows that whatever he can do or think or learn is only because God has given him that ability. This person knows he has value in God's eyes but that everyone else does, too. God has given different abilities to every person.

Today I Will . . .

Think about my opinion of myself. Am I a proud, bragging person? Am I a tear-myself-down kind of person? I'll ask God to just help me understand how he sees me. I'll thank him for the abilities, talents, brains, and appearance he has given me. I am just who he wants me to be.

What Does the Bible Say about Humor?

Humor in the Bible? Really? Laughter is so much fun. There isn't much that feels better than a really good deep-from-inside-you belly laugh. Sharing a good joke or funny situation with someone really bonds you together. But does God care about humor? Yeah, actually, he does. His Word even says that laughter is good for the soul.

What the Bible Says

You make known to me the path of life;
in your presence there is fullness of joy;
at your right hand are pleasures forevermore.

PSALM 16:11

Then our mouth was filled with laughter,
and our tongue with shouts of joy;
then they said among the nations,
"The Lord has done great things for them."

PSALM 126:2

Time to Face the Facts

If you wonder whether God has a sense of humor, look around you at some of his creations. How did he think of long-necked giraffes? What about elephants with their long trunks or insects with their great big eyes? How about the long sweeping branches of weeping willow trees? God's reminder that laughter is good for you is a scientific fact, too.

"Laughter is the best medicine."

Laughter releases endorphins into your blood stream that are good for your health. God wants you to enjoy humor. Go ahead and have a good laugh.

Today I Will . . .

Laugh. And I'll enjoy laughter, as long as I'm laughing with others and not at them. I'll share laughter with others and thank God for humor.

What Does the Bible Say about Hunger?

Real hunger is a gnawing ache in your stomach that is so strong you can't think about anything else. Hopefully you've never experienced true hunger; however, many people around the world live with hunger every day. How does God feel about hunger? It must make him sad. He loves all people and encourages his children to share what they have with others.

What the Bible Says

If your enemy is hungry, give him bread to eat,
and if he is thirsty, give him water to drink.

PROVERBS 25:21

Then the King will say to those on his right, 'Come, you who are blessed by my Father, inherit the kingdom prepared for you from the foundation of the world. For I was hungry and you gave me food. . . .

MATTHEW 25:34–35

Jesus said to them, "I am the bread of life; whoever comes to me shall not hunger, and whoever believes in me shall never thirst.

JOHN 6:35

Time to Face the Facts

God makes a point several times in the Bible to encourage his people to share what they have with others and to take care of people who are hurting. That's a real example of living for him. When you have more than you need, find a way to share it with someone who is hungry. Pay attention to the world and don't get caught up in always wanting more for yourself.

"I would be happy to share with people around the world . . . I'm just not sure how to do it."

Today I Will . . .

Talk to someone in my church or family about how to help people in our city who are hungry. I'll also pay attention to how I could help with hunger problems around the world.

What Does the Bible Say about Idleness?

What's wrong with idleness? It feels good to not have anything to do some-times. It's a nice break from homework or chores, so can't you just enjoy it? Well, maybe . . . for a while. A rest is good, that's for sure. But don't get in the habit of just watching TV or playing video games or whatever. Idleness that is a rest is okay. Idleness that is wasting time is not. God gives each person a certain number of hours to enjoy on this earth, and he gives you work to do for him during those hours.

What the Bible Says

What does the LORD your God require of you, but to fear the LORD your God, to walk in all his ways, to love him, to serve the LORD your God with all your heart and with all your soul, and to keep the commandments and statutes of the LORD. . . .

DEUTERONOMY 10:12–13

Whoever works his land will have plenty of bread, but he who follows worthless pursuits lacks sense.

PROVERBS 12:11

Time to Face the Facts

If you spend a lot of your day wasting time, you'll run out of time to do the things you should be doing, whether that is home-work, chores, or things God wants you to do. An even bigger danger of wasting time is that when you're idle for a while, you can end up getting into trouble by do-

"Cool. I've only seen this one six times."

ing things you shouldn't be doing. There's an old saying that "idle hands are the devil's workshop." You can enjoy a rest, that's okay. But once you're rested, get up and use your time wisely.

Today I will . . .

Not waste time. It's so easy to veg out in front of the TV or get caught up in a video game or something like that. I understand I can enjoy idleness for a rest, but not forever!

What Does the Bible Say about Idolatry?

What's the most important thing in your life? Wait, don't answer that too quickly . . . think about this. What do you spend the most time thinking about? What do you get excited about? What do you spend your time on? If the same activity or thing or person is the answer to all of those questions, then you may have a little problem with idolatry. God has strong feelings about idolatry. He insists on being the most important thing in your life. Anytime something or someone pushes him out of the way, there will be trouble.

What the Bible Says

You shall worship no other god, for the LORD,
whose name is Jealous, is a jealous God.

EXODUS 34:14

The idols of the nations are silver and gold,
the work of human hands.

PSALM 135:15

Little children, keep yourselves from idols.

1 JOHN 5:21

Time to Face the Facts

There will be trouble? What kind of trouble? Like lightning shooting out of the sky and knocking you down? Probably not. Trouble like things won't go well in your life because it's out of balance—the wrong thing is in the number one position. Things become idols in your life without you even knowing it is happening. Maybe friends are too important. Perhaps it's a hobby that becomes number one. Or a habit or addiction. It happens. Nothing and no one should be more important to you than God. Nothing. No one.

Today I Will . . .

Take an honest look at my life. What has the number one place? If it's not God, I'm going to do some rearranging.

What Does the Bible Say about Immortality?

What does immortality even mean? It means never dying . . . living forever. That's probably not something you think about as a kid. Being fifty may seem like living forever. What does God say about immortality? He says you will live forever. That's absolute truth. Where you spend forever is kind of up to you.

What the Bible Says

Turn away from evil and do good;
so shall you dwell forever.

PSALM 37:27

Those who trust in the LORD are like Mount Zion,
which cannot be moved, but abides forever.

PSALM 125:1

They will see his face, and his name will be on their foreheads. And night will
be no more. They will need no light of lamp or sun, for the Lord God
will be their light, and they will reign forever and ever.

REVELATION 22:4–6

Time to Face the Facts

You will live forever. God promises that. So, you do have immortality. It's up to you whether your forever will be spent in heaven with God, worshiping and praising him, or whether it will be spent in hell because you rejected him. Asking Jesus into your heart to be your Savior is your assurance that you will be with God in heaven when you leave this earth . . . forever.

"Wow! He must be
at least 25."

Today I Will . . .

Make sure that I'm assured of spending forever in heaven. If I haven't asked Jesus into my heart, I'll do that now or speak with someone who can guide me along that way. I *will* live forever, and I want it to be with God.

IMPULSIVENESS

What Does the Bible Say about Impulsiveness?

There's a saying that a person who rushes into life is like a "bull in a china shop." That means that person rushes into life and things get broken or people get hurt or wrong decisions are made. How does God feel about impulsiveness? He would prefer that you slow down a bit and seek his guidance and direction in your life.

What the Bible Says

You have led in your steadfast love the people whom you have redeemed;
you have guided them by your strength to your holy abode.

EXODUS 15:13

For you are my rock and my fortress;
and for your name's sake you lead me and guide me.

PSALM 31:3

Be still before the LORD and wait patiently for him;
fret not yourself over the one who prospers in his way,
over the man who carries out evil devices!

PSALM 37:7

Time to Face the Facts

If you seek God's guidance and direction, he will give it. The thing is that you have to slow down and wait for him to show you what he wants. Impulsiveness and waiting on God do not go together. Slow down, ask his guidance, and wait for him. God loves you and has an amazing plan for your life. The best life ever will come your way if you wait to see what his plan is.

"Do now—think later."

Today I Will . . .

Slow down. Just slow down and wait for God to direct me. I know I have to be quiet for a while so I can hear his direction and guidance through all the noise and busyness of life.

INDEPENDENCE

What Does the Bible Say about Independence?

"I'm going to do things my way, when I want to do them, and that's that." Independence is kind of that way. Independent people don't work well on a team. Decisions and life are all about them, and they don't care a lot about how things affect other people. Being too independent is in opposition to how God wants you to live. He is happy when you think of others and show love and concern to them.

What the Bible Says

Incline my heart to your testimonies,
and not to selfish gain!

PSALM 119:36

If you have bitter jealousy and selfish ambition in your hearts, do not boast and be false to the truth. This is not the wisdom that comes down from above, but is earthly, unspiritual, demonic.

JAMES 3:14–15

Beloved, let us love one another, for love is from God, and whoever loves has been born of God and knows God.

1 JOHN 4:7

Time to Face the Facts

There are two ways to look at independence. When independence keeps you from going along with the crowd who is doing things you know that God wouldn't want you to do, then that's a good thing. When independence keeps you from obeying God by caring about others and being kind and considerate of them, that's not a good thing. Independence is not good when it causes you to be self-centered and not submitted to God.

Today I Will . . .

Obey God, no matter what. If I am sometimes too independent to be obedient to him, then I will ask him to help me be more submitted to his will and his guidance. I will think about other people and their feelings more often than I think about mine.

What Does the Bible Say about Ingratitude?

What do you do when people do nice things for you? Everyday normal things such as your mom or dad cooking dinner or driving you to soccer practice. Or extra-special things like getting you that special thing you wanted for your birthday—even though it was maybe a financial stretch. If you act like you deserve anything done for you, then you've fallen victim to ingratitude. Some ingratitude is even directed toward God, shown by never stopping to thank him for all he does.

What the Bible Says

Oh give thanks to the LORD, for he is good;
for his steadfast love endures forever!

1 CHRONICLES 16:34

Let the peace of Christ rule in your hearts,
to which indeed you were called
in one body. And be thankful.

COLOSSIANS 3:15

"Is that all?"

Time to Face the Facts

Ingratitude is really selfish because it shows that deep inside you think people owe you all the kindnesses shown to you. In reality, no one owes you anything. You can change the ingratitude in your life by some simple steps. Stop and appreciate what God and others do for you each day. Then, tell them. Yes, just say, "Thank you, I appreciate all you do for me." That's not hard, and pretty soon, as you notice those nice things and verbalize your thanks, your heart will truly be blessed by seeing how much God and other people love you.

Today I Will . . .

Make an effort to notice each little thing done for me. Then, as I notice them, I will give sincere thanks to the people who are so kind to me. I will also pay attention to all that God does for me each day; I know I take much of that for granted. This will help me know how special I am to him.

What Does the Bible Say about Injustice?

Why do some people seem to have everything they want and to have what appears to be an easy life? Why do others have to struggle for everything? Why is there racial injustice? Why is there any injustice in this world? Doesn't God care? Yes, he does care. He loves all people of all countries, of all colors, both men and women, young and old. Injustices are not his idea.

What the Bible Says

Give justice to the weak and the fatherless;
maintain the right of the afflicted and the destitute.

PSALM 82:3

Do not say, "I will repay evil";
wait for the LORD, and he will deliver you.

PROVERBS 20:22

Time to Face the Facts

There is injustice in this world because of sin. When God created the world, everything was perfect, and there was no room for injustice. But as soon as Adam and Eve sinned against God, evil entered the world and injustice was born. What can you do about injustice? There are times you can refuse to join in crowd actions that are unjust. There are organizations that work toward stopping injustice in the world. Take a stand. Pray. Do all you can to honor God and the people he created.

"That's not fair."

Today I Will . . .

Take a stand in my school or my town against injustice. All people are worth loving, and all people deserve freedom and the chance to make something of their lives. I'll take a stand and do what I can.

INSENSITIVITY

What Does the Bible Say about Insensitivity?

Have your feelings ever been hurt by something people said? Did it hurt even more when they didn't seem to care that they had hurt you? Insensitivity to others' feelings—just not caring when you hurt someone and doing the same hurtful thing over and over—causes a lot of pain. This does not obey God's instructions to love others and to show others his love by how we treat them.

What the Bible Says

Hatred stirs up strife, but love covers all offenses.

PROVERBS 10:12

So whatever you wish that others would do to you,
do also to them, for this is the Law and the Prophets.

MATTHEW 7:12

A new commandment I give to you, that you love one another:
just as I have loved you, you also are to love one another.

JOHN 13:34

Time to Face the Facts

Insensitivity to others' feelings is really selfishness. It shows that you feel that nothing and no one is more important than you, and therefore you don't need to pay attention to how your words and actions make others feel. Sad, huh? If you've been the victim of insensitivity, then you know how it feels. You don't want to do that to anyone, do you? Your goal should always be to show God's love to others by the way you treat them and speak to them.

Today I Will . . .

Think about how my actions and words may make others feel. I don't want to be insensitive. I do want to show God's love to those around me, including my family and friends as well as people I don't know well or don't particularly get along with.

INSIGNIFICANCE

What Does the Bible Say about Insignificance?

Okay, all the students are lined up in gym class and a couple of captains are choosing their team members. If you aren't a humdinger of an athlete, you may be chosen close to the last. Does that make you feel embarrassed? Does it make you feel as though you don't matter? Yeah, that's a feeling of insignificance—a perpetual B-team benchwarmer. Here's something to remember though: you are not insignificant to God.

What the Bible Says

And behold, I am with you always, to the end of the age.

MATTHEW 28:20

I am sure that neither death nor life, nor angels nor rulers, nor things present nor things to come, nor powers, nor height nor depth, nor anything else in all creation, will be able to separate us from the love of God in Christ Jesus our Lord.

ROMANS 8:38–39

See what kind of love the Father has given to us, that we should be called children of God; and so we are. . . .

1 JOHN 3:1

Time to Face the Facts

You may look around you and see people who are really smart or good-looking or talented, and that may make you feel insignificant. It shouldn't, though. God made you just the way he wants you to be, and he gave you the talents and abilities he wants you to have. God loves you completely. You can *know* that because Jesus died and rose again for *you*.

"Helloooo—
do you see me down here?"

Today I Will . . .

Stop comparing myself to others. I'll concentrate on the way God made me and thank him for that. Anytime I start to feel insignificant, I'll remind myself that God loves *me*!

What Does the Bible Say about Integrity?

What makes you uniquely you? How would people describe you? Are you honest, fair, and moral? A person of integrity is all those things. A person of integrity has high standards, which are a part of being obedient to God. Living your life in a way that shows you are becoming more and more like Christ can be done only by living a life of integrity.

What the Bible Says

> He has told you, O man, what is good;
> and what does the LORD require of you
> but to do justice, and to love kindness,
> and to walk humbly with your God?
>
> **MICAH 6:8**

> These are the things that you shall do:
> Speak the truth to one another;
> render in your gates judgments
> that are true and make for peace.
>
> **ZECHARIAH 8:16**

> Blessed are the pure in heart,
> for they shall see God.
>
> **MATTHEW 5:8**

Time to Face the Facts

Some people try to fool others by appearing to be honest, fair, and moral, but on the inside they are not always those things. You may be able to fool people into thinking you have integrity . . . but you can't fool God. He sees your heart and therefore knows your thoughts and intentions. He knows what you are really like. Don't try to fake integrity; let God work in your heart to make you a person who honestly has this character quality.

Today I Will . . .

Be honest with myself and God. I know whether I try to fake these qualities in my life or if they are really a part of me. I want to be a person of integrity. I want to be more Christlike in my attitudes, thoughts, and actions.

What Does the Bible Say about Intelligence?

Maybe you're one of those students who is always at the top of the class. You're considered one of the "smart kids" or perhaps you are the smartest. Or, perhaps you're always right in the middle of the class—average. Or, you may bring up the bottom of the class, in which case you feel like you must have been in the wrong line when intelligence was handed out. How does God feel about this? He knows that real intelligence is not "school smarts." Real intelligence is seeking to know him better and live in obedience to him.

What the Bible Says

Everyone then who hears these words of mine and does them will be like a wise man who built his house on the rock. And the rain fell, and the floods came, and the winds blew and beat on that house, but it did not fall, because it had been founded on the rock.

MATTHEW 7:24–25

If any of you lacks wisdom, let him ask God, who gives generously to all without reproach, and it will be given him.

JAMES 1:5

Time to Face the Facts

Okay, it's understandable if you struggle with how well you do in school or even with pride because of how well you do in school. But don't get too caught up in that thought process. The smartest person in the world as far as book-learning goes is not really smart at all if he or she doesn't know God, read his Word, and seek to obey him. That's real intelligence, and it's available to everyone, regardless of their brainpower.

"I know something about everything."

Today I Will . . .

Not get caught up in what the rest of the world considers to be intelligence. I will follow real intelligence by knowing God better and better and letting his love show in my life.

What Does the Bible Say about Jealousy?

Wanting what someone else has. Spending tons of times wishing you had someone else's abilities or talents. Not being happy with who you are. Jealousy is a green-eyed monster. When you're jealous of someone or something, you are never satisfied with what you have. There is no place for jealousy in God's system. He cares that you feel cheated or sad about what you have in this world. But the bottom line is there is no reason to be jealous of someone else. God made you the way he wants you to be and gave you what you need to do the work he has for you.

What the Bible Says

> A tranquil heart gives life to the flesh, but envy makes the bones rot.
> **PROVERBS 14:30**

> Not that we are sufficient in ourselves to claim anything as coming from us, but our sufficiency is from God.
> **2 CORINTHIANS 3:5**

"I know God didn't make me like him . . . I just wish he made me a little like him."

Time to Face the Facts

Jealousy is consuming. When you're jealous of someone, you can't think about much else. You may feel cheated because of your own abilities, appearance, or place in this world. But that is just wrong. There is no reason to be jealous of others if you keep your focus on God. If you're not living up to the potential God placed in you, then you need to work on that. But if you are following God's plan for your life, be happy with the way God made you. Don't worry about what others have. Just be thankful to God for who you are and what you have.

Today I Will . . .

Stop looking at others and what they have. Jealousy can be so consuming that I can't think of anything else. I want to focus on who I am in God and what work he has for me to do. I can't do that if I'm jealous.

What Does the Bible Say about Joy?

Joy is deeper in your soul than happiness. Joy starts somewhere in your heart and bubbles up through you. It makes you more thankful for everything. Joy makes the world look brighter and happier. Joy is not dependent on circumstances and is deeper than moods. True joy comes from loving and trusting God.

What the Bible Says

The joy of the LORD is your strength.

NEHEMIAH 8:10

I have set the LORD always before me; because he is at my right hand, I shall not be shaken. Therefore my heart is glad, and my whole being rejoices; my flesh also dwells secure.

PSALM 16:8–9

Rejoice in the Lord always; again I will say, Rejoice.

PHILIPPIANS 4:4

Time to Face the Facts

Everyone likes to be happy. But happiness comes and goes depending on your mood or what's happening in your life. Joy is deeper in your heart because it comes from God. It is an appreciation of what he has given you and done for you. Joy remains even when situations become difficult. It is not dependent on what is happening around you. The joy God gives is deep and true and will take you through whatever life brings. Trust him with your life and love him. Joy will come.

"I feel great! I feel wonderful! But why are all the birds and butterflies following me?"

Today I Will . . .

Be quiet. Yes, I will read a verse about joy and just think about it. I want to trust God and love him so much that his joy has a place deep in my heart.

What Does the Bible Say about Judging Others?

When you meet someone new, do you look that person over and make decisions about her? Maybe you think she is not cool enough to be your friend. Perhaps you decide she doesn't have a clue about the right thing to wear. Maybe you even decide that she is too rebellious or weird to have any interest in God. Judging others happens when you don't have all the information to form an opinion of someone—but you do it anyway. God speaks out against judging others. He says you shouldn't ever judge anyone at all but should only love others.

What the Bible Says

But the Lord said to Samuel, "Do not look on his appearance or on the height of his stature, because I have rejected him. For the Lord sees not as man sees: man looks on the outward appearance, but the Lord looks on the heart."

1 SAMUEL 16:7

These also are sayings of the wise.
Partiality in judging is not good.

PROVERBS 24:23

Judge not, that you be not judged.

MATTHEW 7:1

Time to Face the Facts

Judging others will only get you into trouble. For one thing, it isn't fair to form an opinion of someone when you don't have all the information. For another thing (and much more serious) judging is disobedient to God's Word. You may miss making some really good friends because of the opinion you formed. You definitely lose the chance to show God's love to the person you pushed away by your impulsive judgment.

Today I Will . . .

Slow down. When I judge someone else, I usually do it in a hurry. So, I'll slow down and ask God to guide my thoughts and opinions. I will look for ways to show love to others rather than forming opinions about them.

What Does the Bible Say about Justice?

Does it make you crazy when someone gets away with doing something wrong? Do you shout, *"It is not fair!"* Nope, it probably isn't. Life isn't fair. Some people get away with things, and some get caught on the smallest thing. A classic example is when your brother hits you and you hit him back. You're the one Mom catches, and you're the one punished—it isn't fair. Justice is a big deal with God. Someday every wrong that has ever been done will be judged.

What the Bible Says

God is a righteous judge,
and a God who feels indignation every day.

PSALM 7:11

You have heard that it was said, "You shall love your neighbor and hate your enemy." But I say to you, Love your enemies and pray for those who persecute you, so that you may be sons of your Father who is in heaven. For he makes his sun rise on the evil and on the good, and sends rain on the just and on the unjust.

MATTHEW 5:43–45

So whatever you wish that others would do to you, do also to them, for this is the Law and the Prophets.

MATTHEW 7:12

"That will teach you!"

Time to Face the Facts

One day everyone will answer for their actions. They will find out that they haven't really gotten away with anything when they stand before God. He will judge with mercy, love, and fairness. You can learn a lesson from God in that when someone hurts you, treat them with mercy, love, and fairness. That's a way of showing God's love to them.

Today I Will . . .

Oh man, this is hard. When someone hurts me, what I want to do back is not show mercy, love, and fairness. In fact, I know I can't do that by myself. I'll ask God to help me. I know he will.

What Does the Bible Say about Kindness?

Your school, neighborhood, and town are starving for acts of kindness. Acts of selfishness and evil are the things we hear about on the news. Kindness is simply thinking about someone else's feelings or needs. God is your example of showing kindness. He does so each day and encourages you to pay it forward.

What the Bible Says

Love is patient and kind; love does not envy or boast; it is not arrogant.

1 CORINTHIANS 13:4

Be kind to one another, tenderhearted, forgiving one another, as God in Christ forgave you.

EPHESIANS 4:32

But when the goodness and loving kindness of God our Savior appeared, he saved us, not because of works done by us in righteousness, but according to his own mercy, by the washing of regeneration and renewal of the Holy Spirit.

TITUS 3:4–5

Time to Face the Facts

You can begin an "acts of kindness" campaign. Somehow kindness seems to be catching. If you do something kind for someone, there is a chance that they will do something kind for someone else . . . and on and on. Kindness may simply be "hello" and a smile to someone. It might be helping someone pick up their groceries that they dropped. It's simple things that show you care about other people.

Today I Will . . .

Look around and notice ways I can be kind to others. I know kindness shows God's love to them . . . and it's fun to be a bright spot in someone else's day!

KNOWLEDGE

What Does the Bible Say about Knowledge?

Some people have a hunger for knowledge. They want to know how things work and how to build things. They love studying, whether it is history, science, math, or geography. They just love learning new things. That's great, but it's important to remember that the most important knowledge is knowing God and learning from his Word.

What the Bible Says

These words that I command you today shall be on your heart. You shall teach them diligently to your children, and shall talk of them when you sit in your house, and when you walk by the way, and when you lie down, and when you rise. You shall bind them as a sign on your hand, and they shall be as frontlets between your eyes. You shall write them on the doorposts of your house and on your gates.

DEUTERONOMY 6:6–9

Everyone then who hears these words of mine and does them will be like a wise man who built his house on the rock. And the rain fell, and the floods came, and the winds blew and beat on that house, but it did not fall, because it had been founded on the rock.

MATTHEW 7:24–25

Time to Face the Facts

There is certainly nothing wrong with knowledge. Learning uses the brain God gave you and gives an appreciation for all he has created. Be careful to remember that knowledge of God and his Word is the most important thing. View all other knowledge through the truth filter that God made it all!

Today I Will . . .

Read and study and learn. But I'll remember that everything I'm learning about was made by God in the first place. And, I'll put my learning of his Word at the top of my knowledge list!

"Brain like a steel trap."

What Does the Bible Say about Language?

Language? Like Japanese, Spanish, or English? No, that's not exactly what the question is about. It's asking about your choice of language—swearing, taking God's name in vain, unkind words versus kind words. In that sense, language has a lot to do with the Bible. God does care about your language and how you speak to others. Your words should be glorifying to him and loving and kind to others.

What the Bible Says

> You shall not take the name of the LORD your God in vain, for the LORD will not hold him guiltless who takes his name in vain.
>
> **EXODUS 20:7**

> Have nothing to do with foolish, ignorant controversies; you know that they breed quarrels. And the Lord's servant must not be quarrelsome but kind to everyone, able to teach, patiently enduring evil, correcting his opponents with gentleness. . . .
>
> **2 TIMOTHY 2:23–25**

> The tongue is a small member, yet it boasts of great things. How great a forest is set ablaze by such a small fire! And the tongue is a fire, a world of unrighteousness. The tongue is set among our members, staining the whole body, setting on fire the entire course of life, and set on fire by hell.
>
> **JAMES 3:5–6**

Time to Face the Facts

The hard part about this topic is that sometimes the words you choose and the tone with which you deliver them is because you think what you're saying is funny. But if that joke comes at another person's expense, where their feelings or reputation may be hurt, then you need to reevaluate. Language is so important. Choose words that honor God and words that show kindness and love to others. Unkind words lie as a heavy weight on the hearts of others.

Today I Will . . .

Think before I speak. I don't need to use swear words—my vocabulary is bigger than that. I'll think about what I say about others and, even if I think a story is funny, I'll think about how it might make the other person feel.

What Does the Bible Say about Laziness?

So, maybe you think that because you're a kid you don't have to work. Do you think it's okay for you to sleep late, lie around, put off chores and homework to the last minute, then rush through them with a sloppy finish? That's laziness, and God has pretty strong opinions about that. He says you should do the work that's before you and do it to the best of your abilities.

What the Bible Says

The LORD upholds all who are falling
and raises up all who are bowed down.

PSALM 145:14

Whatever you do, in word or deed, do everything in the name of
the Lord Jesus, giving thanks to God the Father through him.

COLOSSIANS 3:17

Whatever you do, work heartily, as for the Lord and not for men.

COLOSSIANS 3:23

Time to Face the Facts

Sluffing off responsibility just because you're not a grown-up doesn't fly with God. Even as a young person you have responsibilities. Right now is a good time to learn responsibility and make it a habit in your life. Take your work seriously and make it a goal to always do your best. Then laziness will not be a problem for you.

Today I Will . . .

Make a list of my responsibilities. Set goals for when to get them done and commit to do them as well as I can. Laziness will not be one of my characteristics.

"I had the urge to do yard work—so I lay down until the urge passes."

What Does the Bible Say about Leadership?

A leader is someone people follow. Usually that's because the leader knows where he's going, and he has some excitement about it that draws other people in. There's nothing really wrong with that unless the leader is leading people away from obeying God. Leadership is a responsibility. Be careful who you follow.

What the Bible Says

Do not look on his appearance or on the height of his stature, because I have rejected him. For the Lord sees not as man sees: man looks on the outward appearance, but the Lord looks on the heart.

1 SAMUEL 16:7

But whoever would be great among you must be your servant.

MATTHEW 20:26

Remember your leaders, those who spoke to you the word of God. Consider the outcome of their way of life, and imitate their faith.

HEBREWS 13:7

Time to Face the Facts

If you are a leader, be aware of what you're leading others to. Do you encourage others to know and obey God and to be kind to others? Do they see that in your actions and attitudes? If you are following others, do they model and encourage those qualities in their followers? Be careful how you lead and who you follow. Don't take either position lightly. Remember that the most important path should lead you to a closer relationship with God.

"I promise longer recesses for everyone!"

Today I Will . . .

Decide whether I am a leader or a follower. Think about whether my leading or my following is leading myself and others to knowing, obeying, and loving God.

What Does the Bible Say about Learning?

Did you know that you are learning things even when you aren't thinking about learning? Yeah, the people you spend time with and the things you do when you're playing or talking are all teaching you things. Learning is a big part of life. Hopefully you are learning things that will help you become a better person and a stronger God-follower.

What the Bible Says

Blessed are you, O LORD;
teach me your statutes!

PSALM 119:12

If you turn at my reproof,
behold, I will pour out my spirit to you;
I will make my words known to you.

PROVERBS 1:23

Everyone then who hears these words of mine and does them
will be like a wise man who built his house on the rock.
And the rain fell, and the floods came, and the winds blew
and beat on that house, but it did not fall, because
it had been founded on the rock.

MATTHEW 7:24–25

Time to Face the Facts

This is a time for an honest evaluation of how you spend your time and with whom you spend it. What are you teaching your mind even in your free time? Focus on learning how to be kinder and more considerate. Learn more about God's Word and how he wants you to live. Make your learning worthwhile.

Today I Will . . .

Pay attention to how I'm spending my time and what that might be teaching me. I want my learning to be worthwhile stuff to make me a better person and a better God-follower.

What Does the Bible Say about Life after Death?

Once you're dead, you're dead, right? That's it, you're gone. Well, some people live like they believe that. But the Bible says there is life after death. You only get one chance for life on earth, but once you leave this planet, life does go on. God says it is your choice whether your life after death is spent in heaven with him or in hell with Satan.

What the Bible Says

For God so loved the world, that he gave his only Son, that whoever believes in him should not perish but have eternal life.

JOHN 3:16

For the wages of sin is death, but the free gift of God is eternal life in Christ Jesus our Lord.

ROMANS 6:23

And the world is passing away along with its desires, but whoever does the will of God abides forever.

1 JOHN 2:17

Time to Face the Facts

There is life after death. That's a fact. Where you live in that life after death is up to you. You can choose heaven by accepting Jesus as your Savior and living for him. If you do that you will be laying up rewards in heaven, which will be ready and waiting when you get there.

Today I Will . . .

Think about life as a bigger picture than the here and now. I'll think about heaven and how I can lay treasures up there now.

What Does the Bible Say about Lifestyle?

What's your idea of the perfect lifestyle? As you look around at adults or teenagers, what kind of lifestyle do you long for? Would you like to be rich and famous—jetting around the world, eating at the finest restaurants? Life would be one big party. Or maybe you're realistic that you won't be one of the "beautiful people" but you still want a party lifestyle, hanging out with friends, and partying every chance you get. God cares about the lifestyle you choose. He wants your lifestyle to honor him.

What the Bible Says

You are a people holy to the LORD your God. The LORD your God has chosen you to be a people for his treasured possession, out of all the peoples who are on the face of the earth.

DEUTERONOMY 7:6

Even a child makes himself known by his acts, by whether his conduct is pure and upright.

PROVERBS 20:11

Blessed are the pure in heart, for they shall see God.

MATTHEW 5:8

Time to Face the Facts

Believe it or not, your lifestyle reflects your opinion of God. It shows how important he is to you. That's kind of scary, isn't it? Even at your age you can begin establishing your lifestyle. Make God the number one thing in your life so that the ways you spend your time, money, and energy reflect that God is most important to you.

"only the best for me!"

Today I Will . . .

Look at the way my choices are guiding me to a specific lifestyle. If I keep going in this direction, will it show that God is number one in my heart? If not, I'll make some changes right now.

What Does the Bible Say about Limitations?

Limitations hold you back from what you think you might be able to accomplish. You can have great strengths, such as incredible musical talent, but your limitation might be that you have great pride in your talent. Limitations and strength sometimes kind of mimic each other and confuse the issue. God gives you certain strengths that are evident in your heart. He wants to you live in those strengths and not put limitations on yourself.

What the Bible Says

The joy of the LORD is your strength.

NEHEMIAH 8:10

I can do all things through
him who strengthens me.

PHILIPPIANS 4:13

For this I toil, struggling with all his
energy that he powerfully works within me.

COLOSSIANS 1:29

Time to Face the Facts

Limitations are character weaknesses that keep you from being the person God wants you to be. They hold your strengths in check, too. Whatever your strength may be, it can't develop to the point it might and it can't bless the people around you in the way it could if your limitations were not tied to it. Sometimes your limitations are your own attitudes that may not believe your strengths are worthwhile or that God could possibly use you.

Today I Will . . .

Ask God to free me from the limitations that hold me back. I'll ask God to help me be realistic about my strengths. I will ask him to use me in any way he chooses.

What Does the Bible Say about Listenings?

This is an interesting topic. How often do your parents or teachers talk to you and you respond with "uh huh," but you haven't really heard a word they have said? It goes both ways. You may talk to your dad but he's busy reading the paper or doing something and he doesn't really listen to what you're saying. Do you sometimes talk to God and wonder if he is really listening? He is. God promises to hear your prayers . . . always.

What the Bible Says

> But know that the LORD has set apart the godly for himself;
> the LORD hears when I call to him.
>
> **PSALM 4:3**

> A new commandment I give to you, that you love one another:
> just as I have loved you, you also are to love one another.
>
> **JOHN 13:34**

Time to Face the Facts

God is your model. He listens to you because he loves you. He cares about what you say to him and how you're feeling. When other people speak to you, whether it's your parents or teachers who are giving instructions, listen. It's important to hear what they say. If it is your friend who is speaking to you, telling you how she feels or what she's worried about, listen. It shows you care about her. Listening to other people gives them worth. It shows they matter to you.

"Hello-Earth to Super Dude. Come in, Super Dude!"

Today I Will . . .

Focus. When someone is speaking to me I will quit thinking about the other stuff happening at that moment and just focus on them. I'll thank God for listening to me, and I'll model his care by listening to others.

LONELINESS

What Does the Bible Say about Loneliness?

Did you know that you can feel lonely even when you're in a crowd of people? It's not the number of people around you that makes you feel loved and accepted, it's the relationships with those people. Loneliness feels like no one really, truly cares about you and what's happening in your life. In reality, though, you are never truly alone. There is someone who is always with you and who cares about you more than you can possibly imagine . . . God.

What the Bible Says

How precious to me are your thoughts, O God!
How vast is the sum of them!

PSALM 139:17

Fear not, for I am with you;
be not dismayed, for I am your God;
I will strengthen you, I will help you,
I will uphold you with my righteous right hand.

ISAIAH 41:10

So we, though many, are one body in Christ,
and individually members one of another.

ROMANS 12:5

Time to Face the Facts

Okay, you may know that God is always with you and he loves you and cares about you. But maybe you feel as though you sometimes need to have people around—live people with skin to give you hugs or a pat on the back. You need to know that others care about you. That's understandable. Look around you and perhaps you'll see someone who is there on the edges of your life who may care about you. Sometimes you need to open yourself up to their care. Be open to share your life with someone. You must be a friend to have a friend.

Today I Will . . .

Reach out to someone. Maybe if I stop thinking about how lonely I am all the time I will notice someone else who may be lonely, too. I'll ask God to show me how to be a friend to someone else. That may take care of two people's loneliness.

What Does the Bible Say about Looks?

Be honest . . . do you judge others by the way they look? Seriously, if a person isn't wearing the right kind of clothes or has a bad haircut, do you kind of dismiss them as not worthy of your time? If a person is obviously poor or wears dirty, torn clothing, then that's even worse, right? That person could not be worthy of your time. God encourages you not to look at outward appearance because that isn't what's important. The inside (or the heart) is most important.

What the Bible Says

But the LORD said to Samuel, "Do not look on his appearance or on the height of his stature, because I have rejected him. For the LORD sees not as man sees: man looks on the outward appearance, but the LORD looks on the heart."

1 SAMUEL 16:7

His delight is not in the strength of the horse,
    nor his pleasure in the legs of a man,
but the LORD takes pleasure in those who fear
him, in those who hope in his steadfast love.

PSALM 147:10–11

"You need to go to
the groomer!"

Time to Face the Facts

God looks at the hearts of people. Their attitude and relationship to him is more important than their looks. He cares about their character. You could miss getting to know some really cool people just because you judge people by their looks rather than looking at their inside. Not everyone is gorgeous and stylish or muscular and good-looking. Take time to get to know a new person and see what he or she is like on the inside.

Today I Will . . .

Go talk to someone that I've ignored because of the way he or she looks. I want to be loving as God commands, and I want to see if I've missed getting to know someone cool because I've judged them by what is on the outside.

What Does the Bible Say about The Lord's Day?

Honesty time: Is Sunday any different for you from any other day of the week? Should it be? Why do we call it "The Lord's Day" if it's just like Tuesday or Friday? God commanded that we set his day aside and treat it special. Maybe we should listen.

What the Bible Says

Remember the Sabbath day, to keep it holy. Six days you shall labor, and do all your work, but the seventh day is a Sabbath to the LORD your God. . . .

EXODUS 20:8-10

You shall keep my Sabbaths and reverence my sanctuary: I am the LORD.

LEVITICUS 26:2

So then, there remains a Sabbath rest for the people of God.

HEBREWS 4:9

Time to Face the Facts

Obviously, Sunday is supposed to be different. God commanded that his children set that day aside as a day of rest, just as he rested on the seventh day of creation. On that day, you should think about him and enjoy the loved ones around you. Wow. Most of the world has gotten off base on that.

Today I Will . . .

Make an effort to keep Sunday free of work. That means doing my homework and chores on Saturday. Spend Sunday hanging out with my family or friends and actually enjoying worshiping God.

"Everyone is so loving and peaceful. I wish every day was Sunday."

What Does the Bible Say about Loss?

Loss is part of life. A stinky part of life, but nevertheless a part of life. It may be the loss of a pet, or a friend moving away, or a parent walking away from the family, or the death of a loved one. Whatever it is, loss hurts. How does God feel about the losses you suffer? He cares. He promises to be right beside you through the pain of loss. He's there, waiting for you to turn to him.

What the Bible Says

Even though I walk through the
valley of the shadow of death,
I will fear no evil,
for you are with me;
your rod and your staff,
they comfort me.

PSALM 23:4

Surely he has borne our griefs
and carried our sorrows.

ISAIAH 53:4

Blessed be the God and Father of our Lord Jesus Christ, the Father of mercies and God of all comfort, who comforts us in all our affliction, so that we may be able to comfort those who are in any affliction, with the comfort with which we ourselves are comforted by God.

2 CORINTHIANS 1:3–4

Time to Face the Facts

God knows that losses hurt, but he often doesn't stop them because they are a part of life in this world wracked by evil, sin, and death. He cares about the pain you feel, though. He cares, too, about what happens in your heart as you experience loss. He cares that you turn to him and grow closer to him through the pain you have. Learn to lean on him, depend on him, and trust him to get you through whatever life brings.

Today I Will . . .

Tell God how I feel about the loss in my life. Instead of feeling deserted or alone, I'll ask him to strengthen me and help me get through the pain. I'll stay close to him.

What Does the Bible Say about Love?

Wow, knowing that someone loves you is the *most* awesome thing. Whether it's a family member or a friend who loves you, there is a confidence that even if you have an argument that person will not walk away. Life is a whole lot better when you can give love and receive love. God is the model of love. His love is unconditional—you have done nothing to deserve it and you can do nothing to stop it.

What the Bible Says

Hatred stirs up strife, but love covers all offenses.

PROVERBS 10:12

Greater love has no one than this, that someone lay down his life for his friends.

JOHN 15:13

Now concerning brotherly love you have no need for anyone to write to you, for you yourselves have been taught by God to love one another.

1 THESSALONIANS 4:9

Time to Face the Facts

God is love. He says that about himself. He also says that if you belong to him, you will be love, too. Being loved is so amazing because it makes you feel worthwhile as a person . . . after all, someone loves you. Giving love is just as amazing because you know how good the one you love feels. Love

"Ain't love grand!"

binds people together. The thing to remember about love is that it cannot just be based on how you feel. Feelings come and go. Love is a commitment to another person, regardless of circumstances or feelings. Love stands strong.

Today I Will . . .

Thank God for his love for me. Thank him for the people in my life who love me. I'll love God right back—stronger and stronger. And I'll love others, too.

What Does the Bible Say about Loyalty?

Do you have a truly loyal friend? If so, stop right now and thank God for that person. A loyal friend stands up for you when others tear you down. A loyal friend gives you the benefit of the doubt when it appears that you have said or done something hurtful. A loyal friend sticks closer than "white on rice." God is loyal. In fact, he is the model for loyalty. He stands beside you, no matter what. He goes before you, leading the way, and comes behind you, protecting you.

What the Bible Says

All the paths of the Lord are steadfast love and faithfulness,
for those who keep his covenant and his testimonies.

PSALM 25:10

Let not steadfast love and faithfulness forsake you; bind them around
your neck; write them on the tablet of your heart.
So you will find favor and good success
in the sight of God and man.

PROVERBS 3:3–4

Time to Face the Facts

Loyalty is a real gift. If you have a loyal friend you have security and trust with that friend. You know that he or she will be there for you no matter what. Are you a loyal friend who stands by and stands up for your friends, regardless of what others say or do? Model your loyalty standards after God who sticks by you at all times and in all situations. Nothing can separate you from his love . . . *nothing*.

"Okay, let's not overdo it."

Today I Will . . .

Examine how loyal I am. Am I willing to take some persecution for standing up for a friend . . . or for God? I will ask God to help me be loyal to him and to my friends. I need his strength to do that.

What Does the Bible Say about Lying?

Maybe you don't tell out-and-out lies. But do you sometimes admit to just part of the truth or tell a version of the truth? Do you do this so you come out looking better or less guilty? Lying is usually a form of protection (false protection). God says honesty is always the best policy. He doesn't lie, and he doesn't want you to, either.

What the Bible Says

Truthful lips endure forever, but a lying tongue is but for a moment.

PROVERBS 12:19

Therefore, having put away falsehood, let each one of you speak the truth with his neighbor, for we are members one of another.

EPHESIANS 4:25

Do not lie to one another, seeing that you have put off the old self with its practices and have put on the new self, which is being renewed in knowledge after the image of its creator.

COLOSSIANS 3:9–10

Time to Face the Facts

Lying to others shows a lack of respect for them—think about how you feel when you learn someone has lied to you. You know others don't trust you enough to tell you the truth. You can't be closely following God and still lie to others. God is truth, so his life inside you should move you to be truthful. Telling the truth means you must take responsibility for your actions rather than lying about them. So, live in a way that makes no lying comfortable.

"Sparky did it."

Today I Will . . .

Think about how often I just tell part of the truth instead of the entire truth. I do that to protect myself. I commit to being truthful, and that means I commit to treating others fairly and behaving in a way that I can admit to.

What Does the Bible Say about Mathematics?

"No, please, no math!" Some people love math. The concepts come easily to them, and they are very good at it. But for others, math is just no fun. It makes no sense, doesn't seem logical, and the concepts just don't stick in their minds. Maybe you are one of these non-math people. Does God really want you to do math? What he wants is for you to work hard and do your work (math homework, for instance) to the best of your ability.

What the Bible Says

He gives power to the faint,
and to him who has no might he increases strength.

ISAIAH 40:29

Be strong in the Lord and in the strength of his might.

EPHESIANS 6:10

I can do all things through him who strengthens me.

PHILIPPIANS 4:13

Time to Face the Facts

Right now is the time in your life when you are developing the habit of good work ethics. That means you work hard on whatever you need to do. In the case of math, it means listening to your teacher explain formulas, studying hard, and spending quality time on your homework. It also means taking responsibility for yourself if you don't understand something. If you need extra help, ask your teacher for it.

"Now let me see ... If I have 5 apples and I give 2 to Sally ..."

Today I Will . . .

Ask for help if I need it. If math is a problem for me, I'll work harder on it. I want to do my best work and develop good study habits.

What Does the Bible Say about Meekness?

First, get this straight: meekness does not equal weakness. Now, what's your definition of meekness? Some mousy little person who is afraid of her own shadow? Well, that's not right. A meek person is one who is not overly impressed with herself—she knows that all she is and all she has is because of God.

What the Bible Says

Blessed are the meek,
for they shall inherit the earth.

MATTHEW 5:5

Beware of practicing your righteousness
before other people in order to be seen
by them, for then you will have no reward
from your Father who is in heaven.

MATTHEW 6:1

Clothe yourselves, all of you, with humility
toward one another, for God opposes
the proud but gives grace to the humble.

1 PETER 5:5

Time to Face the Facts

A meek person who knows she is God's creation and that all her talents, abilities, and position in life come from him does not have to be pushy or loud or proud. Meekness means it's okay with you if someone else gets the attention. You are happy if someone else wins the game. A meek person is content to just be God's person doing what God wants her to do.

Today I Will . . .

Examine my motives and attitudes. If I'm not meek, then I might be the opposite of meek—proud. I don't want to be filled with pride. I want to be a person who seeks the best and highest for other people because I love them.

MENTAL CRUELTY

What Does the Bible Say about Mental Cruelty?

There's no end to the way people hurt each other. One of the ways they do so that doesn't leave any physical bruises or cuts is mental cruelty. It's a sneaky way of tearing another person down and making him feel bad about himself. Mental cruelty is playing with another person's mind. Treating someone this way is in direct opposition to God's instructions to love one another and be kind to one another.

What the Bible Says

Love is patient and kind; love does not envy or boast; it is not arrogant or rude. . . .

1 CORINTHIANS 13:4–5

I am sure of this, that he who began a good work in you
will bring it to completion at the day of Jesus Christ.

PHILIPPIANS 1:6

May the Lord make you increase and abound in love for one another and for all.

1 THESSALONIANS 3:12

Time to Face the Facts

You might not even realize when someone is being mentally cruel to you. It can happen so quietly with just comments about how you look or how dumb you are. Sometimes it is comments about how lousy you are at sports or studies or music. Mental cruelty tears down your own opinion of yourself. It challenges your self-worth and your worth before God. Never believe that God is directing those kinds of statements. He doesn't tear you down. Love doesn't do that.

Today I Will . . .

Not listen to those kinds of unkind words. I know that God would never make me feel that way. He loves me. I'll also be careful about what I say to others. I don't want to be the source of their mental cruelty.

"Your brain is the size of a peanut."

What Does the Bible Say about Mental Maturity?

Maturing is more than just growing taller and stronger. Your body matures without you even thinking about it. Mental maturity shows when you begin making choices and decisions that show you care about other people. Mental maturity grows as God's character grows in you.

What the Bible Says

I will instruct you and teach you in the way you should go;
I will counsel you with my eye upon you.

PSALM 32:8

Finally, brothers, whatever is true, whatever is honorable, whatever is just,
whatever is pure, whatever is lovely, whatever is commendable,
if there is any excellence, if there is anything worthy of praise,
think about these things.

PHILIPPIANS 4:8

Therefore, as you received Christ Jesus the Lord,
so walk in him, rooted and built up in him and
established in the faith, just as you were
taught, abounding in thanksgiving.

COLOSSIANS 2:6-7

Time to Face the Facts

Getting to know God better and better by reading his Word and learning how he wants you to live develops mental maturity. As your mind and thoughts mature, you care most about living the way God wants you to live. You care about other people and choose to make honest and truthful decisions. Maturity in your thought process makes you a better person.

Today I Will . . .

Commit to spend time each day reading God's Word. I understand that to mature in my thought processes I need to know God better and better. I choose to reflect his love and character in my life.

What Does the Bible Say about Mercy?

When you're really sad or hurt, it's nice to have someone come along beside you and share your pain, isn't it? It's good to know you're not alone. Mercy is caring poured out on you by someone who cares. The greatest example of mercy is God himself. His mercy is poured out on us, even when we don't deserve it.

What the Bible Says

The Lord passed before him and proclaimed, "The Lord, the Lord, a God merciful and gracious, slow to anger, and abounding in steadfast love and faithfulness.

EXODUS 34:6

The steadfast love of the Lord never ceases; his mercies never come to an end.

LAMENTATIONS 3:22

Let us then with confidence draw near to the throne of grace, that we may receive mercy and find grace to help in time of need.

HEBREWS 4:16

Time to Face the Facts

God's mercy to you provides love and care. It also provides forgiveness for your sins. There is no greater mercy. His example of mercy should motivate you to pass mercy on to others. How do you do that? Care about the difficult times your friends have. Let them know you care by hanging out with them or making an encouraging card for them. Pray for your friends. When a friend hurts you, forgive him. That's mercy.

"I know you care, I'm just not sure anybody else does."

Today I Will . . .

Thank God for his mercy shown to me.

When I really think about it, I know how amazing it is. I'll ask God to soften my heart toward my friends so I notice their feelings and can show mercy to them.

What Does the Bible Say about Miracles?

Miracles are awesome! Don't you love to read the stories in the Bible of the miracles Jesus did? Have you ever prayed for a miracle in your own life? Miracles are things that happen in supernatural ways. Jesus healed sick people and brought dead people back to life. One time the sun stood still for several hours, another time food fell out of the sky for the people. Does God still do miracles today? Of course, he still loves his children today.

What the Bible Says

> Remember the wondrous works that he has done,
> his miracles and the judgments he uttered.
>
> **1 CHRONICLES 16:12**

> He healed many who were sick with various
> diseases, and cast out many demons.
>
> **MARK 1:34**

"He stubbed that toe three
weeks ago."

Time to Face the Facts

Sometimes it may seem that miracles don't happen anymore or at least not very often. But stop and think about this: We have modern medicine that can cure terrible diseases or treat painful symptoms. Think about the amazing ways people can stay in touch with each other no matter where they are in the world. God sometimes does still do amazing miracles that seem to come from nowhere. But isn't it also miraculous that we have medicine and cell phones and airplanes. . . . Perhaps his miracles today work through the things he has allowed to be in place in our world.

Today I Will . . .

Notice things. I will ask God to help me notice the things that I take for granted each day but that could actually be considered miracles in our world. I'm so thankful for his love and care.

What Does the Bible Say about Missions?

Think about the blessing you have of knowing that God loves you. You have the Bible available to read in your own language—in several different versions in fact, so you can surely understand it. Missions is the effort to make that same blessing available to people around the world. When Jesus left this earth to return to heaven, he instructed his followers to go into all the world and tell of his love.

What the Bible Says

If a man has a hundred sheep, and one of them has gone astray, does he not leave the ninety-nine on the mountains and go in search of the one that went astray? And if he finds it, truly, I say to you, he rejoices over it more than over the ninety-nine that never went astray. So it is not the will of my Father who is in heaven that one of these little ones should perish.

MATTHEW 18:12–14

Go therefore and make disciples of all nations, baptizing them in the name of the Father and of the Son and of the Holy Spirit, teaching them to observe all that I have commanded you.

MATTHEW 28:19–20

We are ambassadors for Christ, God making his appeal through us. . . .

2 CORINTHIANS 5:20

"It's a lot easier to listen with a full stomach."

Time to Face the Facts

There are probably people right in your town who have not heard about God's love. There are people who have not read the Bible. Imagine that; they have never sat down and read the Bible. Some missionaries answer the command of Jesus to leave their homes and go around the world to tell of his love. Some missions happens right in your own country, state, and town. Missions is simply telling others about God.

Today I Will . . .

Support missionaries by praying for them and giving to their financial needs. I will also look around and see how I can be a missionary right here where I live.

What Does the Bible Say about Mistakes?

No one plans to make mistakes. That's why they are called mistakes. However, everyone (yes, *everyone*) makes mistakes. Sometimes the result of a mistake hurts you and sometimes it hurts others, too. That's when forgiveness is a joy. God willingly and lovingly models forgiveness for mistakes. How are you at passing that forgiveness along?

What the Bible Says

Come now, let us reason together, says the LORD:
though your sins are like scarlet,
they shall be as white as snow;
though they are red like crimson,
they shall become like wool.

ISAIAH 1:18

For I am sure that neither death nor life, nor angels nor rulers, nor things present nor things to come, nor powers, nor height nor depth, nor anything else in all creation, will be able to separate us from the love of God in Christ Jesus our Lord.

ROMANS 8:38–39

Not that I have already obtained this or am already perfect, but I press on to make it my own, because Christ Jesus has made me his own. Brothers, I do not consider that I have made it my own. But one thing I do: forgetting what lies behind and straining forward to what lies ahead, I press on toward the goal for the prize of the upward call of God in Christ Jesus.

PHILIPPIANS 3:12–14

Time to Face the Facts

You have made mistakes in your life, and you will again in the future. Sometimes your actions or choices are truly mistakes—bad choices or acting without thinking. Sometimes they may be on purpose to hurt someone or protect yourself. When you've made a mistake, the way to handle it is to apologize to anyone hurt by it, whether it's God or another person. Learn from your mistakes and try not to make the same mistakes over and over.

Today I Will . . .

Admit when I've made a mistake. That's the first step. Then I will apologize for it and ask God to help me learn from it. I don't what to keep making the same mistake over and over.

MONEY

What Does the Bible Say about Money?

If a person has lots of money, then his focus is often on how to spend it and enjoy the finer things in this world. If a person does not have lots of money, then he may constantly be wondering how to get more or how he's going to pay his bills. Making money, spending money, and thinking about money takes up a lot of time. God doesn't want thoughts about money to be your main brain activity. There are more important things to think about.

What the Bible Says

No one can serve two masters, for either he will hate the one and love the other, or he will be devoted to the one and despise the other. You cannot serve God and money.

MATTHEW 6:24

For the love of money is a root of all kinds of evils. It is through this craving that some have wandered away from the faith and pierced themselves with many pangs.

1 TIMOTHY 6:10

Keep your life free from love of money, and be content with what you have, for he has said, "I will never leave you nor forsake you."

HEBREWS 13:5

Time to Face the Facts

Putting more importance on money than you do on people is not a good thing. If you're doing that, then you've got your priorities turned upside down. Money should be important only to the point of getting you stuff you need (not stuff you want) and of helping those less fortunate than you are to get what

"Money! My best friend!"

they need. God said that the two most important commandments are to love him and love others . . . neither of those mention money.

Today I Will . . .

Not put so much emphasis on money and getting more and more stuff. I will focus more on loving God and loving others.

MOODS

What Does the Bible Say about Moods?

Moody people are happy one minute and crabby the next. You never really know what kind of person you'll get when you are with someone like that. It's hard to figure out what makes this person's mood swing from high to low and back again. Sometimes the moody person doesn't know either. The challenge for a moody person is to stay focused on God and others rather than on self.

What the Bible Says

You keep him in perfect peace
whose mind is stayed on you,
because he trusts in you.

ISAIAH 26:3

Be kind to one another, tenderhearted, forgiving
one another, as God in Christ forgave you.

EPHESIANS 4:32

Casting all your anxieties on him,
because he cares for you.

1 PETER 5:7

Time to Face the Facts

Often a person's moods swing back and forth because she is focusing more on herself than on others. She's concerned about how things affect her more than how others may feel. Then she ends up letting her emotions control her attitudes and actions. The sad thing is that this person misses chances to be an encouragement or a help to those around her. She misses the chance to love others because she's too concerned about herself.

Today I Will . . .

Stop thinking only of myself. I never thought about moodiness being selfish. But that makes sense. I want to be more concerned with others than with myself.

MOTIVES

What Does the Bible Say about Motives?

Why do you do what you do? Do you help others so that people will talk about how kind you are? Do you go to church or youth group so that others will think you're really spiritual? Maybe you make a big deal of giving to the food pantry or something so that your friends will think you're super generous. Here's a news flash: the reason you do things is more important to God than what you actually do. He looks at your heart—your motives.

What the Bible Says

But the LORD said to Samuel, "Do not look on his appearance or on the height of his stature, because I have rejected him. For the LORD sees not as man sees: man looks on the outward appearance, but the LORD looks on the heart."

1 SAMUEL 16:7

Every way of a man is right in his own eyes,
but the LORD weighs the heart.

PROVERBS 21:2

Beware of practicing your righteousness before other people in order to be seen by them, for then you will have no reward from your Father who is in heaven.

MATTHEW 6:1

Time to Face the Facts

Does it surprise you that God cares more about your motives for doing things than he cares about what you actually do? Yeah, you can't fool God. He knows if you're doing good things for the wrong reasons. He knows, and it matters to him. If your heart is truly attuned to serving him, your motives will be healthy and pure. Then, the good things you do will be even better!

Today I Will . . .

Think about why I do the things I do. If my motives aren't good, I'll ask God to help me change them. I want to do good things for the right reasons.

What Does the Bible Say about Movies?

Oh, come on, God doesn't care about movies, does he? He certainly does. Want to know why? Because of their content. You have to admit that the morals and values in many of today's movies are not the best. God wants you to be careful about what kinds of things you feed your mind.

What the Bible Says

He has told you, O man, what is good;
and what does the LORD require of you
but to do justice, and to love kindness,
and to walk humbly with your God?

MICAH 6:8

Let there be no filthiness nor foolish talk nor crude joking, which are out of place, but instead let there be thanksgiving.

EPHESIANS 5:4

Time to Face the Facts

Unfortunately, a constant mind diet of swearing, sex, and violence gets imbedded in your mind and those things or attitudes begin creeping into your thoughts, language, and actions. So, yes, God cares about what movies you see. There's nothing wrong with wholesome entertainment except that it's hard to find. Pay attention to what you feed your mind and heart. If the movies you choose to see portray low moral values, bad language, or violence . . . choose something else.

"Do I want to put that in my brain?"

Today I Will . . .

Make some tough choices. I see some movies just because I want to be with my friends, so saying no to some of their choices may be hard. But I want to put good things in my mind and heart. I want to choose values that are honoring to God.

What Does the Bible Say about Music?

Music is mentioned a lot in the Bible. Did you know that the book of Psalms is actually the songbook of the early Christians? Music is a good thing. But there are a lot of different types of music to choose from these days. Just as with the topic of movies, it's important to look at the content of the music you listen to. Music is a gift, but make sure the kind of music you listen to honors and respects God and other people.

What the Bible Says

Praise him with trumpet sound;
praise him with lute and harp!
Praise him with tambourine and dance;
praise him with strings and pipe!
Praise him with sounding cymbals;
praise him with loud clashing cymbals!
Let everything that has breath praise the Lord!
Praise the Lord!

PSALM 150:3–6

Time to Face the Facts

Each generation seems to have its own favorite style of music. Older generations often do not appreciate the music that the younger generation listens to. The most important thing is that the content of the lyrics is moral and respectful to other people and to God. The best music to listen to is music that worships and praises God and encourages you to walk more closely with him.

"Rock on!"

Today I Will . . .

Double-check the content of the music I listen to most often. I will enjoy music that celebrates God's love and power. It's fun to worship him through music.

What Does the Bible Say about Natural Disasters?

Earthquakes, tsunamis, tornadoes, hurricanes . . . natural disasters are powerful and destructive. Thousands of dollars' worth of damage are caused by these occurrences. Thousands of lives are lost each year because of them, too. Why doesn't God stop these natural disasters? Doesn't he care?

What the Bible Says

Even though I walk through the valley of the shadow of death,
I will fear no evil,
for you are with me;
your rod and your staff,
they comfort me.

PSALM 23:4

The LORD is good, a stronghold in the day of trouble;
he knows those who take refuge in him.

NAHUM 1:7

I have said these things to you, that in me you may have peace. In the world you will have tribulation. But take heart; I have overcome the world.

JOHN 16:33

Time to Face the Facts

It is hard to understand why God doesn't stop these terrible natural disasters. You know he cares about the homes and lives lost because he loves people. Perhaps God doesn't stop these things because they are just a part of the natural occurrences in our world. Before sin entered the world, there were no natural disasters; but when God's perfect plan was changed because of sin, it meant that natural disasters, illness, and death became a part of what people must deal with. The good promise, though, is that God is always with you, no matter what you must go through.

Today I Will . . .

Pray for people who have lost their homes and family members because of natural disasters. I'll also thank God for his presence and comfort for all who need it.

What Does the Bible Say about Nature?

Towering, snow-covered mountains; powerful ocean waves; fragrant flowers; beautiful deer; busy hummingbirds; gentle streams . . . what's your favorite part of nature? The record of the creation of all nature is recorded in Genesis. God made it all! He is incredibly creative.

What the Bible Says

In the beginning, God created the heavens and the earth.

GENESIS 1:1

Praise him, sun and moon,
praise him, all you shining stars!
Praise him, you highest heavens,
and you waters above the heavens!

PSALM 148:3

And some of the Pharisees in the crowd said to [Jesus], "Teacher, rebuke your disciples." He answered, "I tell you, if these were silent, the very stones would cry out."

LUKE 19:39–41

Time to Face the Facts

If you look around at the world God made, nature seems to praise him all by itself. The strength of many parts of nature shows God's power. The beauty of nature shows his attention to detail. God made this beautiful world with so much creativity that there is something for all people to enjoy. Praise him for his creation.

"Nature is tweet!"

Today I Will . . .

Thank God for his creation of nature. His creativity is amazing. I love seeing the mountains. I love the oceans. I love flowers and birds and penguins . . . I love it all!

What Does the Bible Say about Neatness?

There is an old saying: "A place for everything and everything in its place." Most kids aren't known for their neatness, especially the closer they get to their teens. Their rooms get pretty messy with clothes, books, CDs, and who knows what else all over the room. When everything is a mess, it is hard to find things and things get lost or broken. This treatment of your "stuff" shows very little respect for the money it took to buy those things.

What the Bible Says

What does the LORD your God require of you, but to fear the LORD your God, to walk in all his ways, to love him, to serve the LORD your God with all your heart and with all your soul.

DEUTERONOMY 10:12

For to everyone who has will more be given, and he will have an abundance. But from the one who has not, even what he has will be taken away.

MATTHEW 25:29

For no good tree bears bad fruit, nor again does a bad tree bear good fruit, for each tree is known by its own fruit. . . .

LUKE 6:43–44

Time to Face the Facts

Now, the emphasis in your life should never be on money. But someone does have to earn the money to buy your clothes and other stuff. You should respect that effort and take care of the stuff. Keep your room neater. Keep your locker at school neater. Think about how much time you will save on looking for your things!

Today I Will . . .

Clean my room, okay? I'll put stuff away and try to always put my things where they belong. I'll respect the stuff I have.

"I don't see my room as a mess—I just have a lot of stuff."

What Does the Bible Say about Neglect?

Neglect is when you don't care enough about another person to help him. It often results in the neglected person being hurt. How do you live with yourself if you've neglected someone and he suffers because of it? It would be difficult, right? Neglecting others is in direct opposition to God's desire that you love others. You can't love people and neglect them, too.

What the Bible Says

And everyone who hears these words of mine and does not do them will be like a foolish man who built his house on the sand. And the rain fell, and the floods came, and the winds blew and beat against that house, and it fell, and great was the fall of it.

MATTHEW 7:26–27

But be doers of the word, and not hearers only, deceiving yourselves.

JAMES 1:22

So whoever knows the right thing to do and fails to do it, for him it is sin.

JAMES 4:17

Time to Face the Facts

Loving people means more than just saying that you love them. Showing that love by being concerned for them and helping them in any way you can is real love. This takes time and effort, and it means that you consider another person more important than yourself. Huh . . . that's just what God said you should do.

Today I Will . . .

Put my love for others into action. I will not knowingly neglect another person. I want to always show God's love to others.

"It's not neglect . . . I fed him last month."

What Does the Bible Say about Obedience?

Don't you get tired of hearing about obedience? Does it seem like there is always someone you have to obey? Can you not wait to grow up so you don't have to obey anyone? Well, don't get your hopes up on that. Even adults have to obey. The most important obedience is to God.

What the Bible Says

Do what is right and good in the sight of the LORD,
that it may go well with you. . . .

DEUTERONOMY 6:18

If you love me, you will keep my commandments.

JOHN 14:15

For this is the covenant that I will make with the house of Israel
after those days, declares the Lord:
I will put my laws into their minds,
and write them on their hearts,
and I will be their God,
and they shall be my people.

HEBREWS 8:10

Time to Face the Facts

If you say you love God, but don't obey what you know he wants you to do, then your love may be only lip service. God doesn't insist that you obey because he wants to run your life. He wants you to obey because obeying him helps you be a better person—more kind, fair, loving, and considerate. Obeying him means obeying others isn't an issue. Obeying puts your love into action.

Today I Will . . .

Not make excuses about obeying. I will study God's Word so I know how to obey God. I know I'll be a nicer person if I'm obeying him.

What Does the Bible Say about Obesity?

Look around you and you will see many large people. Obesity is an epidemic these days. Between unhealthy diets and couch potatoes, people have grown to be very overweight. The scary thing is that obesity impacts your health in very serious ways. There are a couple of reasons why obesity that isn't caused by health issues is a sin. It means you aren't taking care of the body God gave you.

What the Bible Says

There is no soundness in my flesh
because of your indignation;
there is no health in my bones
because of my sin.

PSALM 38:3

Do you not know that your body is a temple of the Holy Spirit within you,
whom you have from God? You are not your own, for you
were bought with a price. So glorify God in your body.

1 CORINTHIANS 6:19–20

Time to Face the Facts

If you suffer from obesity, you probably don't have the energy or strength to do the work God gave you to do. Obesity may also mean that you are not sharing the resources you have with those who do not have enough—that would be your food and money. That means you aren't caring for others. Obesity that is from overeating and lack of exercise shows lack of care for yourself and others. It disrespects the one body God gave you.

"They don't make chairs like they used to."

Today I Will . . .

Get off the couch and go for a walk or play some sports. I'll watch what I eat and make every effort to keep my weight under control. I want to respect the body God gave me and keep it healthy.

What Does the Bible Say about Obstacles?

Have you ever seen those little bumps placed across a road to keep cars from going too fast? They are called speed bumps. Sometimes life has speed bumps—obstacles that you must go over or around in order to keep moving. Life is full of obstacles, and figuring out how to handle them is part of the process of maturing. The wonderful thing is that God will be your wisdom and guide as you face these obstacles.

What the Bible Says

For he who avenges blood is mindful of them;
he does not forget the cry of the afflicted.

PSALM 9:12

We are afflicted in every way, but not crushed;
perplexed, but not driven to despair.

2 CORINTHIANS 4:8

Count it all joy, my brothers, when you meet trials
of various kinds, for you know that the testing
of your faith produces steadfastness.

JAMES 1:2–3

Time to Face the Facts

You can count on obstacles in your life. Learning how to handle them is important. Ask for God's help to stay true to your values of living for him as you maneuver around obstacles. Don't ever sacrifice your commitment to obeying God as you move forward. Trust God to be your guide and your strength throughout all of life.

Today I Will . . .

Ask God to direct my life each day. Then he will show me the way to handle any obstacles that come up in my life.

What Does the Bible Say about the Occult?

This is scary territory. Because of various books and movies that have been popular lately, kids are curious about the spirit world. They perhaps even take it pretty lightly. The world of the occult is real and it is evil. God and the angels he sends to protect you are also real. He will keep you from the dangers of the occult.

What the Bible Says

Put on the whole armor of God, that you may be able to stand against the schemes of the devil. For we do not wrestle against flesh and blood, but against the rulers, against the authorities, against the cosmic powers over this present darkness, against the spiritual forces of evil in the heavenly places.

EPHESIANS 6:11–12

Be sober-minded; be watchful. Your adversary the devil prowls around like a roaring lion, seeking someone to devour.

1 PETER 5:8

Submit yourselves therefore to God. Resist the devil, and he will flee from you.

JAMES 4:7

"Hocus Pocus . . . Help me focus!"

Time to Face the Facts

Fooling around with the occult is dangerous. Don't take it lightly. The spirit world is real—God's Spirit and his angels are real and the evil side of the spirit world is real, too. Satan controls it, and he does not have your best interests in mind. Stay away from the occult. Keep your focus on God and seek his protection in your life.

Today I Will . . .

Not fool around with the occult. My friends may think it is cool and even fun, but I know there is real danger there of letting Satan and his evil into my heart. I'll keep my focus on God and ask for his protection.

What Does the Bible Say about Opportunities?

Big opportunities. Small opportunities. Opportunities come your way every day. You are presented with opportunities to make good choices or bad ones, to try something new or to stay in your comfort zone. Some opportunities present the choice of serving and obeying God or not. God sends opportunities your way to help you learn and grow as you live for him.

What the Bible Says

For I know the plans I have for you, declares the Lord, plans for welfare and not for evil, to give you a future and a hope.

JEREMIAH 29:11

Look carefully then how you walk, not as unwise but as wise, making the best use of the time, because the days are evil.

EPHESIANS 5:15–16

Whatever you do, work heartily, as for the Lord and not for men.

COLOSSIANS 3:23

Time to Face the Facts

Opportunities to hurt other people or do evil things are not opportunities sent by God. When you have an opportunity that you're not sure how to handle, ask God to show you that it is from him. His opportunities will give you the chance to serve him, help others, and try new things that will possibly help you to know what gifts he has given you and what career you should pursue as a grown-up. Opportunities are exciting. Be courageous and try some new things!

Today I Will . . .

Grab opportunities that come my way. I'll be sure that the opportunities I'm grabbing are truly from God. When I know that, I will be willing to take them. This is exciting!

OPPOSITION

What Does the Bible Say about Opposition?

You're trying to do good things, trying to live for God . . . and it feels like every day it gets harder and harder. That's opposition. The more devoted you try to be in living for God, the harder Satan is going to oppose you. His opposition may be sneaky and come in the form of other kids making fun of you. It may come in the form of temptations—strong ones—to do things that are disobedient to God. Opposition can be very strong. You need God to guide you and protect you through it.

What the Bible Says

Blessed is the man
who walks not in the counsel of the wicked,
nor stands in the way of sinners,
nor sits in the seat of scoffers.

PSALM 1:1

Blessed is the man who remains steadfast under trial, for when he has stood the test he will receive the crown of life, which God has promised to those who love him.

JAMES 1:12

Time to Face the Facts

You will have opposition in living your Christian life. You can count on it. It's important to stay alert because sometimes the opposition is sneaky and can appear to be no big deal. Stay close to God. Ask him to guide your thoughts and actions. He will reveal to you when opposition is creeping into your life, and he will help you resist it. You can trust him.

"Hey, look at the Jesus-boy."

Today I Will . . .

Ask God to keep me alert. I don't want to give in to opposition that tempts me to disobey God. It's so easy to do that sometimes. I'll stay close to God by reading his Word and praying. I know he will protect me and guide me.

What Does the Bible Say about Organization?

Life gets pretty chaotic sometimes, doesn't it? If you don't have a schedule for spending time with God, getting homework done, doing your chores, and hanging out with friends, well, it's sometimes hard to fit everything in. Another part of organization is putting stuff away and then knowing where it is when you need it again. Organization of schedules and stuff is pretty necessary to living an organized life. Look around—God created an organized world.

What the Bible Says

Great peace have those who love your law;
nothing can make them stumble.

PSALM 119:165

For God is not a God of
confusion but of peace. . . .

1 CORINTHIANS 14:33

But all things should be done
decently and in order.

1 CORINTHIANS 14:40

Time to Face the Facts

God is not the author of confusion. If your life is chaotic and crazy, it's not God's fault. If you're living life like a ball that bounces against one thing then another and another—just doing whatever activity you bump into or talking to whichever friend you run into—that's not organization. God asks you to be intentional in how you live and what you do. That takes organization.

Today I Will . . .

Slow down. I'll make a list of the things that are important to me and that I believe God wants me to do. Then I'll number them and organize my life so that I'm doing the important things. If I'm organized in what I do and what I have, there will be more time to do the things I want to do.

What Does the Bible Say about Orphans?

Maybe your parents make you crazy once in a while, but imagine how hard life would be without them. Orphans are children whose parents are no longer living. These children depend on the kindness of other family members or sometimes complete strangers. While it may be sad for these people to know they are orphans, a good thing to remember is that God is their Father. He loves and cares for them.

What the Bible Says

Whoever gives one of these little ones even a cup of cold water because he is a disciple, truly, I say to you, he will by no means lose his reward.

MATTHEW 10:42

A new commandment I give to you, that you love one another: just as I have loved you, you also are to love one another.

JOHN 13:34

Religion that is pure and undefiled before God, the Father, is this: to visit orphans and widows in their affliction, and to keep oneself unstained from the world.

JAMES 1:27

Time to Face the Facts

It is sad for a child to not have her parents in her life while she is growing up. God certainly intended for families to be together, but it doesn't always happen that way. But remember that God's love is complete and never-ending. He encourages his children to treat orphans in a special way, too. He knows they need an extra measure of love and care.

"Where do I belong?"

Today I Will . . .

Thank God for my parents or caregivers. I will tell them how much I appreciate them and all they do for me. I will also be especially caring to any kids I know who do not live with their parents.

What Does the Bible Say about Pain?

Being in pain is no fun. When something hurts, it's hard to think about anything else. It's hard to be cheery, and it's hard to concentrate. Being around someone who is in pain takes a lot of compassion and patience. It is also important to pray for that person. Thank God for pain-relieving medications and remember that God is the only true pain reliever.

What the Bible Says

> For he has not despised or abhorred
> the affliction of the afflicted,
> and he has not hidden his face from him,
> but has heard, when he cried to him.

PSALM 22:24

> Blessed be the God and Father of our Lord Jesus Christ, the Father of mercies and God of all comfort, who comforts us in all our affliction, so that we may be able to comfort those who are in any affliction, with the comfort with which we ourselves are comforted by God.

2 CORINTHIANS 1:3–4

Time to Face the Facts

Do you have the patience and care to help a person who is in pain? It's a chance for you to show your love for that person as you look for ways to be a helper or an encourager. If you've ever been in a little pain for a short time, just think about how it would be to feel that way for a long time. It's sometimes hard to understand why God doesn't just stop pain. But even when he doesn't do that, he stays close by and gives comfort and support.

"Help, my thumb's going to fall off!"

Today I Will . . .

Pray for someone I know who is in pain. I will look for ways that I can be an encourager or helper to that person.

What Does the Bible Say about Panic?

You're alone in your room on a dark, windy night. Noises echo in the darkness and fear takes root in your heart. It creeps throughout your body until it becomes full-fledged panic. Fear gone crazy is panic. God says over and over in his Word that he is your protector and helper. He is the antidote to panic.

What the Bible Says

I will give peace in the land,
and you shall lie down, and none
shall make you afraid.

LEVITICUS 26:6

God is our refuge and strength,
a very present help in trouble.

PSALM 46:1

You keep him in perfect peace
whose mind is stayed on you,
because he trusts in you.

ISAIAH 26:3

Time to Face the Facts

When fear begins to take root in your heart, turn to God for help in stopping it from becoming panic. Focus on his love and care and his promises to protect you. Stop your fear by putting your mind on the positive truth of God's care. He will make your panic go from a roaring lion down to a purring kitten.

Today I Will . . .

Tell God what my fears are and which ones grow so quickly into panic. I'll memorize one verse about God's care or protection, and when that fear starts going crazy in my mind, I'll say that verse over and over.

What Does the Bible Say about Parents?

Hopefully you have wonderful parents who teach you about God, take great care of you, and make life a lot of fun. Parents are your earliest influence. They are also most often the people who love you unconditionally. Even if they make you angry sometimes with their rules and chores, parents are a wonderful gift from God.

What the Bible Says

Honor your father and your mother, that your days may be long in the land that the Lord your God is giving you.

EXODUS 20:12

Children, obey your parents in the Lord, for this is right. "Honor your father and mother" (this is the first commandment with a promise), "that it may go well with you and that you may live long in the land."

EPHESIANS 6:1–3

Time to Face the Facts

Believe it or not, it is not completely unexpected that you and your parents have problems sometimes. As you get older, you want to stretch your wings of independence, and then there are issues with your parents. As you get older ,you will realize the value of parents who love you enough to set boundaries. So, thank God for them. Love them back and enjoy them.

Today I Will . . .

Be nice to my parents. I'll help out around the house and be pleasant when I talk with them. I'm really thankful for my parents. I want them to know that.

"Now that I am a little older, it's amazing how much smarter my parents are."

What Does the Bible Say about Patience?

There are things you need patience for, regardless of your age. You may need patience to learn new information in school or to perfect sports skills. Perhaps you need extra patience because of an annoying person in your life. The need for patience never goes away. You will always need it. God promises to help you with patience. In fact, it's tough to have patience without God in your life.

What the Bible Says

The LORD is good to those who wait for him,
to the soul who seeks him.

LAMENTATIONS 3:25

The fruit of the Spirit is love, joy, peace, patience, kindness, goodness, faithfulness, gentleness, self-control; against such things there is no law.

GALATIANS 5:22–23

"Give me patience—NOW!"

Time to Face the Facts

Some people are naturally more patient than others—at least on the outside. But patience is not necessarily a character trait. It is definitely a result of the Holy Spirit working in your life, as the verses above told you. You need patience to wait on God and not rush into life without his direction. You need patience in dealing with other people sometimes and even in dealing with yourself and mistakes you make or things you need to learn. That patience grows and develops with God's help.

Today I Will . . .

Ask God to help me with patience. It doesn't come easily for me. I need the Holy Spirit working in my heart to help me learn to be more patient in waiting for God and in dealing with others.

What Does the Bible Say about Peace?

Being peaceful means you get along well with others. It means you are comfortable with where you are in life. Peace means you are not always thinking about what you would like to be doing or where you would rather be. God is peace, and knowing him brings peace into your heart.

What the Bible Says

You are a hiding place for me;
you preserve me from trouble;
you surround me with shouts of deliverance.
Selah

PSALM 32:7

When you pass through the waters, I will be with you;
and through the rivers, they shall not overwhelm you;
when you walk through fire you shall not be burned,
and the flame shall not consume you.
For I am the LORD your God,
the Holy One of Israel, your Savior. . . .

ISAIAH 43:2–3

Peace I leave with you; my peace I give to you. Not as the world gives
do I give to you. Let not your hearts be troubled, neither let them be afraid.

JOHN 14:27

Time to Face the Facts

Peace is a by-product of trusting God and knowing that he is in control. God working in your heart helps you get along with others and not always be concerned with how things affect you. You can have peace in your heart where God is concerned because you know he is leading you and he wants the very best for you. Trust equals peace.

Today I Will . . .

Not fight with God or anyone else. I want peace in my heart instead of always looking to see what's next or thinking about where I'd like to live or what I'd like to do. I want to get along with others and be a peacemaker, not a troublemaker. I'm sure that's what God wants, too.

What Does the Bible Say about Peer Pressure?

Peer pressure is when your friends push you to do things just like them. Things they want to do—even if you don't. The pressure is "do this, dress like us, think like us, or act like us, and if you don't, then you can't be our friend anymore." It's tough, but God cares a lot about who you allow to influence you.

What the Bible Says

Choose this day whom you will serve, whether the gods your fathers served in the region beyond the River, or the gods of the Amorites in whose land you dwell. But as for me and my house, we will serve the LORD.

JOSHUA 24:15

Even a child makes himself known by his acts,
by whether his conduct is pure and upright.

PROVERBS 20:11

And we all, with unveiled face, beholding the glory of the Lord, are being transformed into the same image from one degree of glory to another. For this comes from the Lord who is the Spirit.

2 CORINTHIANS 3:18

Time to Face the Facts

You belong to God, so no one else should be influencing your actions. Peer groups may try to pull you away from doing what God wants or even what you know is right. It's true that you should want to be transformed, but you should be transformed into the image of God, not the image of a bunch of other kids.

Today I Will . . .

Choose to serve God and him only. It's going to be tough sometimes, but with God's help, I can do it.

"Dude . . . Come join the cool hair club!"

PERFECTION

What Does the Bible Say about Perfection?

Maybe you know someone who seems to have her life all together. Everything goes her direction, she's good-looking, has a great family, gets good grades, is talented, and to top it off, she never seems to make a mistake or have a problem. *She is perfect!* No, she's not. The only perfect Person who ever lived is Jesus. Perfection for the rest of us is possible only in heaven.

What the Bible Says

If my people who are called by my name humble themselves, and pray and seek my face and turn from their wicked ways, then I will hear from heaven and will forgive their sin and heal their land.

2 CHRONICLES 7:14

And you, who once were alienated and hostile in mind, doing evil deeds, he has now reconciled in his body of flesh by his death, in order to present you holy and blameless and above reproach before him, if indeed you continue in the faith, stable and steadfast, not shifting from the hope of the gospel that you heard, which has been proclaimed in all creation under heaven, and of which I, Paul, became a minister.

COLOSSIANS 1:21–23

Time to Face the Facts

Don't kid yourself, perfection is not possible on this earth. Everyone here is sinful. Some people are better at hiding their problems than others are, but they do have them. Thank goodness, God forgives our sins and he actually forgets them. So, in his sight, you are perfect if you've asked Jesus into your heart, because you are forgiven. But in reality . . . you're not perfect, except in him. That's true of *everyone* else, too.

"Can't get any better than . . . Me!"

Today I Will . . .

Cut myself a little slack. I'm not perfect, even though I try hard to be. But I'm thankful that because of Jesus, I can be perfect in God's sight because of forgiveness.

What Does the Bible Say about Persecution?

A lot of people are treated unfairly for various reasons—because they belong to the wrong gang or follow the wrong sports team. Real persecution, though, is often put upon people who choose to follow Christ. Enemies of Christianity persecute, torture, and punish Christians, either out of fear or in an effort to get them to renounce their faith. It's not surprising. Christ said it would happen.

What the Bible Says

Blessed are you when others revile you and
persecute you and utter all kinds of evil against
you falsely on my account.

MATTHEW 5:11

If the world hates you, know that it has hated me before it hated you.
If you were of the world, the world would love you as its own; but
because you are not of the world, but I chose you out
of the world, therefore the world hates you.

JOHN 15:18–19

But rejoice insofar as you share Christ's sufferings, that you may
also rejoice and be glad when his glory is revealed.

1 PETER 4:13

Time to Face the Facts

You may not be tortured or beaten because of your faith, but you may experience verbal persecution. This usually comes in the form of being made fun of because Christ is important to you. Even though it's hard, you can take comfort in the truth that Satan is afraid of your making a difference for God in this world. That's why he motivates the persecution. Stand strong. Trust God to be your strength and protection in times of persecution.

Today I Will . . .

Stand strong. Nothing is too hard to go through when I consider what Jesus went through for me. I will trust God to be my strength and to hold me up in difficult times.

What Does the Bible Say about Perseverance?

Perseverance is when you keep on going no matter how tough things get. Regardless of how scared you are or how tired or how confused, you just keep on doing what you know you're supposed to do. This is real obedience to God, even when life gets tough.

What the Bible Says

If you abide in me, and my words abide in you, ask whatever you wish, and it will be done for you.

JOHN 15:7

We rejoice in our sufferings, knowing that suffering produces endurance, and endurance produces character, and character produces hope, and hope does not put us to shame, because God's love has been poured into our hearts through the Holy Spirit who has been given to us.

ROMANS 5:3–5

For this very reason, make every effort to supplement your faith with virtue, and virtue with knowledge, and knowledge with self-control, and self-control with steadfastness, and steadfastness with godliness, and godliness with brotherly affection, and brotherly affection with love. For if these qualities are yours and are increasing, they keep you from being ineffective or unfruitful in the knowledge of our Lord Jesus Christ.

2 PETER 1:5–8

Time to Face the Facts

Mother Teresa, a famous nun who worked with the desperately poor in India, was a classic example of a person with perseverance. She knew God had called her to this work early in her life, so she just kept doing it day after day after day for her entire life. Toward the end of her life she said there were times when she couldn't sense God's presence or direction, but she kept on doing what God had told her to do. She thought that he would tell her if he wanted her to stop. Do you have the faith to persevere in difficult situations over a long period of time?

Today I Will . . .

Persevere in just one thing. Maybe God hasn't told me what he wants me to do with my whole life yet. But I can find one command to obey and just keep obeying that every day. I can persevere.

PERSONAL HYGIENE

What Does the Bible Say about Personal Hygiene?

Maybe you think God doesn't really care whether you brush your teeth and floss every day. Do you think God has more important things to think about than whether you take a shower and smell all fresh and nice? Surprise, surprise . . . God cares about the image and scent you leave with people.

What the Bible Says

So, every healthy tree bears good fruit,
but the diseased tree bears bad fruit.
A healthy tree cannot bear bad fruit,
nor can a diseased tree bear good fruit.

MATTHEW 7:17–18

Or do you not know that your body is a temple of the Holy Spirit within you, whom you have from God? You are not your own.

1 CORINTHIANS 6:19

For we are the aroma of Christ to God among those who are being saved and among those who are perishing.

2 CORINTHIANS 2:15

Time to Face the Facts

How you take care of yourself reflects your opinion of God. If you're content to be dirty, smelly, and unhealthy, then it shows that deep down inside you don't think much of the health and body God has given you. Other people will see that, too. Not a good thought to leave behind with them.

"Whoa—did an army of cockroaches march through your mouth?"

Today I Will . . .

Begin taking care of my body. It's the only one God gave me, and I want to honor it.

What Does the Bible Say about Physical Education?

Some kids consider physical education class to be a throwaway class—an easy A. Others find it more boring than watching grass grow. Still others think it's the most difficult class in the whole year. What's the benefit of learning physical education? Variety. Yep, through physical education classes you learn different ways of exercising and training the muscles in your body. Just as math, science, and English train your brain, physical education trains your body.

What the Bible Says

They who wait for the LORD shall renew their strength;
they shall mount up with wings like eagles;
they shall run and not be weary;
they shall walk and not faint.

ISAIAH 40:31

While bodily training is of some value, godliness is of value in every way, as it holds promise for the present life and also for the life to come.

1 TIMOTHY 4:8

Time to Face the Facts

It's important to train your entire body—your muscles and your brain. That total body training leads to good health. God made your body to move, not just sit. Your heart and muscles need to move to be healthy, even if it's just taking a walk every day. Through physical education class you may discover a sport or exercise style you really enjoy.

"These days I just jump rope to keep in shape."

Today I Will . . .

Stop complaining about this class. I'll keep an open mind and try to find something I enjoy . . . and get healthier at the same time!

What Does the Bible Say about Physical Fitness?

Sit-ups and jumping jacks? That doesn't have anything to do with the Bible. Well, it kind of does. Physical fitness means you're taking care of your body— the only one you get in this life. Taking care of it shows respect and honor to God.

What the Bible Says

I appeal to you therefore, brothers,
by the mercies of God, to present
your bodies as a living sacrifice,
holy and acceptable to God,
which is your spiritual worship.

ROMANS 12:1

Do you not know that you are God's temple
and that God's Spirit dwells in you?

1 CORINTHIANS 3:16

You yourselves like living stones are being
built up as a spiritual house, to be a holy
priesthood, to offer spiritual sacrifices
acceptable to God through Jesus Christ.

1 PETER 2:5

Time to Face the Facts

You can choose to sit around and be a couch potato while you watch TV or play video games. If you do that, your body will not be physically fit. That doesn't just mean you get fat; it means your heart is not healthy, your blood vessels get clogged up with junk, your muscles get weak, and eventually you get sick. That's *not* taking care of the body God gave you.

Today I Will . . .

Pay attention to my body. I'll exercise and eat right and do all I can to be physically fit.

What Does the Bible Say about Physical Maturity?

God is amazing. When you were born, you were this tiny little person, but everything your body needed to have when you became an adult was already there inside you. Your body grows and develops as you grow up without you even thinking about it. You probably notice things changing in your body each year. God takes care of all this, but you do have a little responsibility—taking care of your body.

What the Bible Says

> For you formed my inward parts;
> you knitted me together in my mother's womb.
> I praise you, for I am fearfully and wonderfully made.
> Wonderful are your works; my soul knows it very well.
>
> **PSALM 139:13–14**

> I press on toward the goal for the prize of
> the upward call of God in Christ Jesus.
>
> **PHILIPPIANS 3:14**

Time to Face the Facts

Yes, God does the maturing. He created your body to grow and develop so that you can grow into an adult. Your responsibility is in taking care of your body. What does that mean? Putting healthy food into it so you have the vitamins and nutrients it needs to stay healthy. Getting enough exercise to keep your heart and muscles strong and working well. Getting enough

"I used to fit just fine."

sleep so your body can rest from the activities and busyness of the day. Take care of your body; God will do his part to bring it to physical maturity.

Today I Will . . .

Wow, I never thought about how my body is growing and changing. That's cool. I'll do my part by watching what I eat and getting enough exercise and rest. God and I are a team in this!

What Does the Bible Say about Planning?

Planning keeps you organized. For example, if you don't have a plan, at least in your mind, of what to do each day, you stand a good chance of not accomplishing the things you need to do. The important things tend to get pushed aside because something else yells for attention. God is organized, and he has plans. In fact, he has plans for you. Follow his example.

What the Bible Says

And you, Solomon my son, know the God of your father and serve him with a whole heart and with a willing mind, for the LORD searches all hearts and understands every plan and thought. If you seek him, he will be found by you, but if you forsake him, he will cast you off forever.

1 CHRONICLES 28:9

Commit your way to the LORD;
trust in him, and he will act.

PSALM 37:5

Trust in the LORD with all your heart,
and do not lean on your own understanding.
In all your ways acknowledge him,
and he will make straight your paths.

PROVERBS 3:5–6

Time to Face the Facts

It's called the "tyranny of the urgent" or the "squeaky wheel gets the oil"—weird expressions that just mean that if you don't have a plan, you could get caught up in doing things that aren't all that important. Some people find it helpful to keep a daily calendar or to make a list of things they need to do. Prioritize your list to show what's the most important. Then stick to your list.

Today I Will . . .

Make a list. That's a good idea. That way I can plan what I need to do each day in order to get the important things done. The top of my list for each day will be spending time with God. This planning will probably mean I actually get more done each day.

What Does the Bible Say about Pleasure?

Pleasure itself is neither good nor bad. Obviously just because something brings you pleasure doesn't mean it's a good thing. In the same way, pleasure itself is not bad. God made a lot of wonderful things in this world to bring you pleasure. He wants you to enjoy this world and experience a lot of pleasure. But he also wants you to keep the right perspective on those pleasures and how important they are to you.

What the Bible Says

> You make known to me the path of life; in your presence there is fullness of joy; at your right hand are pleasures forevermore.
>
> **PSALM 16:11**

> For those who live according to the flesh set their minds on the things of the flesh, but those who live according to the Spirit set their minds on the things of the Spirit. For to set the mind on the flesh is death, but to set the mind on the Spirit is life and peace.
>
> **ROMANS 8:5–6**

Time to Face the Facts

The danger of something that brings pleasure is that it could become more important to you than God himself. For example, if you get great pleasure from playing baseball and want to do nothing else except play baseball, then that pleasure makes your life out of focus. It means more to you than spending time with God, obeying him, or reading his Word. Pleasure at its highest level is pleasure that is pleasing to God.

"Thank you, God, for this bone I am about to receive."

Today I Will . . .

Take a good look at the things that bring me pleasure. I will make sure that none of them are more important to me than God is. I will enjoy the things he put in this world to bring me pleasure. But I will find my greatest pleasure in knowing and serving him.

What Does the Bible Say about Popularity?

Of course I want to be popular. I like it when people want to be around me and when they think I'm funny and cool. What's the big deal? Everyone wants to be popular. God does care about how you feel about being popular. He doesn't want anything to get in the way of how you love him and love other people.

What the Bible Says

You shall not bow down to them or serve them, for I the LORD your God am a jealous God. . . .

EXODUS 20:5

When pride comes, then comes disgrace, but with the humble is wisdom.

PROVERBS 11:2

You shall love the Lord your God with all your heart and with all your soul and with all your mind.

MATTHEW 22:37

Time to Face the Facts

God wants to be number one in your life. He won't share that place with your drive to be Miss or Mister Popularity. Also, God has declared that it's important to love others and make them important in your life. If you're pushing to be popular, then you probably care only about other people based on how important they think you are. Not good.

"Actually, we like her because she has a Playstation 3."

Today I Will . . .

Stop worrying about being popular. I want God to be most important in my life and other people to be in second place.

POSSESSIONS

What Does the Bible Say about Possessions?

What's your view of your "stuff"? Do you spend a lot of time and energy trying to get more "stuff"? Do you make every effort to keep your "stuff" to yourself and not share it with anyone? There's nothing wrong with having possessions. God encourages you to share your possessions with those who do not have what they need. That means your possessions can be a means of serving God.

What the Bible Says

I will say to my soul, "Soul, you have ample goods laid up for many years; relax, eat, drink, be merry." But God said to him, "Fool! This night your soul is required of you, and the things you have prepared, whose will they be?" So is the one who lays up treasure for himself and is not rich toward God."

LUKE 12:19–21

All who believed were together and had all things in common. And they were selling their possessions and belongings and distributing the proceeds to all, as any had need.

ACTS 2:44–45

But if anyone has the world's goods and sees his brother in need, yet closes his heart against him, how does God's love abide in him?

1 JOHN 3:17

Time to Face the Facts

Possessions are a gift from God. Just remember you possess them, they don't possess you. Don't let accumulating more stuff become your focus. Don't be selfish with what you have. Enjoy your possessions, but be free enough with them that you can share them with others.

"He who dies with the most toys, still dies!"

Today I Will . . .

Enjoy what I have. But I won't let my possessions control me. I'll hold them with an open hand and share them with others—or even give them away when that seems like the thing God is telling me to do.

POVERTY

What Does the Bible Say about Poverty?

You can see people on the news or on the Internet anytime who don't have food to eat, clothes to wear, or a home to live in. Poverty around the world is at an epidemic level. Children starve to death every single day. Does God care about this? Yes, of course he does. In fact, he wants his children who have enough to share with those who have nothing. All of us working together is the only way poverty around the world is going to be defeated. Sharing and giving and loving.

What the Bible Says

Whoever has a bountiful eye will be blessed,
for he shares his bread with the poor.

PROVERBS 22:9

Each one must give as he has decided in his heart, not reluctantly
or under compulsion, for God loves a cheerful giver.

2 CORINTHIANS 9:7

They are to do good, to be rich in good works, to be generous and ready to share,
thus storing up treasure for themselves as a good foundation for the future,
so that they may take hold of that which is truly life.

1 TIMOTHY 6:18–19

Time to Face the Facts

If you saved the money from just one snack or soft drink each day and sent that to an organization that is trying to help defeat poverty, it would make a difference. That may not seem like a lot of money to you, but it doesn't really take much to feed a child in a developing country. Poverty can't be defeated unless God's people work together and take action.

Today I Will . . .

Start saving a little each day by not having one snack or soft drink or whatever I choose to give up. I'll save that money and send it to an organization to help fight poverty.

What Does the Bible Say about Power?

People follow powerful people. They listen to their opinions and agree with them. They try to be like the powerful in attitudes and appearance. There is a lot of power in power. In your school it may be the powerful people who decide which kids are in and which kids are out. It is those powerful kids who decide what activities and what styles are acceptable. But remember that God has the only true power in the universe.

What the Bible Says

> Once God has spoken;
> twice have I heard this,
> that power belongs to God.
>
> **PSALM 62:11**

But you will receive power when the Holy Spirit has come upon you, and you will be my witnesses in Jerusalem and in all Judea and Samaria, and to the end of the earth.

ACTS 1:8

Ugh—he needs deodorant!"

Time to Face the Facts

God's power is unequaled by any human. His is the power of creation. He has the power to raise dead people back to life. He has the power to take a heart and change it to be like his heart. Regardless of how powerful the Power Kids at your school seem to be, their power cannot even begin to match God's power. Here's a secret: God's amazing power is available to you because you are his child. Cool, huh?

Today I Will . . .

Access the amazing power of God in my life. His power is available to me because he lives in me. But I won't ask him for his power to be used in any way that does not honor God completely.

What Does the Bible Say about Praise?

Your team comes from behind and the star player scores the winning point. What's your reaction? Praise, right? Praise for the team or for the star player. If you've ever been present when a star athlete, politician, singer, or actor comes into a room, you have heard the praise of men ring out. However, only God is worthy of praise.

What the Bible Says

> Praise the Lord!
> Praise God in his sanctuary;
> praise him in his mighty heavens!
> Praise him for his mighty deeds;
> praise him according to his excellent greatness! . . .
> Let everything that has breath praise the Lord!
> Praise the Lord!

PSALM 150:1–2, 6

> The whole multitude of his disciples began to rejoice and praise God with a loud voice for all the mighty works that they had seen, saying, "Blessed is the King who comes in the name of the Lord! Peace in heaven and glory in the highest!" And some of the Pharisees in the crowd said to him, "Teacher, rebuke your disciples." He answered, "I tell you, if these were silent, the very stones would cry out."

LUKE 19:37–40

Time to Face the Facts

God is the Creator of the universe. He is the Giver of salvation. He is power and strength and love. Only God is worthy of praise. The cheers that some humans receive are for things they have done, with the abilities God gave them. Ultimately all praise should go back to God. The Bible says that even the rocks and stones will cry out in praise to God if people do not.

Today I will . . .

Praise God. I'll limit my adoration of famous people and keep it short of praise for them. Only God is worthy of praise.

What Does the Bible Say about Prayer?

How good does it feel to sit down with a friend and talk for a couple of hours? You can spill your deepest feelings; your worries; your joys; your dreams. Talking with a friend feels good. Prayer is talking with God. You can tell God whatever is on your mind; in fact, he wants you to talk with him.

What the Bible Says

> Ask, and it will be given to you; seek, and you will find; knock, and it will be opened to you.
>
> **MATTHEW 7:7**

> Do not be anxious about anything, but in everything by prayer and supplication with thanksgiving let your requests be made known to God. And the peace of God, which surpasses all understanding, will guard your hearts and your minds in Christ Jesus.
>
> **PHILIPPIANS 4:6–7**

Time to Face the Facts

What a privilege to be able to talk with the God of the universe anytime you want to. Think about that. God asks you to tell him what's on your mind and heart. The difference between talking with a friend and talking with God is that he can do something about the things. He can intervene and give you guidance and direction or even heal the sick. The more you talk with God and listen for his response to you (that quiet voice in your mind or heart) the better you will know him, and then you will trust him more.

"Cool—we can talk to God anytime!"

Today I Will . . .

Tell God the things on my heart. I do want to know him better and trust him more, so I need to be honest with him.

What Does the Bible Say about Prejudice?

Prejudice is just wrong. Disliking people simply because of the color of their skin or the country they are from is just wrong. Prejudice dismisses the possibility that a person could have any worth because of the opinion formed on one aspect of who they are. God said to love one another . . . just love. He said that his children's love for others is one thing that would show the world they belong to him.

What the Bible Says

Do not look on his appearance or on the height of his stature, because I have rejected him. For the LORD sees not as man sees: man looks on the outward appearance, but the LORD looks on the heart.

1 SAMUEL 16:7

If I speak in the tongues of men and of angels, but have not love, I am a noisy gong or a clanging cymbal. And if I have prophetic powers, and understand all mysteries and all knowledge, and if I have all faith, so as to remove mountains, but have not love, I am nothing. If I give away all I have, and if I deliver up my body to be burned, but have not love, I gain nothing.

1 CORINTHIANS 13:1–3

And above all these put on love, which binds everything together in perfect harmony.

COLOSSIANS 3:14

Time to Face the Facts

It's impossible to love someone and be prejudiced toward them at the same time. Love is patient and kind. It overlooks differences and gives others the benefit of the doubt. Prejudice does not do any of that. Think what amazing people you might miss knowing if you give in to prejudice. Don't let it happen. Love others as God wants you to and enjoy getting to know them.

Today I Will . . .

Be fair. Prejudice is not fair. I don't want to miss knowing some amazing people who have had different experiences than I have. I will miss that if I ignore people because of prejudice.

What Does the Bible Say about the Presence of God?

Everything! The Old Testament is story after story of God's presence with his people as he guided, protected, and taught them. The New Testament is a different kind of God's presence. Once Jesus went back to heaven, God's presence came in the form of the Holy Spirit. One way or another, God's presence is always with his people.

What the Bible Says

Be strong and courageous. Do not be frightened, and do not be dismayed, for the LORD your God is with you wherever you go.

JOSHUA 1:9

In the cover of your presence you hide them
from the plots of men;
you store them in your shelter
from the strife of tongues.

PSALM 31:20

Draw near to God, and he will draw near to you.
Cleanse your hands, you sinners,
and purify your hearts, you double-minded.

JAMES 4:8

Time to Face the Facts

This is amazing. You don't have to ask God to be with you or with those you love because he has already promised to be with you. Always. Read through some of the stories in the Old Testament and read God's promises of his presence with you. It's comforting to remember that he is with you when life gets hard. It's also wonderful to remember he's with you in the good times. Celebrate with him!

Today I Will . . .

Memorize one of these verses about God's presence. Then, when life gets tough, I'll recall his words of comfort and care.

What Does the Bible Say about Pride?

Healthy pride causes you to do good work or to be proud of your friends or family's accomplishments. That's okay. Those are things to celebrate. However, unhealthy pride lifts you above others. Pride makes you think you're better than others or more important than they are. Pride-filled people are no fun to be around. Pride damages relationships because the proud person wants all the attention. Remember that God's instructions are to love others.

What the Bible Says

> For you save a humble people,
> but the haughty eyes you bring down.
>
> **PSALM 18:27**

> Whoever exalts himself will be humbled,
> and whoever humbles himself will be exalted.
>
> **MATTHEW 23:12**

Time to Face the Facts

Loving others and having pride in yourself do not go together. Loving others means celebrating when they excel (even when they excel over you). Love seeks the best for other people, not for self. Being a person of pride can make you a pretty lonely person. Who wants to be around someone who only thinks of self and brags about herself all the time? Yeah, there is no love in that and therefore not much chance to help others or even be an encouragement to them.

" . . . and I'm so humble about how great I am!"

Today I Will . . .

Take a hard look at myself. If I am prideful in any area of my life, I will ask God to help me change that pride into a healthy attitude.

What Does the Bible Say about Priorities?

If you made a list of what things are most important to you, would the top things on that list match the things you spend the most time on? Priorities are tough because in your mind you say certain things are your top priorities and you mean it. But other, less important things, get in the way and take up much of your time. God wants your top priority to be knowing and serving him.

What the Bible Says

What does the LORD your God require of you, but to fear the LORD your God, to walk in all his ways, to love him, to serve the LORD your God with all your heart and with all your soul, and to keep the commandments and statutes of the LORD. . . .

DEUTERONOMY 10:12–13

Trust in the LORD with all your heart,
and do not lean on your own understanding.
In all your ways acknowledge him,
and he will make straight your paths.

PROVERBS 3:5–6

Seek first the kingdom of God and his righteousness,
and all these things will be added to you.

MATTHEW 6:33

Time to Face the Facts

God won't settle for second place in your life. Anything that pushes him out of the number one spot actually becomes an idol. One of the sneaky ways Satan works is to squeeze little things into your life that demand attention. You think, *Okay, just this once I'll do this thing and after that God will get my attention.* He keeps doing that and pretty soon, serving and knowing God is waaayyy down your list of activities. Satan has successfully messed up your priorities.

Today I Will . . .

Not let Satan mess up my priorities. I know that sometimes it isn't Satan, though. Sometimes it is simply my choices that are wrong. I want God to be number one always.

What Does the Bible Say about Problems?

Everyone has problems. Yes, everyone. Kids, teens, and adults. If you're alive, you will have problems. Sometimes problems happen because of choices you make that put you in opposition to God's values. Some choices cause problems with other people. Some create situations that are difficult to deal with. Dealing with problems can teach you better how to live in obedience to God and in relationship with other people.

What the Bible Says

The Lord is a stronghold for the oppressed,
a stronghold in times of trouble.

PSALM 9:9

But we have this treasure in jars of clay, to show that the surpassing power
belongs to God and not to us. We are afflicted in every way,
but not crushed; perplexed, but not driven to despair.

2 CORINTHIANS 4:7–8

Humble yourselves, therefore, under the mighty hand of God so that at the proper time he may exalt you, casting all your anxieties on him, because he cares for you.

1 PETER 5:6–7

Time to Face the Facts

Problems can consume a lot of energy, both emotional and mental. God doesn't hide from your problems. He knows you will need his help. He's waiting for you to ask for his guidance and wisdom. He promises to give it to you when you ask. You never need to go through problems alone. God is your comfort, strength, peace, and joy.

"You think you have problems . . . I can't find my bone."

Today I Will . . .

Turn to God for help. Problems are going to be a part of my life, and I know I can't handle them on my own. I'll ask God for help and do my best to follow his lead.

PROCRASTINATION

What Does the Bible Say about Procrastination?

Putting things off can be a form of laziness or even of disobedience. Making excuses is classic to procrastinating because you don't want to take the blame for what doesn't happen. God warns against procrastinating because time runs out and important things don't get done. He has a part for you to play in his work on this earth, and if you put things off, his work is impacted.

What the Bible Says

Know therefore that the LORD your God is God, the faithful God who keeps covenant and steadfast love with those who love him and keep his commandments, to a thousand generations.

DEUTERONOMY 7:9

Look carefully then how you walk, not as unwise but as wise, making the best use of the time. because the days are evil.

EPHESIANS 5:15–16

Whatever you do, work heartily, as for the Lord and not for men, knowing that from the Lord you will receive the inheritance as your reward. You are serving the Lord Christ.

COLOSSIANS 3:23–24

Time to Face the Facts

Do you ever put things off because you just don't want to deal with them? Then you have to make excuses about why things don't get done. If you're procrastinating about something, examine your motives. Are you afraid, disobedient, or lazy? Failure to do what you know you're supposed to do is sin.

"Maybe it will rain."

That's serious. Obeying God and serving him is the most important thing.

Today I Will . . .

Stop putting off things I don't want to do. I know some things must be done even if they aren't fun. I need God's help, but I'll do the important things.

What Does the Bible Say about Productivity?

Productivity is usually measured by how much of something you get done in a given amount of time. Being focused on how much instead of how well something is done can result in poor quality. Rushing through work in order to have big numbers is not a good goal. Being concerned with productivity can also make you so busy that friendships and time with your family suffers. That's not good—God says loving others is more important than numbers.

What the Bible Says

Whoever works his land will have plenty of bread,
but he who follows worthless pursuits lacks sense.

PROVERBS 12:11

For no good tree bears bad fruit, nor again does a bad tree bear good fruit, for each tree is known by its own fruit. For figs are not gathered from thorn bushes, nor are grapes picked from a bramble bush. The good person out of the good treasure of his heart produces good, and the evil person out of his evil treasure produces evil, for out of the abundance of the heart his mouth speaks.

LUKE 6:43–45

The fruit of the Spirit is love, joy, peace, patience, kindness, goodness, faithfulness, gentleness, self-control; against such things there is no law. And those who belong to Christ Jesus have crucified the flesh with its passions and desires.

GALATIANS 5:22–24

Time to Face the Facts

There's nothing wrong with being productive. It's better than being lazy. But if putting up large numbers in some area becomes more important to you than anything else, then productivity is a problem. Don't let productivity become more important than spending time with people. Do your best work, do it as quickly as is reasonable, but don't forget people. Connecting with others is very important. It's obedience to God.

Today I Will . . .

Make sure I stay connected with others. I want to do good work in my responsibilities, but not at the expense of relationships.

What Does the Bible Say about Profanity?

How many actual words do you think you know? Are you intelligent enough to express yourself in language that is not profanity whether you are angry, sad, or happy? Profanity, vulgar language, or using God's name in vain shows disrespect to those you are speaking with and most definitely to God.

What the Bible Says

You shall not take the name of the LORD your God in vain, for the LORD will not hold him guiltless who takes his name in vain.

EXODUS 20:7

Let there be no filthiness nor foolish talk nor crude joking, which are out of place, but instead let there be thanksgiving.

EPHESIANS 5:4

Whatever is true, whatever is honorable, whatever is just, whatever is pure, whatever is lovely, whatever is commendable, if there is any excellence, if there is anything worthy of praise, think about these things.

PHILIPPIANS 4:8

Time to Face the Facts

Some people think using profanity makes them look cool. But in reality it makes them sound less than intelligent, as though they don't have enough words in their vocabulary to express themselves. God warned against using profanity or foolish language. There are better ways to express yourself.

"He really needs to learn how to express himself."

Today I Will . . .

Be careful with what words I use. I would never use God's name in a foolish way, even though I hear it used that way about a hundred times a day. I don't want to dishonor God in that way. I'll be careful about vulgar or foolish language, too.

PROMISES

What Does the Bible Say about Promises?

Has anyone ever broken a promise to you? It hurts, doesn't it? Have you ever broken a promise? It doesn't feel good because you know you are disappointing someone. Promises are supposed to be kept. Unfortunately, they aren't always, except in one case. God has made many promises to you in his Word. He promises to love you always, to take care of you, and to guide you. He never breaks his promises. You can count on that.

What the Bible Says

Let not your hearts be troubled. Believe in God; believe also in me. In my Father's house are many rooms. If it were not so, would I have told you that I go to prepare a place for you?

JOHN 14:1–2

Let us hold fast the confession of our hope without wavering, for he who promised is faithful.

HEBREWS 10:23

Time to Face the Facts

Most people don't plan to break their promises. Perhaps they make a promise without really thinking about it. Or, once the promise is made, situations change and it becomes difficult to keep it. Doesn't matter though, right? It still hurts. It's good to know there is someone you can always trust. God will never disappoint you. Put your trust in him. Trust his promises.

"You can trust me."

Today I Will . . .

First of all, forgive anyone who has broken a promise to me. I know they didn't mean to do it, and I do it myself sometimes. Then, I will put my trust in God. I know he will always keep his promises.

What Does the Bible Say about Prophecy?

Wouldn't you love to be able to know the future? Well, you can. Okay, maybe not stuff like where you'll go to college or who you will marry, but you can know a part of the future—the important part. The Bible is filled with prophecy that talks about the future of God's work on earth. It promises that God will triumph over evil and that your future in heaven with him can be certain.

What the Bible Says

Let not your hearts be troubled. Believe in God; believe also in me. In my Father's house are many rooms. If it were not so, would I have told you that I go to prepare a place for you? And if I go and prepare a place for you, I will come again and will take you to myself, that where I am you may be also.

JOHN 14:1–3

They are to do good, to be rich in good works, to be generous and ready to share, thus storing up treasure for themselves as a good foundation for the future, so that they may take hold of that which is truly life.

1 TIMOTHY 6:18–20

Behold, I am coming soon. Blessed is the one who keeps the words of the prophecy of this book.

REVELATION 22:7

Time to Face the Facts

Some prophecy is hard to understand because of the images used to describe it. But the important thing is that prophecy says Jesus will come back one day and will take the people who have asked him into their hearts back to heaven with him. Prophecy says that Satan will be defeated and thrown into a lake of fire. The people who haven't followed God will go with Satan . . . forever. Prophecy for Christians is a wonderful promise for eternity. Prophecy for non-Christians is not so wonderful.

Today I Will . . .

Thank God for the promises of prophecy for me . . . if I have asked Jesus into my heart. If I haven't done that, I think it's time to get serious about making sure I know him. I should also be telling those I know who aren't Christians about him.

PROTECTION

What Does the Bible Say about Protection?

Rich and famous people have bodyguards surrounding them. Their "people" make sure that no one gets too close to them and that they are safe. Even in the Bible there were kings who were protected by servants who tasted their food and wine to make sure there was no poison in it. Would you like to know you have protection from the dangers of this world? You do. Maybe not the kind you think, but God is always with you, and since he loves you so very much, you know he will protect you.

What the Bible Says

How precious is your steadfast love, O God!
The children of mankind take refuge in the shadow of your wings.

PSALM 36:7

But the Lord is faithful. He will establish you and guard you against the evil one.

2 THESSALONIANS 3:3

Time to Face the Facts

Perhaps you're thinking about a time when you got hurt—or thinking about the terrible things that happen in the world where people are injured or killed. Yes, those things happen. God's protection is sometimes physical protection. Often his protection is of your heart. God cares that your heart is pure and that the things that happen to you don't make your heart become selfish or angry. Still, when you are afraid, ask God for his protection and for an awareness of his presence going with you always.

"Here I am to save the day!"

Today I Will . . .

Not be afraid. I know that nothing will happen to me that God doesn't know about. I'll ask for physical protection, and I will know that he is with me, no matter what.

What Does the Bible Say about Provision?

Do you have food to eat, clothes to wear, and a bed to sleep in? Those are provisions. Your definition of what you actually need may differ from what your parents or caregivers think. In this materialistic world needs and wants get easily confused. All that you have is provided by God. Ultimately he is the giver of all things.

What the Bible Says

All things come from you, and of
your own have we given you.

1 CHRONICLES 29:14

Whoever gives one of these little ones even a cup of cold
water because he is a disciple, truly, I say to you,
he will by no means lose his reward.

MATTHEW 10:42

But if anyone has the world's goods and sees
his brother in need, yet closes his heart against
him, how does God's love abide in him?

1 JOHN 3:17

Time to Face the Facts

Many people in this world do not have all they need, others seem to have all they want. It's hard to understand this lack of balance. The bottom line is that what anyone has is provided by God. God may motivate those who have much to give to those who don't have anything. Realize that in praying for provisions for the poor, you may be part of the answer to your own prayer. God tells his children to help the poor and share what they have. It all came from God anyway.

Today I Will . . .

Thank God for what I have and be truly appreciative. Pray for those who don't have enough to survive and look for ways to be part of their provision solution.

PUBERTY

What Does the Bible Say about Puberty?

"What's happening to me?" Have you ever thought that? Okay, you knew that as you grow up your body would change and grow. That was to be expected. But maybe you're surprised by the emotions that race through you. Anger and frustration one minute and confusion and pain the next. What's going on? Puberty. Yep, your emotions grow and change as you mature just as your body does. Hang on to God through this experience.

What the Bible Says

> The LORD is near to all who call on him, to all who call on him in truth.
>
> **PSALM 145:18**

> Draw near to God, and he will draw near to you. Cleanse your hands, you sinners, and purify your hearts, you double-minded.
>
> **JAMES 4:8**

Time to Face the Facts

Everyone goes through it, but that doesn't help much, does it? Sometimes grown-ups forget how hard it is, too. Emotions that seem out of control sometimes are frustrating. You struggle for independence but are afraid when it comes, even though you'd never tell your parents that. You want to try new things—some that aren't safe—and in this emotional uproar you can be pulled away from your faith. Don't

"Dad. I need to borrow your razor."

let that happen. Decide to stay close to God. Choose to keep reading your Bible and talking with him each day. Let him guide you through puberty.

Today I Will . . .

Stop and think. If these emotions described as puberty are things I'm struggling with . . . well, at least I know what's going on. I'll make every effort to stay close to God and to let him guide me through this. On the other side of puberty I want to still be a kind, loving God-follower.

What Does the Bible Say about Punishment?

Being punished stinks. However, when you do something wrong, your parents must punish you in order for you to learn that choices have natural consequences. Believe it or not, they are trying to help you learn to be a better person. Disobeying God has a price, too. He loves you and will punish you. But his punishment doesn't come from anger. It comes from a desire to help you become a better person.

What the Bible Says

Whoever loves discipline loves knowledge,
but he who hates reproof is stupid.

PROVERBS 12:1

The wages of sin is death, but the free gift of God
is eternal life in Christ Jesus our Lord.

ROMANS 6:23

For the moment all discipline seems painful rather
than pleasant, but later it yields the peaceful fruit
of righteousness to those who have been trained by it.

HEBREWS 12:11

Time to Face the Facts

No one enjoys punishment—usually not even the people who must give it. Unfortunately, punishment is what it often takes in order for you to learn not to do something or to do something. No doubt God does not enjoy punishing you. It's a kind of tough love to punish you in order help you learn. God sees the end result of punishment, which is you becoming a better person who reflects his love to others.

Today I Will . . .

Not complain about punishment. No, I don't like it, but I see now that there is a reason behind it. My parents are not just being mean, and God isn't just ignoring me. I want to learn my lessons and move forward.

What Does the Bible Say about Purpose?

Have you ever played with one of those goofy little balls that are not balanced so when you bounce it the silly thing flies around like crazy? You never know which direction it will go or where it will stop. Well, my friend, that is kind of how a life without purpose is. If you have no purpose in your life, you will flit from one thing to another, sometimes not finishing any of them. The Bible says you should have purpose and stay focused on it.

What the Bible Says

But this command I gave them: "Obey my voice, and I will be your God, and you shall be my people. And walk in all the way that I command you, that it may be well with you."

JEREMIAH 7:23

For I know the plans I have for you, declares the LORD, plans for welfare and not for evil, to give you a future and a hope.

JEREMIAH 29:11

It is my eager expectation and hope that I will not be at all ashamed, but that with full courage now as always Christ will be honored in my body, whether by life or by death.

PHILIPPIANS 1:20

"I just don't know where to focus."

Time to Face the Facts

Your primary purpose should be to obey and serve God. Under that umbrella comes obeying parents, loving others, and using the gifts and talents God gave you. Knowing your purpose is not easy, especially if you have a lot of different interests. But the great thing is that if you ask God to help you focus on your purpose, he will!

Today I Will . . .

Actively seek to know what my purpose is. I'll make a list of the top five things that are important to me, then look at how much time I spend on those things. Wherever I spend most of my time will tell me a lot about what my purpose is.

What Does the Bible Say about Quitting?

There is an old saying that goes something like this: "Quitters never win and winners never quit." Quitting is admitting defeat. It is giving up. People learn that they can't count on a consistent quitter to finish things, so they don't trust him and don't expect much from him. God will be your strength and encouragement when you feel like quitting. Turn to him.

What the Bible Says

Be strong and courageous. Do not be frightened, and do not be dismayed, for the LORD your God is with you wherever you go.

JOSHUA 1:9

Therefore, my beloved brothers, be steadfast, immovable, always abounding in the work of the Lord, knowing that in the Lord your labor is not in vain.

1 CORINTHIANS 15:58

Let us not grow weary of doing good, for in due season we will reap, if we do not give up.

GALATIANS 6:9

Time to Face the Facts

Everyone wants to quit sometimes. It's important to keep your focus on a goal when you feel like quitting. That goal may be just the encouragement you need to keep you going. Instead of giving up and quitting when things get tough, look at your goal and ask God to give you strength and perseverance to keep on going, even through the rough times. He will help you, and he will send other people around you to encourage you.

"An open-air birdhouse is good enough."

Today I Will . . .

Not quit, even when I want to more than anything else. Quitting is the easy way out sometimes. So, I'll ask God to give me strength, and I'll ask him to keep me trying and working and growing.

What Does the Bible Say about Racism?

Racists judge people based on the color of their skin or the language they speak. They feel their own race is superior, and any other race is less valuable. In extreme cases of racism, hatred spills out and people are hurt or killed. God created all people, and nowhere in the Bible is one race more valued than another.

What the Bible Says

> For God so loved the world, that he gave his only Son, that whoever believes in him should not perish but have eternal life.
>
> **JOHN 3:16**

> By this all people will know that you are my disciples, if you have love for one another.
>
> **JOHN 13:35**

> Here there is not Greek and Jew, circumcised and uncircumcised, barbarian, Scythian, slave, free; but Christ is all, and in all.
>
> **COLOSSIANS 3:11**

Time to Face the Facts

Racism exists on many levels. Often it is expressed in crude jokes or name-calling directed at certain races. In these cases, the hurt is emotional not physical. In some situations racism keeps people from getting jobs or being able to live where they would like. No good comes from racism. It's unfair and unkind and in direct opposition to God's instruction to love one another.

Today I Will . . .

Pay attention to the jokes I hear or the nicknames used to refer to some people. If they even hint of racism, I'll speak up and try to put a stop to it. I'll take a stand by loving people of all races and treating them equally.

What Does the Bible Say about Rebellion?

Rebellion can get ugly. It may start as a little yearning in your heart to do things your own way and when you want to do them. Then it grows to getting "mouthy" with your parents. From there it may expand to breaking rules on purpose and stubbornly refusing to conform. Rebellion can lead to an all-out battle with parents, teachers, and . . . God. He insists on obedience, so, rebellion against him is serious.

What the Bible Says

Know therefore that the LORD your God is God, the faithful God who keeps covenant and steadfast love with those who love him and keep his commandments, to a thousand generations.

DEUTERONOMY 7:9

If you love me, you will keep my commandments.

JOHN 14:15

Time to Face the Facts

Rebellion is evidence of self-centeredness and stubbornness. It is two forces pulling against one another. No good can come from it. Time and effort are wasted in this struggle. Rebellion against God will bring you only pain and regret. God doesn't insist on obedience because he is a dictator; he insists on it because He can see your whole life. He knows what's ahead and what is possible if you obey. He loves you and wants the best for you.

"You can't make me do that."

Today I Will . . .

Stop pulling away from God. I do sometimes, but I don't want to do that. I want to trust him completely with my life and my future. I believe he loves me.

RECONCILIATION

What Does the Bible Say about Reconciliation?

When you've had a big fight with a friend, you cannot make up until one of you takes the first step toward reconciliation. That's what brings healing and restores the relationship. Reconciliation is a big topic in the Bible, on two levels. One is being at peace with other people, and the other is reconciliation with God.

What the Bible Says

All this is from God, who through Christ reconciled us to himself and gave us the ministry of reconciliation; that is, in Christ God was reconciling the world to himself, not counting their trespasses against them, and entrusting to us the message of reconciliation.

2 CORINTHIANS 5:18–19

Put on then, as God's chosen ones, holy and beloved, compassionate hearts, kindness, humility, meekness, and patience, bearing with one another and, if one has a complaint against another, forgiving each other; as the Lord has forgiven you, so you also must forgive.

COLOSSIANS 3:12–13

Time to Face the Facts

Reconciliation with God is important because sin has broken your relationship with him. It separates you from God. But because of his amazing love for you, God made reconciliation possible by the death and resurrection of Jesus for you! His model of love encourages reconciliation for human relationships, too. It takes a lot of negative energy to be mad at someone. Just reconcile and enjoy the friendship!

"I'm sorry, let's be friends again."

Today I Will . . .

Think about whether I need to reconcile with anyone. Am I holding any grudges? I want my friendships to be healthy. I'll thank God, too, for making reconciliation with him possible.

What Does the Bible Say about Regrets?

Living with feelings of *I should have . . . or I could have . . .* is not fun. Regretting things you did do or things you shouldn't have done can outweigh the most pleasant of memories. Often the regrets are the things that stand out in your mind. God won't change what you did or didn't do, but he will help wipe away the regret and help you move forward.

What the Bible Says

Restore us to yourself, O Lord, that we may
be restored! Renew our days as of old.

LAMENTATIONS 5:21

Create in me a clean heart, O God,
and renew a right spirit within me.
Cast me not away from your presence,
and take not your Holy Spirit from me.
Restore to me the joy of your salvation,
and uphold me with a willing spirit.

PSALM 51:10–12

Time to Face the Facts

Regrets are a good reason to stop and think before you speak or do anything. Think about how your words or actions will make others feel. When there are opportunities ahead of you, think about how you will feel later based on whether you take the opportunity or not. Regrets can weigh heavy on your heart. The best way to handle this emotion is to turn to God and confess what's causing the regret. Then ask him to take it away and help you focus on positive things.

Today I Will . . .

Be honest with myself and God. If I've got regret buried in my heart, I'll admit it. Then, I'll ask God to help me forget the thing I cannot change and move forward with my life.

What Does the Bible Say about Rejection?

Being rejected feels like being thrown away. It hurts. It means you aren't good enough or loved enough or wanted enough. Sometimes rejection comes when a parent walks away from a family. Sometimes it is when a group of friends turns on one person and pushes her out of its circle. Sometimes rejection is a result of race or appearance. Whatever the reason, rejection is painful and downright wrong.

What the Bible Says

You have heard that it was said, "You shall love your neighbor and hate your enemy." But I say to you, Love your enemies and pray for those who persecute you, so that you may be sons of your Father who is in heaven. For he makes his sun rise on the evil and on the good, and sends rain on the just and on the unjust.

MATTHEW 5:43–45

Now may our God and Father himself, and our Lord Jesus, direct our way to you, and may the Lord make you increase and abound in love for one another. . . .

1 THESSALONIANS 3:11–12

Time to Face the Facts

No one likes to be rejected. Pay attention to your world and whether anyone is being rejected for any reason. God says to love one another and encourage and support one another. You can't do that and still reject people. You just can't; it is an either/or choice. You can rest assured in the truth that God will never reject you. He loves you.

Today I Will . . .

Think about how I treat others. If I'm showing rejection to anyone for any reason, I will ask his or her forgiveness and God's help in being kinder and more accepting.

"At least I know God will never reject me."

What Does the Bible Say about Relationships?

They have a lot to do with the Bible. God puts a lot of emphasis on relationships and treating one another with kindness and love. Relationships with others bring joy and laughter. They give support and encouragement. Other people can often be God's messengers—his love with skin on.

What the Bible Says

Love bears all things, believes all things, hopes all things, endures all things.

1 CORINTHIANS 13:7

Put on then, as God's chosen ones, holy and beloved, compassionate hearts, kindness, humility, meekness, and patience, bearing with one another and, if one has a complaint against another, forgiving each other; as the Lord has forgiven you, so you also must forgive. And above all these put on love, which binds everything together in perfect harmony.

COLOSSIANS 3:12–14

Time to Face the Facts

Life is much more pleasant when you share it with others. Sometimes you are the giver of encouragement and love and sometimes it is given to you. Relationships are give and take. Relationships begin with family members who love you unconditionally. Friends come next with their heartfelt concern for you. You must be a friend to have a friend; in other words, be kind and caring. Don't always be focused on yourself. Show God's love to others by the way you treat them. Build strong relationships.

Buddies for life!

Today I Will . . .

Thank God for the relationships in my life. Each day is a lot more fun because I get to share it with others. I am also very thankful for my relationship with God. That's the best one of all!

What Does the Bible Say about Repentance?

Okay, you know that everyone sins—everyone. The Bible tells you that. You can confess your sin and even be sorry for it. But repentance is deeper than just being sorry for sin. It's being so sorry that you do a turn-around and head in the opposite direction. You change because of sorrow for the sin in your life. Repentance is important because it puts action to being sorry for sin.

What the Bible Says

For you will not delight in sacrifice, or I would give it;
you will not be pleased with a burnt offering.
The sacrifices of God are a broken spirit;
a broken and contrite heart, O God, you will not despise.

PSALM 51:16–17

Repent therefore, and turn again, that your sins may be blotted out,
that times of refreshing may come from the presence of the Lord,
and that he may send the Christ appointed for you, Jesus.

ACTS 3:19–20

Time to Face the Facts

You can say you are sorry for something until you are blue in the face. But if your actions don't change, no one is going to believe that you are truly sorry. Repentance changes your actions. If you are really sorry, you will want to change your actions. Repenting from your sins shows you have learned a lesson and are trying to improve your obedience and your actions.

"Enough already. I forgive you for stepping on my tail."

Today I Will . . .

Repent. I tell God I'm sorry all the time, but then I turn around and do the same thing over again. I want to repent—change my actions—and be more obedient to him.

REPUTATION

What Does the Bible Say about Reputation?

Your reputation is what you're known by. Everyone has one—either a good one or a bad one. Most people try to project a good reputation, which means they have strong values and are honest and kind. Other people want a reputation of being a troublemaking rebel. God encourages you to work for a reputation of honesty, fairness, and respect of people and him.

What the Bible Says

I have taught you statutes and rules, as the LORD my God commanded me, that you should do them in the land that you are entering to take possession of it. Keep them and do them, for that will be your wisdom and your understanding in the sight of the peoples, who, when they hear all these statutes, will say, "Surely this great nation is a wise and understanding people."

DEUTERONOMY 4:5-6

If then you have been raised with Christ, seek the things that are above, where Christ is, seated at the right hand of God. Set your minds on things that are above, not on things that are on earth.

COLOSSIANS 3:1-2

Time to Face the Facts

Interestingly, people tend to hang out with those who have a reputation much like their own. It's kind of a "birds of a feather flock together" thing. It gets uncomfortable when your reputation is not a true reflection of who you are. Build your reputation on solid character traits so that you are comfortable with who you are and so others know that they can trust you. Build a reputation of honoring and loving God.

"I got a news flash for you—that look went out in the 50's."

Today I Will . . .

Be honest about what my reputation is. I want to know if it matches who I am inside. I will work toward building a strong, honest reputation of loving, honoring, and obeying God and being fair and honest with other people.

RESENTMENT

What Does the Bible Say about Resentment?

Resentment is an ugly little emotion. It wiggles into your heart and drives a wedge between you and the person you are resenting. It has its roots in bitterness and envy with a little anger thrown in. When you resent people, you don't really care about them because you can't forgive them for whatever they have done.

What the Bible Says

Hatred stirs up strife,
but love covers all offenses.

PROVERBS 10:12

Let not sin therefore reign in your mortal body, to make you obey its passions. Do not present your members to sin as instruments for unrighteousness, but present yourselves to God as those who have been brought from death to life, and your members to God as instruments for righteousness.

ROMANS 6:12–13

Have this mind among yourselves, which is yours in Christ Jesus, who, though he was in the form of God, did not count equality with God a thing to be grasped, but made himself nothing, taking the form of a servant, being born in the likeness of men. And being found in human form, he humbled himself by becoming obedient to the point of death, even death on a cross.

PHILIPPIANS 2:5–8

Time to Face the Facts

Resentment will cause all kinds of problems in your relationships. When you're resenting someone for what he has or what he has done, then you don't want your other friends to be nice to that person either. It just grows and grows. Resentment defeats any opportunity to live in obedience to God's command to love one another. Love and resentment can't live in the same heart.

Today I Will . . .

Be honest with myself about feelings of resentment. If I'm feeling that way about anyone, I need to confess it and repent of it. I need God's help to get over these feelings. I'll ask him.

What Does the Bible Say about Respect?

Maybe you're heard your whole life, "Respect your elders." What does that mean? Respecting someone means you recognize his worth and you honor him for things he has done or for the kind of person he is. Respect shows that you value a person. It's not only elders you should respect. In reality you should respect all people as valuable and as worthy of being treated with kindness and fairness. Begin your respect with God and let it trickle down.

What the Bible Says

> Do nothing from rivalry or conceit, but in humility
> count others more significant than yourselves.
>
> **PHILIPPIANS 2:3**

> Let us not become conceited, provoking one another, envying one another.
>
> **GALATIANS 5:26**

Time to Face the Facts

God deserves your respect. He has incredible power that is filtered in love. God can do anything he chooses, and yet he chooses to love and care for you. As far as other people, it seems that respect is sadly missing in our world today. Too many people are focused only on themselves and how to make themselves look important. Respect means you can let other people shine while you step back because you care about them and their lives.

"Grandpa, you're the best!"

Today I Will . . .

Think about whether or not I truly respect others or if I'm always more concerned about myself. I will ask God to help me put others first by respecting and caring for them.

RESPONSIBILITY

What Does the Bible Say about Responsibility?

Not taking responsibility for your actions is a major problem in the world today. Making excuses for your mistakes or failures to try to push the responsibility off on someone else doesn't really fool many people, and it definitely doesn't fool God. He knows your heart, and he sees your actions. He will give you the strength to take responsibility for your actions and be honest with others and with him.

What the Bible Says

Well done, good and faithful servant. You have been faithful over a little; I will set you over much. . . .

MATTHEW 25:21

Having gifts that differ according to the grace given to us, let us use them: if prophecy, in proportion to our faith; if service, in our serving; the one who teaches, in his teaching; the one who exhorts, in his exhortation; the one who contributes, in generosity; the one who leads, with zeal; the one who does acts of mercy, with cheerfulness.

ROMANS 12:6–8

Do not be deceived: God is not mocked, for whatever one sows, that will he also reap. For the one who sows to his own flesh will from the flesh reap corruption, but the one who sows to the Spirit will from the Spirit reap eternal life.

GALATIANS 6:7–8

Time to Face the Facts

Each person is truly responsible for her own actions, choices, behaviors, and decisions. You are accountable to your family and friends or anyone else your actions affect. You are also accountable to God. When you mess up, admit it, apologize for it, and learn from it. Everyone makes mistakes sometimes. How you behave after the mistake shows your character. Take responsibility and be honest about your actions.

Today I Will . . .

Admit it if I make excuses for my behavior in order to shove responsibility for my actions onto someone else. I'll be honest with myself, others, and God.

What Does the Bible Say about Rest?

These days most people are so busy that they don't have time for rest. Even kids your age are rushing from school to music lessons to soccer practice to youth group to . . . well, whatever your schedule includes. Sometimes people even brag about how busy they are so others will be impressed with how important they are. But is God impressed with your busy schedule? No, not so much.

What the Bible Says

Thus the heavens and the earth were finished, and all the host of them. And on the seventh day God finished his work that he had done, and he rested on the seventh day from all his work that he had done. So God blessed the seventh day and made it holy, because on it God rested from all his work that he had done in creation.

GENESIS 2:1–3

Come to me, all who labor and are heavy laden, and I will give you rest. Take my yoke upon you, and learn from me, for I am gentle and lowly in heart, and you will find rest for your souls. For my yoke is easy, and my burden is light.

MATTHEW 11:28–30

Time to Face the Facts

God is the Creator of the universe. He made everything there is—talk about busy. But he still set aside a day to rest. If rest was good for God, then it must be good for people. Your body and mind need time to recuperate and rejuvenate from all your activities. Rest is a good thing. Time off from your busy schedule gives your body and mind rest, but it also gives your soul a chance to connect with God.

"Cool your heels."

Today I Will . . .

Stop. I'll make sure my schedule includes rest. An evening of relaxing is good for me. Making sure I connect with God and let my soul be fed is as important as resting my body, too.

RESTLESSNESS

What Does the Bible Say about Restlessness?

An insect bite itches and itches and as much as you know you shouldn't . . . you scratch. It makes it feel better at least for a while. What do you do, though, when the itch seems to be inside . . . in your soul? Restlessness makes you discontent with where you are and what you're doing. You have no peace, and peace is found only in God.

What the Bible Says

Be still, and know that I am God.
I will be exalted among the nations,
I will be exalted in the earth!

PSALM 46:10

Therefore, since we have been justified by faith, we have peace with God through our Lord Jesus Christ. Through him we have also obtained access by faith into this grace in which we stand, and we rejoice in hope of the glory of God.

ROMANS 5:1-2

Do not be anxious about anything, but in everything by prayer and supplication with thanksgiving let your requests be made known to God. And the peace of God, which surpasses all understanding, will guard your hearts and your minds in Christ Jesus.

PHILIPPIANS 4:6-7

Time to Face the Facts

Sometimes God uses restlessness to tell you it's time to move from one type of service to another. But once you have done that, the restlessness is gone and you feel satisfied again. Other forms of restlessness come because your focus is wrong. Perhaps you're thinking about yourself instead of others, or perhaps you're resisting doing something you know you should be doing. That itch inside is only satisfied by being obedient. God will give you peace when you follow him and trust him.

Today I Will . . .

Ask God to show me why I have this restlessness inside. When I know what's going on, I'll obey him and follow his will for me. I know my restlessness will be satisfied only by obeying him.

What Does the Bible Say about Restrictions?

If you've ever walked an energetic puppy that is attached to a leash, you understand restrictions. The puppy jumps and pulls and tries with all his strength to go places that the leash will not allow. He even seems to choke himself, but doesn't understand that if he just accepts the restrictions of the leash (because it will keep him safe), his walk will be much easier.

What the Bible Says

Obey my voice, and I will be your God, and you shall be my people.
And walk in all the way that I command you, that it may be well with you.

JEREMIAH 7:23

Now the Lord is the Spirit, and where the Spirit of the Lord is, there is freedom.

2 CORINTHIANS 3:17

Time to Face the Facts

Does the image of a puppy on a leash make you smile? It's hard to walk a puppy who doesn't understand the leash restrictions. But, really, maybe you don't understand restrictions either. If it seems to you that restrictions keep you from doing things you want, perhaps you need to take a step back. Restrictions put on you by parents, teachers, and even God are not to keep you from things; they are to protect you from things. There is a difference there. Restrictions actually give you freedom to enjoy your life . . . in safety.

"Foiled again!"

Today I Will . . .

Try to change my viewpoint on restrictions. I usually think of them as rules to keep me from having fun. I'll try to understand what they are protecting me from. Then, I'll thank God that someone loves me enough to give me restrictions.

What Does the Bible Say about Results?

Much of the world is results-focused these days. The winners of games and contests are celebrated. Test results in school are emphasized. Everything from diets to finances look at the "bottom line"—results. In a sense, God is results-focused, too. But his focus is on the results of how your heart is growing and changing to make you more like Christ.

What the Bible Says

For this reason I bow my knees before the Father, from whom every family in heaven and on earth is named, that according to the riches of his glory he may grant you to be strengthened with power through his Spirit in your inner being, so that Christ may dwell in your hearts through faith—that you, being rooted and grounded in love, may have strength to comprehend with all the saints what is the breadth and length and height and depth, and to know the love of Christ that surpasses knowledge, that you may be filled with all the fullness of God.

EPHESIANS 3:14–20

Therefore, as you received Christ Jesus the Lord, so walk in him, rooted and built up in him and established in the faith, just as you were taught, abounding in thanksgiving.

COLOSSIANS 2:6–7

If any of you lacks wisdom, let him ask God, who gives generously to all without reproach, and it will be given him.

JAMES 1:5

Time to Face the Facts

Results in most things are important because they show that you are applying yourself and doing your best work. Results in following God are the most important. It's tempting sometimes to say the words that make it sound like you're following God very obediently, but your life may not show the results. You can fool people for a while . . . but you can never fool God. He sees your heart and knows whether the results are there or not. Results in following God are that you become more loving and kind to others and more obedient to him.

Today I Will . . .

Focus on God-results. My goal is to be more and more like Christ in how I live. If I focus on that result, all the other things will fall into place.

What Does the Bible Say about Revenge?

Revenge is a basic reaction to feeling that you have been treated wrongly. Revenge and forgiveness cannot go together. If you're busy figuring out how to get even with someone or make them pay for what they have done to you . . . well, no forgiveness is happening.

What the Bible Says

You shall not take vengeance or bear a grudge against the sons of your own people, but you shall love your neighbor as yourself: I am the LORD.

LEVITICUS 19:18

Whoever digs a pit will fall into it, and a stone will come back on him who starts it rolling.

PROVERBS 26:27

Repay no one evil for evil, but give thought to do what is honorable in the sight of all. If possible, so far as it depends on you, live peaceably with all. Beloved, never avenge yourselves, but leave it to the wrath of God, for it is written, "Vengeance is mine, I will repay, says the Lord."

ROMANS 12:17–19

Time to Face the Facts

God makes it pretty clear in the Bible that revenge is pointless. Forgiveness and love are the goal. Leave it to him to deal with the person who treated you badly. He will. Eventually, everyone answers for his behavior. Don't add revenge to the list of things you will have to give an account of. Forgive and move on. Forget about revenge. It just creates an endless loop of hurt and revenge.

"I can hardly wait to . . ."

Today I Will . . .

Let go of any hurt I've been holding onto. I'll give up thinking about getting revenge and ask God to help me forgive the person and get on with life. I'll trust God to take care of my angry, hurt feelings and to work in the heart of the person who hurt me, too.

REWARDS

What Does the Bible Say about Rewards?

When you think of rewards, do you think of something like finding a lost wallet and returning it to the owner? Then the grateful owner rewards you with a hundred dollars? Another kind of reward comes when you give information to the police to help solve a crime, and you get a cash reward for that. The truth is that most actions have consequences. Good consequences are rewards and bad ones are called by a different name. The most amazing reward is the one God gives.

What the Bible Says

Blessed is everyone who fears the LORD,
who walks in his ways!

PSALM 128:1

Blessed is the man who remains steadfast under trial, for when he has stood the test he will receive the crown of life, which God has promised to those who love him.

JAMES 1:12

Time to Face the Facts

Rewards are a prize for something you have done well or for honesty displayed. The possibility of being rewarded can be a motivation for hard work and honesty. However, rewards do not always come immediately. The greatest reward to think about is heaven. God's reward of spending forever with him, however, is actually a gift. You can do nothing to earn it. All you have to do is receive it.

"No reward, son. You just found your own dog."

Today I Will . . .

Appreciate any rewards I've been given, especially ones I've worked hard for. But, most importantly, I'll thank God for the promise of my reward of eternity with him. It is truly a gift.

What Does the Bible Say about Right and Wrong?

You know the difference between right and wrong, right? Wrong? Okay, on most things you do. Knowing the difference between the two is what your parents and teachers have been trying to teach you since day one of your life. God is also interested in your understanding of right and wrong. Knowing that is basic to obeying him.

What the Bible Says

Whoever is wise, let him understand these things;
whoever is discerning, let him know them;
for the ways of the LORD are right,
and the upright walk in them,
but transgressors stumble in them.

HOSEA 14:9

I know that nothing good dwells in me, that is, in my flesh. For I have the desire to do what is right, but not the ability to carry it out. For I do not do the good I want, but the evil I do not want is what I keep on doing.

ROMANS 7:18–19

So whoever knows the right thing to do
and fails to do it, for him it is sin.

JAMES 4:17

Time to Face the Facts

Just because you know the difference between right and wrong does not mean you always do the right thing. Between the pressure from friends to do wrong things and the temptation to fit in with those friends, and just plain old bad choices . . . wrong things happen. But you probably know when you've done something wrong. That knowledge lies like a heavy weight on your heart. Learn from your mistakes, and choose right over wrong next time.

Today I Will . . .

Choose right. I know the difference between right and wrong even though I may not always choose right. I want to be more and more obedient to God, so I'll ask him to help me choose right more and more often.

RIGHTS

What Does the Bible Say about Rights?

"Rights? I'm a kid, I don't have any rights!" Is that how you feel? The whole issue of rights gets confused with issues of pride and feeling as though the world owes you something. That would be something like, "I have the right to be wealthy. I have the right to designer clothes." Yeah, that's not so true. The rights you do have are the right of access to God and of being treated with kindness and value.

What the Bible Says

For you were called to freedom, brothers. Only do not use your freedom as an opportunity for the flesh, but through love serve one another.

GALATIANS 5:13

But we urge you, brothers, to do this more and more, and to aspire to live quietly, and to mind your own affairs, and to work with your hands, as we instructed you, so that you may walk properly before outsiders and be dependent on no one.

1 THESSALONIANS 4:10–12

Time to Face the Facts

Just because you're young doesn't mean you don't have the basic rights owed to any person. That means others should treat you kindly. You shouldn't be mistreated or abused. No one should dismiss you because of your race, sex, or financial status. You are a child of God, and he loves you. His desire is that

"I'll give you the right to a warm bed for two weeks."

all people be treated kindly and with respect. That's your right. It is also the way you should treat others.

Today I Will . . .

Stand up for myself if I need to do so. I do have the right to be treated with respect. So, if necessary, I'll kindly and respectfully ask for that. I'll also be sure I treat others that way.

What Does the Bible Say about Risk?

Are you a thrill-seeker? Do you love stuff like roller coasters? The higher and faster the better, right? Are you willing to try new things that get you out of the comfort zone of what you always do? Risk-takers live life on the edge. That gives an interesting perspective to how these people live their Christian life. Risk-taking faith is what takes the message of God's love around the world.

What the Bible Says

Be strong and courageous. Do not be frightened, and do not be dismayed, for the LORD your God is with you wherever you go.

JOSHUA 1:9

In peace I will both lie down and sleep; for you alone, O LORD, make me dwell in safety.

PSALM 4:8

Time to Face the Facts

Jesus' disciples were risk-takers. They risked being persecuted because of their faith. They followed Jesus even though it meant giving up their jobs or their families turning against them. Risk can be a bad thing or a good thing. Taking a risk can get you out of a rut and give you new ways to serve God and share his message of love. Taking a risk is not easy, but the rewards can be amazing.

"It seemed like a good idea at the time."

Today I Will . . .

Think about how courageous I am and whether I'm brave enough to take a risk. I believe it's important for the message of God's love to be spread around the world. If I can help that happen by taking some risks, I'll ask God to help me with the strength and courage I need.

ROLE MODELS

What Does the Bible Say about Role Models?

Who is your "hero"? There is probably someone you watch and think how awesome it would be to model your life after her. It may be someone famous such as a professional athlete or other celebrity. It may be someone you know who is older than you are. Something about that person makes you want to be like her. Wow, choosing a role model is a big deal.

What the Bible Says

You are the salt of the earth, but if salt has lost its taste, how shall its saltiness be restored? It is no longer good for anything except to be thrown out and trampled under people's feet.

MATTHEW 5:13

Be imitators of me, as I am of Christ.

1 CORINTHIANS 11:1

Show yourself in all respects to be a model of good works, and in your teaching show integrity, dignity, and sound speech that cannot be condemned, so that an opponent may be put to shame, having nothing evil to say about us.

TITUS 2:7–8

Time to Face the Facts

Does your role model truly show the values that are important in life? Just because a person can play a sport or sing a song doesn't mean he or she also lives a life that honors God. It doesn't mean that person is kind to others or treats people fairly and with honesty. It doesn't mean he or she has good moral values. Be careful about choosing a role model. The best role model is Jesus. Study his life and learn to live as he lived.

Today I Will . . .

Read the gospel stories of Jesus when he was on earth. I'll study how he treated others and how serious he was about serving and obeying God. He's the best role model.

What Does the Bible Say about Sacrifice?

One definition of sacrifice is "giving up something." For example, if you play baseball or softball sometimes you sacrifice the chance to get a hit by making a sacrifice hit to move your teammate from one base to the next. You also make a sacrifice when you help a friend to shine in some way while stepping back into the shadows so you don't take any attention from him. Sacrificing to help someone else is done because you care about them. The ultimate sacrifice was Jesus' death on the cross. He gave this sacrifice because he loves you.

What the Bible Says

Greater love has no one than this,
that someone lay down his life for his friends.

JOHN 15:13

God shows his love for us in that while
we were still sinners, Christ died for us.

ROMANS 5:8

Walk in love, as Christ loved us and gave himself up for us,
a fragrant offering and sacrifice to God.

EPHESIANS 5:2

Time to Face the Facts

Sacrificing shows love and concern for another person. It's a way to show you are following God and willing to have attention on someone else, not on you. Sacrificing costs something, whether it's time, money, energy, or humility. Sacrificing does not come cheaply. Jesus' sacrifice certainly didn't. It cost him suffering and persecution and ultimately his death. He gave this sacrifice willingly because he loves you.

Today I Will . . .

Thank Jesus for his sacrifice because it changes my whole life and gives me the promise of heaven. I'll also follow his example by being willing to make sacrifices for my friends and family.

What Does the Bible Say about Sadness?

Your heart is hurting so much that you can't find much joy in life. There seems to be a gray cloud floating above everything in your world. Sadness is a filter that everything else is seen through. When you sink into a pit of sadness, it is hard to get out. Reaching out for God is the only way to find hope.

What the Bible Says

Weeping may tarry for the night, but joy comes with the morning.

PSALM 30:5

He will wipe away every tear from their eyes, and death shall be no more, neither shall there be mourning, nor crying, nor pain anymore, for the former things have passed away.

REVELATION 21:4

Time to Face the Facts

Sadness happens because of disappointment or loss, things that unfortunately are normal parts of life. It's okay to be sad about these things. You feel joy when you're happy, so it's normal to feel sadness when you are hurt or disappointed. Healthy sadness lasts for a while, then it passes, and you get involved in other things. Sadness becomes unhealthy when it takes over your life and you can't get out from under the feeling. Then it may be a good idea to talk to someone like a parent or

"I think I'll go eat worms!"

your pastor about why you're so sad. Of course you should always turn to God for comfort and encouragement to get past the pain of sadness.

Today I Will . . .

Think about the sadness I feel. If it has gone beyond the healthy level, I will talk to someone to get help. I will also read God's Word for comfort and encouragement and let it reach deep into my heart.

What Does the Bible Say about Safety?

Okay, face it—the world is a pretty scary place these days. It seems like people are doing more and more mean things to others. The big, wide world is dangerous, but safety is needed even in your own town or school. Safety has become a hot topic. All kinds of rules and barriers are in place to protect you. Your parents do their best to keep you safe, and God protects you more often than you even realize.

What the Bible Says

For he will command his angels concerning you to guard you in all your ways.

PSALM 91:11

But I am not ashamed, for I know whom I have believed, and I am convinced that he is able to guard until that Day what has been entrusted to me.

2 TIMOTHY 1:12

Time to Face the Facts

"When I'm safe, I feel secure!"

In a perfect world all people would treat others with kindness and respect. There would be no murders or fights and no one would cheat or lie or any of those ugly things. However, the world is not perfect, so bad things do happen, and unfortunately, they sometimes happen to good people. There are probably hundreds of times a week when God protects you and you don't even realize it. But when bad things happen, it doesn't mean God isn't paying attention. That's the price of sin in the world. Ultimately, you will be safe in heaven with him someday. In the meantime, certainly ask him for protection, and follow the rules and guidelines that will help you be safe.

Today I Will . . .

Be serious about safety. I know the rules my parents and God have given me are for my safety. I'll follow them and use good sense about where I go and what I do.

What Does the Bible Say about Salvation?

Salvation is one of the main messages of the Bible, so don't take it lightly. If you and your family attend church a lot, you've heard about salvation your whole life. Perhaps you're so used to it that your brain just kind of shuts off when you hear the word. After all, you've accepted Jesus, so you know you have salvation. That's all that matters, right?

What the Bible Says

For God so loved the world, that he gave his only Son, that whoever believes in him should not perish but have eternal life.

JOHN 3:16

There is salvation in no one else, for there is no other name under heaven given among men by which we must be saved.

ACTS 4:12

Everyone who calls on the name of the Lord will be saved.

ROMANS 10:13

Time to Face the Facts

Okay, so you know your salvation is settled, but hey, look around you. What about your family, friends, neighbors, the people in your town, state, and even in the whole world? Just because you are saved doesn't mean the topic is settled. Take the message of the Bible seriously . . . the day is coming when Jesus will return and take his followers to heaven. All other people—all those who do not have salvation—will not be allowed in heaven. Their forever will not be pleasant. The opportunity for salvation needs to be offered to all people. What's your part in that?

Today I Will . . .

Be serious about sharing Christ with others. Salvation is an important thing, and I don't want anyone to miss their chance to have it.

What Does the Bible Say about Sarcasm?

Oh, come on, the Bible doesn't really talk about sarcasm, does it? Sarcasm is just good old fun—sharp comments that make people laugh. Is it? Is sarcasm just victimless comments? Not usually. Sarcasm is snide, sharp comments about someone else or some activity. Yes, it may make people laugh, but does it hurt someone's feelings or reputation? Is there any level of love in sarcasm?

What the Bible Says

Let no corrupting talk come out of your mouths, but only such as is good for building up, as fits the occasion, that it may give grace to those who hear.

EPHESIANS 4:29

Let your speech always be gracious, seasoned with salt, so that you may know how you ought to answer each person.

COLOSSIANS 4:6

Time to Face the Facts

Victims of your sarcastic comments may laugh along with you . . . on the outside. But you may never know how your words make them feel on the inside. At least you won't if you've never been the victim of sarcasm yourself. The hurtful words make the victim wonder if you really mean what you said, even a little bit. The negative feelings can lie on her heart for a long time, tearing down her own self-image and making her feel pretty ugly. The Bible's encouragement to treat others with love and to watch your speech gets lost in the language of sarcasm.

"Keep your words sweet—you may have to eat them."

Today I Will . . .

Watch what I say. I thought my sarcasm was just making people laugh. I never thought about how it might make others feel.

SATISFACTION

What Does the Bible Say about Satisfaction?

"I need that pair of $200 sneakers!" If you've approached your parents with that statement, you might have heard this response, "You *need* them, or you *want* them?" What does it take to satisfy you? The answer to that question is different for different people. Some refuse to be satisfied with anything less than their "wants" even though other people around the world must be satisfied with less than their "needs." It is possible, believe it or not, to be satisfied with exactly what God has given you and to share any excess of what you have with others.

What the Bible Says

Two things I ask of you;
deny them not to me before I die:
Remove far from me falsehood and lying;
give me neither poverty nor riches;
feed me with the food that is needful for me,
lest I be full and deny you
and say, "Who is the LORD?"
or lest I be poor and steal
and profane the name of my God.

PROVERBS 30:7–9

Not that I am speaking of being in need, for I have learned
in whatever situation I am to be content.

PHILIPPIANS 4:11

Time to Face the Facts

Satisfaction is contentment with what you have and where you are. It is feeling okay with life. It's a good place to be. Of course, it is a good thing to keep learning and growing, but it is not a good thing to keep grabbing for more and more stuff or more power or more attention. Showing God's love to others is possible when you're satisfied with what you have in those areas and your energy is put toward helping others have what they need.

Today I Will . . .

Be satisfied. I'll try to stop wanting what I don't need. Instead I'll look for ways to put my energy into helping others.

What Does the Bible Say about School?

School is either something you *have* to do or something you *love* to do. Really, whether you love school or not, there are some good things about it, right? Maybe there is one subject you enjoy, or perhaps you like hanging out with your friends. But does the Bible say anything about school? Yes, in a way, it does.

What the Bible Says

> Blessed are you, O Lord;
> teach me your statutes!
>
> **PSALM 119:12**

> Whatever you do, work heartily, as for the
> Lord and not for men.
>
> **COLOSSIANS 3:23**

> I am sure of this, that he who began
> a good work in you will bring it to
> completion at the day of Jesus Christ.
>
> **PHILIPPIANS 1:6**

Time to Face the Facts

The Bible says that you should work at your job with honesty and integrity. You should give it your best. Well, right now your job is going to school. So, yes, the Bible says something about school. If you're applying yourself to this "job," you will learn all you can and do your best on homework. You'll pay attention in class and treat your teachers with respect. You'll live your Christian life in school so that all will know God is important in your life.

Today I Will . . .

Have a good attitude about school. I'll work hard and do my best. I know I can't separate my Christian life from my school life. I'm a Christian all the time, and I want that to show to others.

What Does the Bible Say about Science?

In some people's minds science and the Bible are direct opposites. For example, there are hot debates between those who teach evolution and those who believe in God-based creation. Is it possible that science and faith can walk hand-in-hand?

What the Bible Says

In the beginning, God created the heavens and the earth.

GENESIS 1:1

In the beginning was the Word, and the Word was with God, and the Word was God. He was in the beginning with God. All things were made through him, and without him was not any thing made that was made.

JOHN 1:1–3

Time to Face the Facts

It could be tough for science and the Bible to co-exist. But if you take the viewpoint that God created science, that helps some. The Bible tells us that God created everything, and that includes science. The cool things that science has discovered about medicines and plants and . . . well, everything . . . is stuff that God made. He made all the things science is discovering, and he gave the intelligence to scientists to learn all they have learned.

"By George, I think I've got it."

Today I Will . . .

Thank God for science. It's comforting to know that science and the Bible can co-exist. God has made such a complicated world, and the details that come out as science discovers things is just amazing!

What Does the Bible Say about Second Chances?

There are times when knowing you get a second chance is a big relief. For example, when you fail a test and the teacher allows a do-over so you get a chance to bring your grade up. Another do-over that is a comfort is when you hurt a friend and she gives you a second chance instead of walking away from the friendship. Second chances are a gift. The biggest second chances come from God. He gives second, third, fourth, and on and on chances.

What the Bible Says

For I am sure that neither death nor life, nor angels nor rulers, nor things present nor things to come, nor powers, nor height nor depth, nor anything else in all creation, will be able to separate us from the love of God in Christ Jesus our Lord.

ROMANS 8:38–39

And you, who once were alienated and hostile in mind, doing evil deeds, he has now reconciled in his body of flesh by his death, in order to present you holy and blameless and above reproach before him . . .

COLOSSIANS 1:21–22

Time to Face the Facts

The Bible is filled with stories of second chances. Sometimes it is a second chance to obey God or a second chance to trust him. Jonah is a classic example of that. Read his story to understand. God wants your obedience and trust. He wants you to love and trust him because you love him, so he will give you many chances to show that love. God's example is a good model for your life.

"But officer, please!"

Give the people around you second chances to be good friends or good siblings. Everyone needs second chances sometimes!

Today I Will . . .

Thank God for second chances. I really need them sometimes. Realizing that helps me be willing to give others second chances.

What Does the Bible Say about Security?

Things in our world seem to change day by day. Some of the changes may make you feel a little worried about the future. It's harder than it used to be to have security about safety and jobs and finances. Your parents have these responsibilities to deal with more than you, of course. But the desire for security is something everyone has. There is only one thing in this world that is absolutely secure. Do you know what that is?

What the Bible Says

> I waited patiently for the LORD;
> he inclined to me and heard my cry.
> He drew me up from the pit of destruction,
> out of the miry bog,
> and set my feet upon a rock,
> making my steps secure.

PSALM 40:1–2

Do not be anxious about anything, but in everything by prayer and supplication with thanksgiving let your requests be made known to God. And the peace of God, which surpasses all understanding, will guard your hearts and your minds in Christ Jesus.

PHILIPPIANS 4:6–7

Time to Face the Facts

The only secure thing in life is God. He never changes. His love for you is secure. His care for you is secure. His guidance in your life is secure. You can count on God totally and completely.

"Try being just a little more mature about this."

The other securities—safety, jobs, finances, etc.—are things you can ask God for. But regardless of what happens in those areas, God is right there with you as your strength and comfort. That's real security.

Today I Will . . .

Talk to God about the things I worry about. I will remember that real and lasting security is in him.

What Does the Bible Say about Self-confidence?

Do you beat yourself up because you feel that you are not good enough? You aren't pretty or handsome? You aren't a good athlete? You aren't smart . . . you just put yourself on the level of pond scum? Here's news for you: God made you, and he thinks you're very special.

What the Bible Says

> Then God said, "Let us make man in our image, after our likeness."
>
> **GENESIS 1:26**

> Are not two sparrows sold for a penny? And not one of them will fall to the ground apart from your Father. But even the hairs of your head are all numbered. Fear not, therefore; you are of more value than many sparrows.
>
> **MATTHEW 10:29–31**

> Having gifts that differ according to the grace given to us, let us use them: if prophecy, in proportion to our faith; if service, in our serving; the one who teaches, in his teaching; the one who exhorts, in his exhortation; the one who contributes, in generosity; the one who leads, with zeal; the one who does acts of mercy, with cheerfulness.
>
> **ROMANS 12:6–8**

Time to Face the Facts

God made you just the way he wants you to be. He gave you abilities and talents that make you special (even if you don't know what those are yet). He loves you more than you can possibly imagine. So, stop beating yourself up. God likes you; like yourself!

Today I Will . . .

Make a list of things I actually think I'm good at. Make another list of things I'd like to learn. Thank God for both of those lists. Thank him for making me who I am.

What Does the Bible Say about Self-control?

Can you eat just one potato chip? How about only half of a cookie? Are you able to watch half of a television show, then go on to doing something more profitable? When you're really upset with someone, can you control your speech by not spouting angry words? These things all require self-control and are important in your relationship with God and in how you relate to other people.

What the Bible Says

I appeal to you therefore, brothers, by the mercies of God, to present your bodies as a living sacrifice, holy and acceptable to God, which is your spiritual worship. Do not be conformed to this world, but be transformed by the renewal of your mind, that by testing you may discern what is the will of God, what is good and acceptable and perfect.

ROMANS 12:1–2

But put on the Lord Jesus Christ, and make no provision for the flesh, to gratify its desires.

ROMANS 13:14

Time to Face the Facts

Self-control is important for things like eating healthily and not overeating. It's necessary for choices on how you spend your time. Self-control is very important in how you relate to other people, because controlling outbursts and temper tantrums accomplishes a lot more than when you explode at others. Self-control comes from a growing relationship with God. It's one of the evidences of the Holy Spirit working in your heart. He teaches you how to be self-controlled.

"I'll just eat one ... bag!"

Today I Will . . .

Think about how self-controlled I am. I know I don't have self-control in all areas of my life, so I'll ask God to teach me about it, and I'll let him guide me into good self-control.

What Does the Bible Say about Self-defense?

Self-defense is being able to protect yourself from danger. It most often refers to situations where you may be attacked by someone wanting to hurt you. Hopefully, you will never need to use self-defense, but should you be prepared? Do you wonder how God feels about self-defense?

What the Bible Says

One man of you puts to flight a thousand, since it is the Lord your God who fights for you, just as he promised you.

JOSHUA 23:10

Many are the afflictions of the righteous, but the Lord delivers him out of them all.

PSALM 34:19

Time to Face the Facts

God gave you a good brain, and he wants you to use it. Of course, he would prefer that you never be in danger or be hurt. But it makes sense to use your brain and learn all you can about self-defense. It also makes sense to be aware of dangerous situations and places and stay out of them. Don't put yourself in harm's way on purpose, then ask God to protect you. Be smart about things like this. Keep your body strong and your mind alert, and be smart about where you go and the people you hang out with.

"My legs always were my best defense."

Today I Will . . .

Learn some self-defense techniques. I will also make smart choices about the places I go and the people I spend time with. I want to be safe, and I know I have a part in that.

SELF-ESTEEM

What Does the Bible Say about Self-esteem?

What you think of yourself plays a big part in your relationship with God and in the way you get along with others. Did you know that? It's true. If you feel that you're no more special than the green foam of pond scum, then that will show in your attitudes. Okay, maybe that's a little extreme. But your self-esteem reflects in how you accept God's love in your life and in how you believe others feel about you.

What the Bible Says

For you formed my inward parts;
you knitted me together in my mother's womb.
I praise you, for I am fearfully and wonderfully made.
Wonderful are your works;
my soul knows it very well.

PSALM 139:13–14

For by the grace given to me I say to everyone among you not to think of himself more highly than he ought to think, but to think with sober judgment, each according to the measure of faith that God has assigned.

ROMANS 12:3

Time to Face the Facts

Too much self-esteem is pride. Too little self-esteem is a criticism of what God created. He made you. Your responsibility is to develop the brain, body, and talents he gave you. But comparing yourself to others and criticizing yourself for not being like them is just wrong. Notice your abilities and talents. Need some help? Maybe you're a really loyal friend, a good artist, a gifted singer, or you're good at listening to others . . . talents come in many forms. Healthy self-esteem recognizes that you are important to God and to your family and friends. You matter. God made you just the way he wants you to be. Your friends and family love you, so love yourself, too!

Today I will . . .

Stop criticizing myself. I'll accept God's love for me and be honest about the abilities and talents he gave me.

What Does the Bible Say about Selfishness?

"I am most important! Whatever anyone else does or whatever happens, the most important thing is how it affects me!" That is selfishness. If you've been around someone who is selfish, you know that it is no fun. After a while you realize that you don't matter much to that person except in whatever way you can help him. If you are selfish, you may want to take a good, long look at yourself.

What the Bible Says

Do nothing from rivalry or conceit, but in humility count others more significant than yourselves. Let each of you look not only to his own interests, but also to the interests of others.

PHILIPPIANS 2:3–4

For God is not unjust so as to overlook your work and the love that you have shown for his name in serving the saints, as you still do.

HEBREWS 6:10

But if anyone has the world's goods and sees his brother in need, yet closes his heart against him, how does God's love abide in him?

1 JOHN 3:17

Time to Face the Facts

Selfishness is not nice. It damages relationships with others and goes against what God teaches about caring for others and putting their feelings before your own. Generosity and love are strong evidences of God's presence in your heart. He even said in the Bible that his children will be known by the fact that they love others. Selfishness and love are opposite emotions that will have a lot of trouble living together in the same heart.

Today I Will . . .

Admit to myself and God if selfishness is something I struggle with. I know how it feels to be around someone who is selfish, and I don't like it. So, I don't want to make my friends and family feel that way.

SENSITIVITY

What Does the Bible Say about Sensitivity?

Trying to be friends with an insensitive person is kind of like being friends with a brick—she couldn't care less about your feelings. Sensitivity is caring about others' feelings and being sympathetic to them. You can't solve others' problems, but you can care about how they feel and show that by listening to them talk through their feelings. Sensitivity is evidence of love for others, which is exactly what God wants his children to have.

What the Bible Says

No one has ever seen God; if we love one another,
God abides in us and his love is perfected in us.

1 JOHN 4:12

Religion that is pure and undefiled before God, the Father, is this: to visit orphans and widows in their affliction, and to keep oneself unstained from the world.

JAMES 1:27

"Sorry you have to go through this."

Time to Face the Facts

Sensitivity is dulled by selfishness. Being concerned about yourself way more than others replaces sensitivity in your heart. The best way to build good relationships with others is to connect with them by caring about their feelings and problems. In response, they will care about you and your feelings and problems. This creates relationships like a web where people are caring for one another and working together to encourage each other. God's love is flowing back and forth from person to person.

Today I Will . . .

Care about others. I see the importance of God's love flowing between me and others. We can encourage and help and strengthen each other. I will ask God to help me be more sensitive to others.

What Does the Bible Say about Service?

What does service mean? Serving others may mean doing some jobs that might not be your favorite thing to do. It's doing jobs that aren't "assigned" to you. Serving others means noticing things that you could do to help someone else, then doing them. Jesus was the prime example of serving others. He even said that he came to earth to be a servant.

What the Bible Says

But whoever would be great among you must be your servant, and whoever would be first among you must be your slave, even as the Son of Man came not to be served but to serve, and to give his life as a ransom for many.

MATTHEW 20:26–28

Have this mind among yourselves, which is yours in Christ Jesus, who, though he was in the form of God, did not count equality with God a thing to be grasped, but made himself nothing, taking the form of a servant, being born in the likeness of men. And being found in human form, he humbled himself by becoming obedient to the point of death, even death on a cross.

PHILIPPIANS 2:5–8

Time to Face the Facts

Some people want to be the person who is served, and the idea of serving others is not very appealing to them. Jesus taught that serving others shows God-inspired love. What are some ways you could serve someone? Weeding a neighbor's flower garden, loading the dishwasher without being asked, playing with a toddler while his mom does housework, washing the car for your parents . . . simple things that really help people or that others can't do for themselves. Serving takes time, energy, and effort, and there is no room for selfishness and pride in the process. Don't serve someone, then brag about it—that makes it all about you. Serve out of love.

Today I Will . . .

Look around and see what I can do to help someone who really needs to be served. I'll try to serve secretly. This will be fun!

What Does the Bible Say about Sex?

Are you curious about sex things? It's hard not to be since the topic is thrown at you on TV, magazine covers, songs, and just about everywhere else! Sex is a very public topic these days. So, how should you approach this at your age? It's okay to be curious about it. God created sex, and it's a beautiful thing, but keep it in perspective for what's appropriate at your stage in life.

What the Bible Says

No temptation has overtaken you that is not common to man. God is faithful, and he will not let you be tempted beyond your ability, but with the temptation he will also provide the way of escape, that you may be able to endure it.

1 CORINTHIANS 10:13

For this is the will of God, your sanctification: that you abstain from sexual immorality; that each one of you know how to control his own body in holiness and honor, not in the passion of lust like the Gentiles who do not know God.

1 THESSALONIANS 4:3-4

"Is this for real?"

Time to Face the Facts

Sex, as God created it, is meant to be between a husband and a wife. It's a beautiful expression of their love for one another. However, the media, Hollywood, and some music have made the topic of sex the focus of much of what they do. That means the moral values of many in the world have cheapened sex. Read God's feelings about how his creation of man and woman and the expression of that love should be handled. Make a decision right now as to how you will view sex and whether you will keep yourself pure until marriage.

Today I Will . . .

Make that decision. I will not engage in sexual activity until I am married. I don't what to do anything to cheapen what God made to be a beautiful thing.

What Does the Bible Say about Shame?

Shame often follows guilt, or it is an accusation of something done wrong, as in, "Shame on you." Shame is feeling bad about yourself for what you've done. Shame lies on your heart and pulls your self-image down. Is there any good thing about shame? Yes, it can lead you to confession and repentance. Those are necessary steps in restoring your relationship with God and sometimes with others.

What the Bible Says

For all have sinned and fall short of the glory of God.

ROMANS 3:23

If we confess our sins, he is faithful and just to forgive us our sins and to cleanse us from all unrighteousness.

1 JOHN 1:9

Time to Face the Facts

Shame can be very painful because you know that something you have done has hurt another person and broken your relationship with God. The good thing about shame is that, if you act on it, you are led to admit the wrong you've done, confess it, and then repent from it, which means you will make every effort to never do it again. You feel shame because you're sorry for your action. Shame does not have to settle on your heart and affect your self-image. When you feel shame, do what you need to in order to move past it. God forgives and restores your relationship. Hopefully the loved ones in your life will, too.

"Why didn't I think before I said that?"

Today I Will . . .

Figure out why I feel shame—what did I do? When I know what it is, I'll follow the correct actions of confessing, apologizing, and repenting. I don't want to live under the blanket of shame, and I'm thankful that I don't have to.

What Does the Bible Say about Sharing?

Is this how you feel: *What's mine is mine!* You have stuff and the money to do what you want because your mom and dad work hard, so let other people work hard, too. You don't see why you should have to share. Sorry, God doesn't agree with you. You have stuff because of him, and God says the right thing to do is share with others.

What the Bible Says

Whoever has a bountiful eye will be blessed,
for he shares his bread with the poor.

PROVERBS 22:9

Now the full number of those who believed were of one heart and soul,
and no one said that any of the things that belonged to him
was his own, but they had everything in common.

ACTS 4:32

Each one must give as he has decided in his heart, not reluctantly
or under compulsion, for God loves a cheerful giver.

2 CORINTHIANS 9:7

Time to Face the Facts

The main characteristic of God's children is that they love others. So, how do you show love to others if you won't share with them? Especially if they are hungry or cold or just don't have the fun things to do that you do? Show God's love (and yours) by being generous.

"What's mine is yours—I'll share it!"

Today I Will . . .

Look around for someone I can share something with, and do it willingly.

What Does the Bible Say about Sibling Rivalry?

One of the best things in life is being part of a family. One of the hardest things in life is being part of a family. Of course you love your brothers and sisters, but there may be tension once in a while between you and your siblings. Sometimes kids feel like their parents favor one child over another. That creates even more tension between siblings.

What the Bible Says

Love is patient and kind; love does not envy or boast; it is not arrogant or rude. It does not insist on its own way; it is not irritable or resentful; it does not rejoice at wrongdoing, but rejoices with the truth.

1 CORINTHIANS 13:4–6

Rejoice in the Lord always; again I will say, Rejoice. Let your reasonableness be known to everyone.

PHILIPPIANS 4:4

Count it all joy, my brothers, when you meet trials of various kinds, for you know that the testing of your faith produces steadfastness.

JAMES 1:2–3

Time to Face the Facts

The important thing to remember is that God put your family together with exactly who he wants to be in it. You may have trouble getting along with your brothers or sisters once in a while. That's okay. Can you put aside rivalry and celebrate your siblings' successes? Remember that even when you don't like your siblings, you can still love them.

Today I Will . . .

Celebrate good news with my siblings. Love them no matter what. Family is important, and I want to get along with my siblings.

What Does the Bible Say about Sickness?

Sickness kind of takes over your life. When you are sick, it's hard to think about much else and even harder to care about other people. It's hard to think about anyone except yourself. Why does there have to be sickness anyway? Why doesn't God just take all sickness out of the world? Well, he would probably like to. After all, he loves you and all people very much.

What the Bible Says

> Bless the LORD, O my soul,
>   and all that is within me,
>   bless his holy name!
> Bless the LORD, O my soul,
>   and forget not all his benefits,
>   who forgives all your iniquity,
>   who heals all your diseases.

PSALM 103:1–3

> Hope deferred makes the heart sick,
>   but a desire fulfilled is a tree of life.

PROVERBS 13:12

Time to Face the Facts

Sometimes God heals sickness in answer to prayers for a person. Sometimes he doesn't. It's hard to understand. One of God's names is the Great Physician, which means he has the power to heal any sickness. But ever since Adam and Eve brought sin into our world, things have been less than perfect. Unfortunately, we have to live

"Chicken soup doesn't cure everything."

with the evidences of that, and one of those is sickness in our world. However, you're never alone in sickness. God is your comfort and strength.

Today I Will . . .

Pray for some people who are sick. I'll pray for their healing and for God's comfort to be very real to them.

What Does the Bible Say about Sin?

Everyone sins. You can try with all your might not to sin and you will anyway. The Bible says everyone is a sinner. Sin is more than big things like robbery or murder. Sin is also selfishness, bad attitudes, pride . . . things like that. The only sinless Man who ever lived on earth is Jesus.

What the Bible Says

Let not sin therefore reign in your mortal body, to make you obey its passions. Do not present your members to sin as instruments for unrighteousness, but present yourselves to God as those who have been brought from death to life, and your members to God as instruments for righteousness.

ROMANS 6:12–13

For we know that the law is spiritual, but I am of the flesh, sold under sin. For I do not understand my own actions. For I do not do what I want, but I do the very thing I hate. Now if I do what I do not want, I agree with the law, that it is good. So now it is no longer I who do it, but sin that dwells within me.

ROMANS 7:14–17

At one time you were darkness, but now you are light in the Lord. Walk as children of light (for the fruit of light is found in all that is good and right and true).

EPHESIANS 5:8–9

"Wow—sin is everywhere!"

Time to Face the Facts

The Bible teaches how to avoid sin. Obeying God and following the Bible's teachings take some sin from your life. Obeying its teachings will help you become more and more like Jesus. In the meantime, God forgives sin. Isn't that wonderful? When you confess sin and repent from it, he promises to forgive you. He will also give you strength to resist sin and keep focused on living for him.

Today I Will . . .

Confess and repent. I want to get as much sin out of my life as possible. I want to be more and more like Jesus.

SINCERITY

What Does the Bible Say about Sincerity?

Saying the right things is pretty easy. "Sorry you're sick." "I'll pray for you." "I know God loves you." Those are all nice, kind things to say. But when you say them, do you mean them? What about when you talk to God and confess your sins or pray for others? Do your prayers come from your heart or are they just the "right things to say"? Sincerity puts meaning and power behind your words.

What the Bible Says

Know the God of your father and serve him with a whole heart and with a willing mind, for the LORD searches all hearts and understands every plan and thought. If you seek him, he will be found by you, but if you forsake him, he will cast you off forever.

1 CHRONICLES 28:9

Prove me, O LORD, and try me;
test my heart and my mind.

PSALM 26:2

When you give to the needy, sound no trumpet before you, as the hypocrites do in the synagogues and in the streets, that they may be praised by others. Truly, I say to you, they have received their reward. But when you give to the needy, do not let your left hand know what your right hand is doing, so that your giving may be in secret. And your Father who sees in secret will reward you.

MATTHEW 6:2–4

Time to Face the Facts

If you aren't sincere about the words you say, who will know? If you're even a half-decent actress, you can make people think you mean what you say. Yeah, you can fool people . . . but you can't fool God. He sees your heart and knows whether or not you are sincere. If you're not—don't bother saying the words. Even other people will eventually see that you don't mean your apologies or your concerns because your actions won't follow up your words. God's love will flow through you when your heart sincerely means the words you speak.

Today I Will . . .

Think about this. Maybe I think I am sincere, but when I look at my motives, I see that I'm really not—I just want to look caring to others. I want to honestly love others, so I need to be sincere.

What Does the Bible Say about Singing?

Singing is fun! Music expresses joy or sorrow. It can express praise and worship to God or love to another person. Singing says things that are hard to find words for. But what if you don't have an awesome singing voice? What if you can't stay on tune? Should you just sing in the shower and not put others through the pain of listening to you? God says the sound of praise to him is a joy—maybe it's a joyful "noise," but it's still a joy!

What the Bible Says

Oh come, let us sing to the LORD;
let us make a joyful noise to the rock of our salvation!

PSALM 95:1

Make a joyful noise to the LORD, all the
earth; break forth into joyous song
and sing praises!

PSALM 98:4

Praise the LORD!
Sing to the LORD a new song,
his praise in the assembly of the godly!

PSALM 149:1

"That's a joyful NOISE alright."

Time to Face the Facts

Music can soothe the hurting soul and, no, you don't have to sing like an angel to enjoy music. One thing to be careful of with music is the kind of songs you choose to sing. There are plenty of songs out there that are inappropriate because the words are about things that do not honor God or about things that shouldn't be public information. Sing songs that make you smile and feel good. Sing songs of praise to God— even as a joyful noise. Praise him with your voice—and enjoy it!

Today I Will . . .

Sing my love to God. I'll sing loud and with energy and from my heart. Even if every note isn't perfect, the feelings from my heart will be sincere!

What Does the Bible Say about Slang?

Stop and think about how many of the words you speak each day are slang—words that have been made up or words whose meanings have been changed to mean something new. Sometimes slang words become such a part of conversation that they are added to dictionaries and become accepted language. Sometimes they do not because their meanings are unkind to others or are vulgar. Some slang is just a substitute for swear words. Language is important because it's how you communicate with others.

What the Bible Says

Come, let us go down and there confuse their language,
so that they may not understand one another's speech.

GENESIS 11:7

Better is a poor person who walks in his integrity
than one who is crooked in speech and is a fool.

PROVERBS 19:1

Let your speech always be gracious, seasoned with salt, so
that you may know how you ought to answer each person.

COLOSSIANS 4:6

Time to Face the Facts

When you use slang that is understandable only to your group of friends, it is hard to communicate with other people. Remember the story of the Tower of Babel in the Bible? Those people couldn't communicate, so they couldn't have relationships, friendships, or do business with one another. Be careful how you speak. Some slang is okay, but make sure people know what you're talking about. Remember in your choice of language that you are instructed to love others. Make sure others can understand that.

Today I Will . . .

Think about the words I use. If any of my slang is unkind to any group of people or in any other way inappropriate, I will drop it out of my vocabulary.

What Does the Bible Say about Sleep?

Health professionals generally agree that a person your age needs about eight to nine hours of sleep each night. How are you doing on that? Do you get too much sleep or too little? Why is sleep important? Think about it: your body works hard all day. Your muscles are in constant motion, your heart is pumping blood throughout your body, your lungs are working to keep oxygen flowing, and your brain is making constant decisions and choices . . . it's a lot of work. Sleep gives your body a chance to slow down and rest. Sure, some things are still working—your heart and lungs—but at a slower pace. The human body is an amazing machine. God put a lot of thought into it!

What the Bible Says

> The LORD is my shepherd; I shall not want.
> He makes me lie down in green pastures.
> He leads me beside still waters.
> He restores my soul.
> He leads me in paths of righteousness
> for his name's sake.

PSALM 23:1–3

> Come to me, all who labor and are heavy laden, and I will give you rest. Take my yoke upon you, and learn from me, for I am gentle and lowly in heart, and you will find rest for your souls. For my yoke is easy, and my burden is light.

MATTHEW 11:28–30

Time to Face the Facts

Sleep is important for your physical health and your mental attitudes. God designed your body to need rest each day so it can power up for the next day. Remember that even God rested after six days of creating the world. Make sure you get enough rest so that your body and brain can work at full capacity. It's hard to be patient, loving, and obedient to God when you're tired. Take care of your body—it's the only one you get!

Today I will . . .

Turn off the computer, video games, or TV . . . whatever keeps me up too late at night. I'll be organized enough to get my homework done early so I can get to bed on time.

SMOKING

What Does the Bible Say about Smoking?

Maybe you think God doesn't care whether you take a puff or two. After all, a lot of your friends smoke. It's cool, and you want to fit in.   God cares about what you put into your body and how you take care of it. Check it out. . . .

What the Bible Says

So God created man in his own image,
in the image of God he created him;
male and female he created them.

GENESIS 1:27

Put to death therefore what is earthly in you: sexual immorality, impurity, passion, evil desire, and covetousness, which is idolatry.

COLOSSIANS 3:5

For if you live according to the flesh you will die, but if by the Spirit you put to death the deeds of the body, you will live.

ROMANS 8:13

Time to Face the Facts

Okay, think about it. You're created in God's image. Would you offer him a smoke? Yeah, I didn't think so. God gave you one body to use for his service on earth. He expects you to take care of it. Does putting nicotine in your lungs sound like a good way to do that?

Today I Will . . .

Not smoke. Plain and simple. It's not good for my body, so I won't do it.

"The movies make this look way cool."

What Does the Bible Say about Snacks?

Cookies, chips, cupcakes, pizza rolls . . . what's your favorite snack? Snacks are a treat, aren't they? The problem with most snacks is that they aren't really healthy. That means they have too much sugar or salt and no real food value. So what, huh? They still taste good. Yes, but what are they doing to your body, and how does that fit with taking care of the body God gave you?

What the Bible Says

I appeal to you therefore, brothers, by the mercies of God, to present your bodies as a living sacrifice, holy and acceptable to God, which is your spiritual worship. Do not be conformed to this world, but be transformed by the renewal of your mind, that by testing you may discern what is the will of God, what is good and acceptable and perfect.

ROMANS 12:1-2

Be exalted, O Lord, in your strength!
We will sing and praise your power.

PSALM 21:13

Time to Face the Facts

Snacks are okay . . . in moderation. Of course, healthy snacks are best, but if you enjoy the unhealthy ones, at least try to keep them to a minimum. If you crave those sugary or salty things, make them a special treat. That way you can still have them . . . but not every day. It's important to take care of your health, and excessive snack food will just make you heavier and full of bad stuff that adds nothing to your health.

"I read on the Internet that doughnuts are 97% protein."

Today I Will . . .

Write down everything I eat. That's the only way I'm going to get a realistic view of whether I eat a lot of junk food. I'll probably be surprised.

SORROW

What Does the Bible Say about Sorrow?

Sorrow comes from a very sad heart. It usually means you've lost something—a friend, family member, or pet, for example. Sorrow colors pretty much everything else. It is kind of hard to be happy or funny when you feel sorrow. When you're feeling sorrow, you need to know that God cares.

What the Bible Says

Cast your burden on the LORD,
and he will sustain you;
he will never permit
the righteous to be moved.

PSALM 55:22

Blessed be the God and Father of our Lord Jesus Christ, the Father of mercies and
God of all comfort, who comforts us in all our affliction, so that we may
be able to comfort those who are in any affliction, with the comfort
with which we ourselves are comforted by God.

2 CORINTHIANS 1:3–4

He will wipe away every tear from their eyes, and death shall be no more,
neither shall there be mourning, nor crying, nor pain anymore,
for the former things have passed away.

REVELATION 21:4

Time to Face the Facts

Sorrow is part of life, unfortunately. We lose loved ones, either from moving away or from death. We lose animals. We lose dreams. Sorrow is the natural response to those circumstances. How does God help you? In a couple of different ways. Notice the people around you when you need comfort. Your friends and family comforting you and loving you are God's comfort with skin on. God also comforts your heart himself. Tell him exactly why you're hurting and ask him for comfort. Read his Word and see what he says. Be still and wait for his comfort to surround you.

Today I Will . . .

Appreciate the people around me who give me comfort and support. I'll read my Bible and tell God why I'm sad. Then, I'll experience his comfort, too.

What Does the Bible Say about Speech ?

The Bible says that your tongue is a powerful instrument. You can use it for good or bad. If you speak kind, loving words to other people—that's good. If you speak mean words that tear down other people—that's bad. What kind of words do you think God wants you to speak?

What the Bible Says

Let no corrupting talk come out of your mouths, but only such as is good for building up, as fits the occasion, that it may give grace to those who hear.

EPHESIANS 4:29

Let the word of Christ dwell in you richly, teaching and admonishing one another in all wisdom, singing psalms and hymns and spiritual songs, with thankfulness in your hearts to God. And whatever you do, in word or deed, do everything in the name of the Lord Jesus, giving thanks to God the Father through him.

COLOSSIANS 3:16–17

Have nothing to do with foolish, ignorant controversies; you know that they breed quarrels. And the Lord's servant must not be quarrelsome but kind to everyone, able to teach, patiently enduring evil, correcting his opponents with gentleness.

2 TIMOTHY 2:23–25

Time to Face the Facts

Well, of course you know the answer. God wants you to speak kind, loving words that build other people up and make them feel good about themselves. He wants you to use the power of speech in a good way. Use it to encourage, help, and support others. Use speech that glorifies his name and that you wouldn't be afraid for him to hear.

Today I Will . . .

Think about the words I say and how they will make other people feel. I will try to say words that I wouldn't mind God hearing. I want to honor and glorify him with my speech.

What Does the Bible Say about Sports?

Do you enjoy sports? What's your favorite? Playing sports is a lot of fun. Being on a sports team is good for you, too, because you get lots of exercise. Does the Bible say anything about sports? Well, maybe not about baseball, basketball, or soccer. But it does mention some of the cool things you learn from sports.

What the Bible Says

Iron sharpens iron, and one man sharpens another.

PROVERBS 27:17

Two are better than one, because they have a good reward for their toil. For if they fall, one will lift up his fellow. But woe to him who is alone when he falls and has not another to lift him up! Again, if two lie together, they keep warm, but how can one keep warm alone? And though a man might prevail against one who is alone, two will withstand him—a threefold cord is not quickly broken.

ECCLESIASTES 4:9–12

May the God of endurance and encouragement grant you to live in such harmony with one another, in accord with Christ Jesus, that together you may with one voice glorify the God and Father of our Lord Jesus Christ.

ROMANS 15:5–6

Time to Face the Facts

There is nothing wrong with sports, of course. In fact, sports are good because they keep you active and exercising. They give you an opportunity to excel at something and to enjoy being a part of a team. Being on a sport teams teaches you to work together with your teammates and to celebrate when your teamate does something awesome. Sports teach you discipline and perseverance, too. There are a lot of life lessons to be learned from sports!

"Maybe I should go back to pitching marbles."

Today I Will . . .

Enjoy the sports I play. I never thought about the cool things I'm learning. I just love playing. Thank you, God, for sports!

STEALING

What Does the Bible Say about Stealing?

Taking something from someone else and making it your own is wrong. However, it happens every day in every city, state, and country. Some people think they have the right to take things from other people. Why do they feel that way? The Bible has the answer to that question.

What the Bible Says

You shall not steal.

EXODUS 20:15

For out of the heart come evil thoughts, murder, adultery, sexual immorality, theft, false witness, slander.

MATTHEW 15:19

Let the thief no longer steal, but rather let him labor, doing honest work with his own hands, so that he may have something to share with anyone in need.

EPHESIANS 4:28

Time to Face the Facts

Stealing is a result of a sinful heart. It shows selfishness and lack of concern for other people. God says it is wrong to take things that do not belong to you. It doesn't matter how small or big the stolen item is; it's still wrong. Stealing has always been wrong—one of the Ten Commandments says that stealing is wrong. Disobeying God by stealing breaks your relationship with him and hurts other people.

"I'm only borrowing it—
permanently."

Today I Will . . .

Be careful about stealing. I don't want to steal even little things from someone else. I don't want to disappoint God or hurt others.

STRANGERS

What Does the Bible Say about Strangers?

"A stranger is a friend you haven't met yet." That saying has been around forever. What does it mean? Well, think about new kids in your class—kids who have just moved to your town. You don't know the new students. You can judge them based on their race or their appearance, then walk away from them. Or, you can take the opportunity to turn these strangers into friends by getting to know them.

What the Bible Says

> For I was hungry and you gave me food, I was thirsty and you gave me drink, I was a stranger and you welcomed me.
>
> **MATTHEW 25:35**

> A new commandment I give to you, that you love one another: just as I have loved you, you also are to love one another.
>
> **JOHN 13:34**

> Now may our God and Father himself, and our Lord Jesus, direct our way to you, and may the Lord make you increase and abound in love for one another and for all, as we do for you.
>
> **1 THESSALONIANS 3:11–12**

"Welcome to the neighborhood."

Time to Face the Facts

Does it sound scary to talk to someone you don't know? Well, think how the new kid feels. He's in a new town and new school, and it probably seems like the rest of the class knows each other already. The opportunity to make a stranger into a friend is a God-given chance to show Christ's love to someone who really needs it. Yes, it may be a bit scary to get out of your comfort zone, but making a stranger into a friend is a pretty cool thing!

Today I Will . . .

Talk to someone new at school or at church. It doesn't have to be a new student, just someone I've never talked with before. Maybe I'll make a new friend!

STRENGTH

What Does the Bible Say about Strength?

You develop physical strength by exercising, lifting weights, and training your muscles to be stronger. Physical strength is pretty cool, and you can do some awesome things when your muscles are strong. But there is an even more important kind of strength: spiritual strength. This is the strength to stay close to God and live for him, the strength to obey him and do his work in the world.

What the Bible Says

The joy of the LORD is your strength.

NEHEMIAH 8:10

That you may know what is the hope to which he has called you, what are the riches of his glorious inheritance in the saints, and what is the immeasurable greatness of his power toward us who believe, according to the working of his great might that he worked in Christ when he raised him from the dead and seated him at his right hand in the heavenly places, far above all rule and authority and power and dominion, and above every name that is named, not only in this age but also in the one to come.

EPHESIANS 1:18–21

Time to Face the Facts

How do you develop spiritual strength? Well, physical strength takes an effort to develop and so does spiritual strength. It doesn't happen by just sitting in a chair and wishing for it. Spiritual strength comes from reading God's Word and talking with him every day. It grows by living for him and obeying him, even when you fail and have to get up and try again. Especially then. Spiritual strength is very important, and it will be a blessing in your life and to those around you.

"I think I can. I think I can!"

Today I Will . . .

Start doing the "exercise" needed to be spiritually strong. I know this growth takes work, just like exercising my physical body. But it's important, and I want to do it.

What Does the Bible Say about Stress?

What causes you to feel stressed? Homework? Tests? Fights with friends? Parents arguing? Stress comes from a lot of different directions. Regardless of where it comes from, it can make you feel like a rubber band that is stretched so tight that it is in danger of breaking. Trying to handle your problems on your own will just make the stress worse. Turn to God for help. He really cares.

What the Bible Says

Cast your burden on the LORD,
and he will sustain you;
he will never permit
the righteous to be moved.

PSALM 55:22

In the day of my trouble I call upon
you, for you answer me.

PSALM 86:7

Let not your hearts be troubled.
Believe in God; believe also in me.

JOHN 14:1

Time to Face the Facts

God can give you peace and rest in the middle of your stresses. Trust him to help you. When you feel major stress, spend some time alone and let your mind concentrate on a verse of comfort—a promise of God's love and help. Take a break from your work and rest your mind and heart. Staying in the middle of the stress will only cause more stress. Take a break and let God give you rest. Let his love surround you.

Today I Will . . .

Figure out what it is that makes me feel stressed. I'll memorize a verse about God's love and care, and then I'll just take a half an hour or so each day and be quiet while I let God fill my heart with his love and care.

What Does the Bible Say about Stubbornness?

Definition of stubbornness: stubbornness is insisting on doing things your way; having your way; not giving in. Stubbornness is all about you, and it's not pretty. Try to be friends with a stubborn person or work on a team with one. It's not easy and, again, it's not pretty. Stubbornness resists anyone else's ideas or thoughts . . . even God's.

What the Bible Says

> Those who know your name will trust in you,
> for you, LORD, have never forsaken those who seek you.
>
> **PSALM 9:10**

> By insolence comes nothing but strife,
> but with those who take advice is wisdom.
>
> **PROVERBS 13:10**

Time to Face the Facts

It's impossible to have a healthy relationship with God when you stubbornly refuse to obey him and do things his way. It is also unlikely that a stubborn person has healthy friendships, because he doesn't care about others' feelings or let them choose things for them to do as friends. Being stubborn may make you think that you always get your way, but it comes at the price of friendships and a relationship with

"I'm not stubborn, I'm determined!"

God. The opposite of stubbornness is openness to direction from God and a desire to serve him and care and concern for your friends and serving them.

Today I Will . . .

Listen to my friends. When they have ideas of things to do, I'll go along with it. I don't always need to have my way. I'll obey God, too. I believe his way is best, but stubbornness comes naturally to me, so I need to work on that.

What Does the Bible Say about Submission?

Submission is a willingness to yield or surrender to an authority. It means you don't always get your way. Submission is not the same as weakness, though some people think of it that way and fight submitting to anyone. There is always someone in authority to submit to—parents, teachers, police officers, and, of course, God. Unwillingness to submit to any of those will only cause problems for you.

What the Bible Says

Agree with God, and be at peace;
thereby good will come to you.

JOB 22:21

Giving thanks always and for everything to God the Father in the name of our Lord Jesus Christ, submitting to one another out of reverence for Christ.

EPHESIANS 5:20–21

Submit yourselves therefore to God.
Resist the devil, and he will flee from you.

JAMES 4:7

Time to Face the Facts

If you do not submit to the authority of your parents and teachers, you will constantly be in trouble. Lack of submission shows a lack of respect and trust. It says, "You're trying to control my life, and I won't let you!" In reality they aren't trying to control you, they are trying to teach you about life. And not submitting to God? Well, that's just insulting. It shows that you don't think much of him, and that is pretty scary. God has a wonderful plan for your life; submitting to him reveals it to you.

Today I Will . . .

Think about how I feel about submission. It isn't easy sometimes. It feels like there is always someone telling me what to do. I get tired of it. I'll ask God to deepen my trust in him and in the people I must submit to.

What Does the Bible Say about Success?

What does success mean to you? Making the pros as an athlete? Writing a best-selling book? Owning lots of stuff? Making lots of money? Success is different things to different people. The world says success is making lots of money, having power, and making it to the top of your field. There is another definition of success, though. It relates to God. How does God view success?

What the Bible Says

> Depart from me, you evildoers,
> that I may keep the commandments of my God.
>
> **PSALM 119:115**

> It shall not be so among you. But whoever would be
> great among you must be your servant.
>
> **MATTHEW 20:26**

> You shall love the Lord your God with all your
> heart and with all your soul and
> with all your mind.
>
> **MATTHEW 22:37**

Time to Face the Facts

How does success look from God's viewpoint? It doesn't have much to do with money and power. Success from God's viewpoint is related to serving him, obeying him, submitting to him, and doing his work. That doesn't mean you can't be wealthy and powerful, too. But success from God's perspective is based on the heart and its relationship to him.

"Here I am World—
Mr. Wonderful!!"

Today I Will . . .

Think about what success means to me. I want to be successful in life, but I want the basis of all my other successes to be that my heart is loving and serving God.

SUFFERING

What Does the Bible Say about Suffering?

At some time in life you will suffer. That's a cheerful comment, isn't it? It is true, though. At some point you will suffer because of illness, pain, a broken heart, lack of money, loss of a loved one . . . something will cause suffering. It's a part of life. How will you handle suffering? Will you be able to find God in the midst of it?

What the Bible Says

Behold, blessed is the one whom God reproves;
therefore despise not the discipline of the Almighty.
For he wounds, but he binds up;
he shatters, but his hands heal.

JOB 5:17–18

More than that, we rejoice in our sufferings, knowing that suffering produces endurance, and endurance produces character, and character produces hope, and hope does not put us to shame, because God's love has been poured into our hearts through the Holy Spirit who has been given to us.

ROMANS 5:3–5

For the moment all discipline seems painful rather than pleasant, but later it yields the peaceful fruit of righteousness to those who have been trained by it.

HEBREWS 12:11

Time to Face the Facts

Some reasons for suffering are things you bring on yourself, such as a fight with a friend or punishment for being disobedient. Other suffering comes because of things that are out of your control. The important thing is your reaction to the suffering. Will you get depressed and negative as you turn away from God and others? Or will you stay kind and caring and reach out to others for encouragement and turn to God for help and comfort?

Today I Will . . .

Think about what my reaction is when I'm suffering. Does my heart stay obedient and submitted to God? If not, I need to work on that.

What Does the Bible Say about Swearing?

You hear *&%^# swear words all the time at school and maybe even at home. Pretty soon they creep into your own vocabulary. No big deal, right? Everyone talks that way, and you feel cool when you do, too. It should be no surprise that God has definite rules about the kind of words you use.

What the Bible Says

You shall not take the name of the LORD your God in vain, for the LORD will not hold him guiltless who takes his name in vain.

EXODUS 20:7

Let there be no filthiness nor foolish talk nor crude joking, which are out of place, but instead let there be thanksgiving.

EPHESIANS 5:4

Finally, brothers, whatever is true, whatever is honorable, whatever is just, whatever is pure, whatever is lovely, whatever is commendable, if there is any excellence, if there is anything worthy of praise, think about these things.

PHILIPPIANS 4:8

Time to Face the Facts

Okay, just because everyone else swears doesn't mean you should. You are God's child, so you should be different from everyone else. God wants the words that come out of your mouth to honor him and not to hurt anyone else.

Today I Will . . .

Think about what I say. I'll choose my own words and make sure they do honor God and that they aren't just stupid, foolish words.

"I thought he was kidding about the soap."

What Does the Bible Say about Sympathy?

Having a sympathetic friend is the coolest thing. When you're hurting for any reason at all, a friend who cares enough to just sit with you and listen to you talk about why you hurt is priceless. A sympathetic friend reminds you that you're not alone in your pain or hurt. This sympathy is God's love in action, and it encourages you and helps you to keep on going.

What the Bible Says

As a father shows compassion to his children,
so the LORD shows compassion to those who fear him.

PSALM 103:13

Blessed be the God and Father of our Lord Jesus Christ, the Father of mercies and God of all comfort, who comforts us in all our affliction, so that we may be able to comfort those who are in any affliction, with the comfort with which we ourselves are comforted by God.

2 CORINTHIANS 1:3–4

Finally, all of you, have unity of mind, sympathy, brotherly love,
a tender heart, and a humble mind.

1 PETER 3:8

Time to Face the Facts

You don't have to go through any problems by yourself. God has placed friends and family around you who will be sympathetic and caring to any problem you have. God himself will send his love overflowing to you. He cares about your pain, and whether he shows that by surrounding you with caring people or flooding your heart with his love, he will do something. Let people comfort you with their sympathy, and let God fill your heart with his love.

Today I Will . . .

Let others help me. That's hard sometimes, but I really need their sympathy. I also will let God's love flow in my heart. I know he loves me, and I need to feel that right now.

What Does the Bible Say about Talent?

Talent? I don't have any talent . . . unless there is a category for Olympic Shoe-tying. Yeah, there isn't much I'm good at. If you're looking around at others and comparing yourself to them, you will never see your own talent. There's no need to compare yourself to others. You will always come up short. God created you just the way he wants you, and your talents are a very special mix that he made just for you. And he has a plan for how you can use your talents.

What the Bible Says

Having gifts that differ according to the grace given to us, let us use them: if prophecy, in proportion to our faith; if service, in our serving; the one who teaches, in his teaching; the one who exhorts, in his exhortation; the one who contributes, in generosity; the one who leads, with zeal; the one who does acts of mercy, with cheerfulness.

ROMANS 12:6–8

And he gave the apostles, the prophets, the evangelists, the shepherds and teachers, to equip the saints for the work of ministry, for building up the body of Christ.

EPHESIANS 4:11–12

"Pure skill—I've got it!"

Time to Face the Facts

There is a temptation to compare yourself to others. There are probably certain talents that you wish you had. But that isn't the way the gifts of God work. Stop and look at your abilities with an honest eye. Don't worry about being proud. You are good at some things: encouraging others, chatting with lonely people, singing, running, helping others. . . . Whatever it is, you do have talents. God gave them to everyone. He has special plans for how everyone's abilities and talents can be used in his work. Look for his plan.

Today I Will . . .

Stop comparing myself to others. I'll do an honest evaluation of my abilities. There must be some things I'm good at. I'll ask others what they see as my strengths and talents. Then, I'll see how I can use my talent to serve God.

TEACHERS

What Does the Bible Say about Teachers?

Teachers play an important part in your life, whether you know it or not. Did you know that teaching happens in places you might not expect, though? It's not just in the classroom or at church. Your soccer coach is a teacher, older kids teach you things on the playground, TV teaches you things . . . it happens in lots of places. Anything that affects the choices you make and the way you learn is teaching. God warns his children to be careful of what teachers they listen to.

What the Bible Says

Command and teach these things. Let no one despise you for your youth, but set the believers an example in speech, in conduct, in love, in faith, in purity.

1 TIMOTHY 4:11–12

So flee youthful passions and pursue righteousness, faith, love, and peace, along with those who call on the Lord from a pure heart.

2 TIMOTHY 2:22

Show yourself in all respects to be a model of good works, and in your teaching show integrity, dignity, and sound speech that cannot be condemned, so that an opponent may be put to shame, having nothing evil to say about us.

TITUS 2:7–8

Time to Face the Facts

Teaching is a big responsibility because it helps form lives. People who teach things that do not agree with the Bible are teachers you shouldn't pay attention to. Be careful which teachers you follow. Choose teachers who teach things you need to know—reading, writing, math—and teachers who model Christian lives by the way they walk closely to God and study his Word. These teachers will guide you into a healthy lifestyle and encourage a good relationship with God.

Today I Will . . .

Thank God for my good teachers. Choose teachers to follow who will help me live for God and grow stronger in my faith.

TEAMWORK

What Does the Bible Say about Teamwork?

A team is only as successful as its weakest member. It's just like a chain that needs to be strong: if one link in the chain is defective, the whole chain will be broken. A successful team is made up of players who work together, help each other, and encourage one another. There is no place on a team for a "star attitude." Teamwork is the key.

What the Bible Says

We, though many, are one body in Christ, and individually members one of another.

ROMANS 12:5

May the God of endurance and encouragement grant you to live in such harmony with one another, in accord with Christ Jesus, that together you may with one voice glorify the God and Father of our Lord Jesus Christ.

ROMANS 15:5–6

For the body does not consist of one member but of many. If the foot should say, "Because I am not a hand, I do not belong to the body," that would not make it any less a part of the body. And if the ear should say, "Because I am not an eye, I do not belong to the body," that would not make it any less a part of the body. If the whole body were an eye, where would be the sense of hearing? If the whole body were an ear, where would be the sense of smell? But as it is, God arranged the members in the body, each one of them, as he chose. If all were a single member, where would the body be? As it is, there are many parts, yet one body.

1 CORINTHIANS 12:14–20

Time to Face the Facts

A star attitude means that one team member (the weak link) doesn't help or encourage the others. She thinks she needs to be the star and that she's more important to the team than anyone else. Teamwork calls for a willingness to let teammates shine. It calls for cooperation and submission. The lessons learned from teamwork are excellent examples of living the way God teaches—putting others first.

Today I Will . . .

Be a team player. In whatever way I can, I will encourage others and cheer for them when they shine. I want to help others enjoy success, and I know my teammates will do that for me, too.

What Does the Bible Say about Tears?

There are tears of sorrow, tears of joy, and tears of laughter. Sometimes it feels good to cry. It kind of cleanses your emotions by getting things out in the open. Tears are an outward show of your inward emotion. When your tears are from sorrow, they are a sign to those around you that you are hurting, and that gives them a chance to support and encourage you.

What the Bible Says

Let your steadfast love comfort me
according to your promise to your servant.

PSALM 119:76

Blessed be the God and Father of our Lord Jesus Christ, the Father of mercies and God of all comfort, who comforts us in all our affliction, so that we may be able to comfort those who are in any affliction, with the comfort with which we ourselves are comforted by God. For as we share abundantly in Christ's sufferings, so through Christ we share abundantly in comfort too.

2 CORINTHIANS 1:3–5

"Someone—turn off the faucet!"

Time to Face the Facts

You may not like to cry. Most people don't. But remember that tears are a way God has made for your body to relieve some of the stress inside from whatever you are feeling. Isn't your body amazing? God is good. Tears remind others to give you care and comfort. God made humans to need each other and work together. Tears are a motivation to make that happen.

Today I Will . . .

Not be embarrassed by my tears. When I see someone else crying, I'll step up to show love and encouragement and to pray for whatever is causing my friend so much pain.

What Does the Bible Say about Telephone?

Oh come on, the Bible doesn't mention telephones. After all, they weren't invented yet when the Bible was written. No, the telephone wasn't invented yet—especially not cell phones. The next time you walk down a street, notice how many people are talking on their cell phones. Sometimes even people who are walking side by side are each on their phones—not even talking to one another. The telephones of today may be breaking relationships instead of drawing people closer.

What the Bible Says

And now, Israel, what does the LORD your God require of you, but to fear the LORD your God, to walk in all his ways, to love him, to serve the LORD your God with all your heart and with all your soul, and to keep the commandments and statutes of the LORD, which I am commanding you today for your good?

DEUTERONOMY 10:12–13

This is my commandment, that you love one another as I have loved you.

JOHN 15:12

Time to Face the Facts

Telephones are great for staying in touch with others, and that is certainly something that God wants you to do. However, when you're staying in touch with some people but ignoring the person who is right beside you, that isn't a good thing. Once in a while a phone call is important, but it is also important to talk with the person who is right beside you . . . face-to-face. Connections are what God encourages, and the best ones are where you can look a person in the eye and have a conversation.

"She should have used duct tape . . . on her mouth!"

Today I Will . . .

Turn my phone off and just use it for emergencies. I'll talk with the people I'm physically with and find out how they're doing.

What Does the Bible Say about Television?

Television is just mindless entertainment, right? *Wrong.* You may think your TV time gives your brain a recess, but that's not true. The values you learn, the language you hear, and the violence toward others you see all find a place in your mind and then wiggle down to your heart. Does God care? Yeah, God cares a lot about what you feed your brain.

What the Bible Says

For out of the heart come evil thoughts, murder, adultery, sexual immorality, theft, false witness, slander.

MATTHEW 15:19

But that is not the way you learned Christ! . . . put off your old self, which belongs to your former manner of life and is corrupt through deceitful desires, and . . . be renewed in the spirit of your minds, and . . . put on the new self, created after the likeness of God in true righteousness and holiness.

EPHESIANS 4:20–24

Whatever is true, whatever is honorable, whatever is just, whatever is pure, whatever is lovely, whatever is commendable, if there is any excellence, if there is anything worthy of praise, think about these things.

PHILIPPIANS 4:8

Time to Face the Facts

Junk food in the body makes you overweight and unhealthy. Junk food in the mind makes your heart and mind unhealthy and filthy. That kind of heart doesn't honor God.

Today I Will . . .

Carefully evaluate my TV time. Choose programming that doesn't fill my mind with unhealthy violence, sex, or just plain old junk.

What Does the Bible Say about Telling the Truth?

Of course the truth is important, but come on, a little white lie is no big deal, right? Sometimes it's just easier to fudge the truth a little bit. Does it really matter that much? Doesn't God just care about the big stuff? Sorry to burst your bubble, but God cares a lot about truthfulness—complete truthfulness.

What the Bible Says

Truthful lips endure forever,
but a lying tongue is but for a moment.

PROVERBS 12:19

Therefore, having put away falsehood, let each one of you speak the truth with his neighbor, for we are members one of another.

EPHESIANS 4:25

There are six things that the LORD hates,
seven that are an abomination to him:
haughty eyes, a lying tongue,
and hands that shed innocent blood,
a heart that devises wicked plans,
feet that make haste to run to evil,
a false witness who breathes out lies,
and one who sows discord
among brothers.

PROVERBS 6:16–19

"He can't fool everyone always!"

Time to Face the Facts

God cares a lot about you being truthful with others and with him. That doesn't mean you can't be kind in how you say things. Don't pad the truth to make yourself look better. The bottom line is that you treat others with love and honesty . . . the way you would like to be treated.

Today I Will . . .

Ask God to help me be honest with others, even when it's hard. Honest and kind is the best way.

TEMPER

What Does the Bible Say about Temper?

Are your family and friends afraid to tell you the truth because you explode with angry temper? Do they feel as though they have to walk around you like they are walking on eggshells, watching every word they say? Whew! That's tiring. People who have a bad temper take a lot of energy from other people. God has instructions for how to deal with temper in a way that will not damage relationships.

What the Bible Says

Refrain from anger, and forsake wrath! Fret not yourself; it tends only to evil.

PSALM 37:8

Be angry and do not sin; do not let the sun go down on your anger.

EPHESIANS 4:26

Time to Face the Facts

If your temper is so explosive that it causes problems for others, you need to do something about that. Temper happens because you look at life as all about you; your main concern with everything that happens is what it means to you. If you feel scared or unhappy about how things happen, then your temper explodes. God reminds you that life is not all about you. The most important thing is your relationship with him and with other people. If your temper is damaging any relationships, you need to get some help.

"What are you talking about? I don't have a temper. You always . . ."

Today I Will . . .

Be honest with myself about how my temper is. If I need help, I'll talk to a parent or to my pastor about it. I will also talk to God. I know he can change my heart and calm me down so that my temper is under control.

What Does the Bible Say about Temptation?

Temptation stinks. Seriously, once you start feeling tempted by something, it seems to be around every corner. It's so constant! Does God have any idea how hard it is to fight off temptation? Yeah, he does. Jesus went through some serious temptation. God knows temptation is . . . well . . . tempting, and he will help you fight it.

What the Bible Says

> Then Jesus was led up by the Spirit into the wilderness to be tempted by the devil.
>
> **MATTHEW 4:1**

> No temptation has overtaken you that is not common to man. God is faithful, and he will not let you be tempted beyond your ability, but with the temptation he will also provide the way of escape, that you may be able to endure it.
>
> **1 CORINTHIANS 10:13**

> For we do not have a high priest who is unable to sympathize with our weaknesses, but one who in every respect has been tempted as we are, yet without sin.
>
> **HEBREWS 4:15**

Time to Face the Facts

Jesus knows what it's like to face temptation. Read his story sometime in Matthew 4:1–11. He is right there with God telling him when you need extra strength and help. He knows what it's like. Trust him.

"This food is calling my name."

Today I Will . . .

Tell God what is tempting me. It's not like he doesn't already know anyway. I'll ask for his help, and I'll use his strength to fight temptation.

What Does the Bible Say about Tests?

There are all kinds of tests. Students are tested to see what they have learned in school. Potential buyers test-drive cars. Advertisements, new TV programs, and products are all tested with the public to see what people like. Testing gives results. It helps the testers get information they want to know. There are tests in your Christian walk, too, which test the depth of your commitment to God.

What the Bible Says

And lead us not into temptation, but deliver us from evil.

MATTHEW 6:13

In this you rejoice, though now for a little while, if necessary, you have been grieved by various trials, so that the tested genuineness of your faith—more precious than gold that perishes though it is tested by fire—may be found to result in praise and glory and honor at the revelation of Jesus Christ.

1 PETER 1:6–7

Count it all joy, my brothers, when you meet trials of various kinds, for you know that the testing of your faith produces steadfastness. And let steadfastness have its full effect, that you may be perfect and complete, lacking in nothing.

JAMES 1:2–4

Time to Face the Facts

These verses show that testing helps you become stronger in your relationship to God. It's not fun, that's for sure, but problems help you learn to keep on going through the difficulties of life. They help you realize that God is with you through the good times and the hard times. They show you what you can endure and how strong you are. That knowledge helps you the next time to know you can make it because you did the last time. Tests also give you the chance to see that God is always with you. He will help you through any test that comes.

Today I Will . . .

Not give up. When things get tough, I'll realize I'm in a test, and I'll call on God for strength and help.

What Does the Bible Say about Texting?

Some kids would rather text message a friend than talk to them face-to-face or even on the phone. Texting is less personal; it can be answered whenever the person wants. Texting is fun once in a while, but like IMing and e-mailing, it is communication without being with a person. It's less personal and not good for actual relationships where you are with your friends and communicate face-to-face. God says over and over in the Bible that relating to others is very important. Texting is relating, but in an impersonal way.

What the Bible Says

Love one another with brotherly affection.
Outdo one another in showing honor.

ROMANS 12:10

Now concerning brotherly love you have no need for anyone to
write to you, for you yourselves have been taught
by God to love one another.

1 THESSALONIANS 4:9

Let brotherly love continue.

HEBREWS 13:1

Time to Face the Facts

God puts so much importance on personal relationships. Texting is communication, but the personal touch of looking into another's eyes and talking and laughing is lost. The encouragement and caring of relationships is very important. God mentions it often in the Bible. People are to help one another and show love to one another. Don't lose that because personal conversations are lost.

Today I Will . . .

Lay my phone and computer aside and talk with my friends face-to-face.

THANKFULNESS

What Does the Bible Say about Thankfulness?

Some people seem to have the attitude that the world owes them things. With this attitude, when they are given gifts or when nice things are done for them, they don't even say "thank you," let alone feel any gratitude. Have you ever thanked your parents for their hard work to provide a home for you, do your laundry, cook your meals, and take care of you? How often do you thank God for the basic things you enjoy each day?

What the Bible Says

Oh give thanks to the Lord, for he is good;
for his steadfast love endures forever!

1 CHRONICLES 16:34

And let the peace of Christ rule in your hearts, to which indeed
you were called in one body. And be thankful.

COLOSSIANS 3:15

Continue steadfastly in prayer, being watchful in it with thanksgiving.

COLOSSIANS 4:2

Time to Face the Facts

Thankfulness is important because it shows that you are thinking about someone besides yourself. Thanking others for what they do for you is a basic courtesy. Respecting their efforts and appreciating them is a nice thing to do. Thankfulness to God is a celebration of who he is and what he does for you. It recognizes his love for you. Taking the time and making the effort to be thankful creates relationships and bonds you together with others.

"Mom—thanks for making dinner . . . except for the green beans."

Today I Will . . .

Thank my parents for all they do for me. Thank others who go out of their way to help me and do things for me. Thank God every day for his love and care for me.

What Does the Bible Say about Thoughts?

Letting your mind think about things that are unhealthy is a waste of good thinking time. The things you put into your mind create healthy or unhealthy thoughts just as the food you put into your body makes it healthy or unhealthy. What kinds of thoughts are not healthy? You know the answer to that: thoughts of violence, sex, cheating, stealing . . . anything that dishonors another person or God.

What the Bible Says

For out of the heart come evil thoughts, murder, adultery,
sexual immorality, theft, false witness, slander.

MATTHEW 15:19

Finally, brothers, whatever is true, whatever is honorable, whatever is just, whatever is pure, whatever is lovely, whatever is commendable, if there is any excellence, if there is anything worthy of praise, think about these things.

PHILIPPIANS 4:8

Time to Face the Facts

Your thought life is tricky because unhealthy thoughts can sneak in so quietly. If you let them live in your mind and even grow to fantasies about how you could do things that are not right, then your thought life is being controlled by sin. The Bible says to let pure and healthy thoughts live in your mind. Thoughts that move you to kindness and love and to treat others with respect. Think on those kinds of things.

Today I Will . . .

Kick bad thoughts out of my mind. I will keep positive, loving thoughts in mind.

"Dude—you'd better do a rewind and clean up your mind."

What Does the Bible Say about Time?

There are twenty-four hours in a day and sixty minutes in each hour. Every person on the planet gets the same number of minutes and hours in his day. Each person must choose how to spend his time. The hours of a day that are wasted are gone, just gone. You can never get them back. Choosing how to spend your time is a freedom you have. God will direct you and guide you, but ultimately the choice is up to you.

What the Bible Says

If you seek him, he will be found by you, but if you forsake him, he will cast you off forever.

1 CHRONICLES 28:9

You guide me with your counsel, and afterward you will receive me to glory.

PSALM 73:24

Time to Face the Facts

Priorities are the name of the game here. How you choose to spend your time reflects what is truly important to you. You may say that one thing is important, like doing a quality job on your homework, but if you spend your time watching TV or goofing off and cram your homework into a half hour at the end of the day, then it doesn't appear to be important at all. You have the freedom to choose how to spend your time. Choose wisely.

"Time flies when you're doing something fun."

Today I Will . . .

Make a list of the things that are important to me. I will use my time in a way that reflects the important things on that list.

TIREDNESS

What Does the Bible Say about Tiredness?

Falling asleep in class can be pretty embarrassing . . . especially if you fall out of your desk. What makes you so tired? Obviously, it's not getting enough sleep. But there may be some other things playing into that tiredness, too, like boredom. When you're always tired, you can't learn well, you can't do good work, and it's even hard to have a good attitude so that you can be a good friend. Tiredness needs to be taken care of.

What the Bible Says

Awesome is God from his sanctuary;
the God of Israel—he is the one who gives power
and strength to his people. Blessed be God!

PSALM 68:35

He gives power to the faint,
and to him who has no might he increases strength.
Even youths shall faint and be weary,
and young men shall fall exhausted;
but they who wait for the Lord shall renew their strength;
they shall mount up with wings like eagles;
they shall run and not be weary;
they shall walk and not faint.

ISAIAH 40:29–31

And let us not grow weary of doing good, for in due
season we will reap, if we do not give up.

GALATIANS 6:9

Time to Face the Facts

Get enough sleep. That's the first thing to do to get rid of tiredness. Then, if you're still really tired, maybe you need a change of pace, such as a vacation. It might help to change your routine or change your activities so you're not in a rut. Remember that to be a loving and kind person who can give your best to the things you need to do, you must be rested.

Today I Will . . .

Get more sleep. I know I'm crabby when I'm tired, and I'm not reflecting God's love when I feel that way.

What Does the Bible Say about Tithes and Offerings?

What's the difference between a tithe and an offering? A tithe is what the Bible instructs should be given to God's work. It is to be 10 percent of a person's income. An offering is what is given to God's work above and beyond the tithe. Money given to God's work is used to support the pastor of your church, pay the bills there for electricity, gas, and other supplies, support missionaries, and just do what needs to be done to get the message of God's love out.

What the Bible Says

Honor the LORD with your wealth
and with the firstfruits of all your produce;
then your barns will be filled with plenty,
and your vats will be bursting with wine.

PROVERBS 3:9–10

Give, and it will be given to you. Good measure, pressed down,
shaken together, running over, will be put into your lap. For
with the measure you use it will be measured back to you.

LUKE 6:38

Time to Face the Facts

Giving to God's work, whether you give to your church or to another place or person who serves God, is important. Helping support a ministry gives you a part in that ministry. So, when a missionary you help support in Africa does God's work, you are a part of that ministry across the world. That's cool, huh? God's work cannot be done without his people supporting the ministries through their tithes and offerings.

"Can I make change?"

Today I Will . . .

Set aside part of my allowance to give to God's work. I'll establish the habit of tithing right now.

What Does the Bible Say about Traditions?

Your family probably has traditions—things you do together each year. Many families have certain holiday traditions—certain activities you always do or meals you always have. There are summer vacation traditions or traditions related to how you celebrate birthdays. Traditions are fun because you can look forward to them. They are things you share as a family so they bind you together. Traditions connect you to the past, too.

What the Bible Says

This day shall be for you a memorial day, and you shall keep it as a feast to the LORD; throughout your generations, as a statute forever, you shall keep it as a feast.

EXODUS 12:14

See to it that no one takes you captive by philosophy and empty deceit, according to human tradition. . . .

COLOSSIANS 2:8

Time to Face the Facts

Family traditions are important as well as fun. Your family traditions are things that only your family understands so they connect you in a special way. The Bible also speaks of spiritual traditions. Does that sound strange? Think of these as things that remind you of how God has worked in the lives of his people and perhaps even in your own life. Traditions that help you remember his work can help to get you through difficult times. It is always good to remember what God has done in the past and that he is taking care of things now.

"This tradition of pouring water over the candles has got to stop."

Today I Will . . .

Enjoy remembering our family traditions. Think about spiritual traditions and how they remind me of God's love and care.

What Does the Bible Say about Tragedy?

Bad things happen to good people. It may not seem fair, but it's true. A tragedy is more terrible than your run-of-the-mill bad day. Tragedies are unexpected deaths, or terrible natural disasters such as hurricanes or earthquakes, or fires that burn a home to the ground taking all a family's possessions. Tragedies are hard to understand and painful to go through. How do you find God in the midst of a tragedy?

What the Bible Says

For he has not despised or abhorred
the affliction of the afflicted,
and he has not hidden his face from him,
but has heard, when he cried to him.

PSALM 22:24

Those who sow in tears
shall reap with shouts of joy!
He who goes out weeping,
bearing the seed for sowing,
shall come home with shouts of joy,
bringing his sheaves with him.

PSALM 126:5–6

If one member suffers, all suffer together; if one
member is honored, all rejoice together.

1 CORINTHIANS 12:26

Time to Face the Facts

You may wish that God would just stop all tragedies—just keep them from happening. That would be nice, but he probably will not do that. He doesn't typically stop the natural events of our world. So, where do you find God when you've had a tragedy? Right where he has always been. God may not stop the terrible events, but he will be right with you, guiding, comforting, and loving you through whatever you must go through.

Today I Will . . .

Not turn away from God when there is a tragedy. I will turn to him for comfort and peace. I will pass his love and care along to others so they can hold on to him, too.

What Does the Bible Say about Travel?

What is your dream vacation? Where is someplace you would love to see? It's fun to see places where the landscape is totally different from where you live and to visit countries where you see how other cultures live. Travel usually means vacation—a time of rest and togetherness as a family. It's good to get away from your normal responsibilities and have family time for just fun.

What the Bible Says

Come to me, all who labor and are heavy laden, and I will give you rest.

MATTHEW 11:28

Draw near to God, and he will draw near to you. . . .

JAMES 4:8

Time to Face the Facts

Traveling together can bring out the worst in people. The stress of lugging your suitcases, making it to the airport on time, fighting crowds of people, always being together, and doing what the rest of the family wants can make travel kind of stressful. But remember that God puts a lot of importance on relationships, and being part of a family is a gift from him. Try to keep a relaxed attitude about all these things and enjoy just being together and seeing new things. Thank God for the beautiful world he created for you to see. Appreciate different cultures and different people. Travel opens your eyes to the rest of the world.

"This part wasn't in the brochure."

Today I Will . . .

Appreciate family togetherness when we travel. I'll thank God for this whole awesome world he made!

What Does the Bible Say about Trinity?

The answer to that question is . . . everything. The Trinity is the three parts of God's Personhood. Okay, it's kind of hard to understand so maybe you just need to accept by faith that God is three Persons. The Trinity is God the Father, God the Son, and God the Holy Spirit. These three parts of God's personality work together to take care of you, love you, and guide you.

What the Bible Says

At that time Jesus declared, I thank you, Father, Lord of heaven and earth, that you have hidden these things from the wise and understanding and revealed them to little children; yes, Father, for such was your gracious will. All things have been handed over to me by my Father, and no one knows the Son except the Father, and no one knows the Father except the Son and anyone to whom the Son chooses to reveal him. Come to me, all who labor and are heavy laden, and I will give you rest.

MATTHEW 11:25–28

Go therefore and make disciples of all nations, baptizing them in the name of the Father and of the Son and of the Holy Spirit.

MATTHEW 28:19

But you will receive power when the Holy Spirit has come upon you, and you will be my witnesses in Jerusalem and in all Judea and Samaria, and to the end of the earth.

ACTS 1:8

Time to Face the Facts

Each part of the Trinity has certain work to do. God the Father is the Creator and power and strength of the world. God the Son is Jesus who came to earth, lived, died, and rose again to make a way for you to be able to know God. God the Holy Spirit lives in your heart and is God with you. The three parts of the Trinity are different, yet the same. They can't be separated. Yes, it's hard to understand, so for right now, just thank God for each part of the Trinity and for how they each work for you and in your heart.

Today I Will . . .

Not fret about trying to figure out the Trinity. I'm just so glad that each of these parts of God's character are taking care of me and watching out for me and loving me.

What Does the Bible Say about Trouble?

You've been in trouble, right? You get into trouble because of your choice to break rules or disobey. That brings trouble, and that brings punishment. Ugh. Sometimes trouble happens even if you've done nothing wrong. Maybe the dog really does eat your homework and you get in trouble. Trouble happens. Fair or unfair. How you handle the trouble is the really important thing.

What the Bible Says

> Who shall ascend the hill of the Lord?
> And who shall stand in his holy place?
> He who has clean hands and a pure heart,
> who does not lift up his soul to what is false
> and does not swear deceitfully.
> He will receive blessing from the Lord
> and righteousness from the God of his salvation.

PSALM 24:3–5

> Either make the tree good and its fruit good,
> or make the tree bad and its fruit bad, for
> the tree is known by its fruit.

MATTHEW 12:33

Time to Face the Facts

If you are in trouble because you've messed up, admit it, confess it, and promise to do better. Then do better. Some trouble can be avoided by making better choices, taking your time to evaluate a situation, or setting priorities so you get things done on time. Regarding the things that happen which

"Just when I got my math all done."

are out of your control . . . turn to God. Trust him to get you through the trouble. He will be your comfort and strength if you just ask him.

Today I Will . . .

Make better choices to stop trouble I bring on myself. I will also keep learning to trust God more and more.

What Does the Bible Say about Trust?

Who do you trust? Hopefully you trust your parents to take good care of you and provide for you and keep you safe. You may have friends you trust with your secrets and dreams. Trust is important to relationships. If you can't trust a person, then you won't be completely honest with him. Trust is also important in your relationship with God. In fact, it's basic to that relationship.

What the Bible Says

For our heart is glad in him,
because we trust in his holy name.

PSALM 33:21

You keep him in perfect peace
whose mind is stayed on you,
because he trusts in you.

ISAIAH 26:3

Though you have not seen him, you love him. Though you do not now see him, you believe in him and rejoice with joy that is inexpressible and filled with glory.

1 PETER 1:8

Time to Face the Facts

Trust is a two-way street in friendships. You trust your friends, and they trust you. That means you can tell each other anything, and you can know your friend will always stand up for you and be loyal to you. Trusting God with your life and your heart is the very foundation of your relationship with him. If you don't trust his love for you and that he has a plan for your life, then you won't submit to him. Trust comes from experience—look back at how he has cared for you, loved you, and guided you in the past. If it's hard for you, start with a small thing and see how God handles it, then that will lead to bigger trust.

Today I Will . . .

Make sure I'm worthy of my friends' trust. I will be loyal to them and keep their secrets. It's hard to learn to trust God with my whole life, so I'll trust him with one thing and when I see how he takes care of me there, I'll trust more next time.

What Does the Bible Say about Truth?

Do you always tell the truth? The whole truth? If you do, good for you. It's important to be honest. If anyone has ever lied to you (or about you) then you know how much it hurts when a dishonest person disrespects you. Telling the truth is respectful, and the honesty of truth is the way God wants you to relate to other people.

What the Bible Says

> Your righteousness is righteous forever,
> and your law is true.
> Trouble and anguish have found me out,
> but your commandments are my delight.
> Your testimonies are righteous forever;
> give me understanding that I may live.

PSALM 119:142–144

Jesus answered, "You say that I am a king. For this purpose I was born and for this purpose I have come into the world—to bear witness to the truth. Everyone who is of the truth listens to my voice."

JOHN 18:37

"I cannot tell a lie. George Washington did it."

Time to Face the Facts

Truth is God's way. His Word is truthful and honest, and that's what God expects from you. Be truthful with him. You can't fool him, anyway; he knows your thoughts and your heart. Be truthful with others so they know you respect them. If being truthful means you have to admit when you've done something wrong, that's okay. It's better to admit it honestly than to lie about it and be found out later.

Today I Will . . .

Be honest and truthful about my actions and my attitudes. I want others to know that I can be trusted, and I want them to be honest with me.

What Does the Bible Say about Unbelief?

Do you believe God is real? Do you believe that Jesus, God's Son, came to earth as a baby, that he taught people how to live for God, was crucified, died, and rose back to life? Do you believe he did that because he loves you and that his actions made a way for you to be able to live in heaven forever with God? If you don't believe those truths, then you suffer from unbelief.

What the Bible Says

Truly, truly, I say to you, whoever hears my word and believes him who sent me has eternal life. He does not come into judgment, but has passed from death to life.

JOHN 5:24

That which was from the beginning, which we have heard, which we have seen with our eyes, which we looked upon and have touched with our hands, concerning the word of life—

1 JOHN 1:1

Time to Face the Facts

The problem with unbelief is that it blocks your relationship with God. It's not possible to know him in a personal way if you suffer from unbelief. There is no more important decision that you will make in your life than the decision to believe in God and all that he does for you. God loves you very much, and he truly wants you to believe. He wants everyone in the world to have the chance to believe and hopes that each person will choose belief rather than unbelief.

"Are you sure?"

Today I Will . . .

Change things if I have suffered with unbelief. I want to believe in God and his love for me. Then, I will tell others about his love so they can get rid of their unbelief, too.

UNBORN CHILDREN

What Does the Bible Say about Unborn Children?

This is a hot topic these days. Elections are won or lost because of opinions as to when life actually begins. Does God have an opinion about when life begins? Of course he does. God loved you and knew all about you before you even saw the light of this world.

What the Bible Says

For you formed my inward parts;
you knitted me together in my mother's womb.
I praise you, for I am fearfully and wonderfully made.
Wonderful are your works;
my soul knows it very well.
My frame was not hidden from you,
when I was being made in secret,
intricately woven in the depths of the earth.

PSALM 139:13–15

Your eyes saw my unformed substance;
in your book were written, every one of them,
the days that were formed for me,
when as yet there was none of them.

PSALM 139:16

Before I formed you in the womb I knew you,
and before you were born I consecrated you;
I appointed you a prophet to the nations.

JEREMIAH 1:5

Time to Face the Facts

The Bible says that God knows people and even has plans for them before they are ever born. It's hard then to say that life begins at birth, isn't it?

Today I Will . . .

Think about how I feel about abortion. I will also think about how I treat other people, who are God's creations.

"If it's a boy, can you send it back?"

What Does the Bible Say about Understanding?

There is a difference between believing something and understanding it. Having head knowledge of God's plan and his love is one thing, but understanding it allows it to get into your heart. That makes all the difference.

What the Bible Says

You make known to me the path of life;
in your presence there is fullness of joy;
at your right hand are pleasures forevermore.

PSALM 16:11

Open my eyes, that I may behold
wondrous things out of your law.

PSALM 119:18

Your word is a lamp to my feet
and a light to my path.

PSALM 119:105

Time to Face the Facts

Understanding God's love and the sacrifice of Jesus allows it to settle into your heart. That makes it possible for you to have a personal relationship with Jesus. What does that mean? It's like the relationship you have with a friend. You can talk with your friend, and you can listen to her talk about her life and problems. You care about each other, so you want to do all you can for each other. A personal relationship with Jesus means you can talk with him (prayer). You can listen for him to talk to you. You can read his Word—his special instructions to you. All this is possible because you gained understanding of his love.

Today I Will . . .

Ask God to open my mind to be able to understand more of his love and care for me. I want to grow in my understanding so I can know him better and better.

What Does the Bible Say about Unity?

Imagine your school band playing a song. Every instrument in that band has an assigned part. Each musician must be playing the same song at the same tempo. They must be in unity. Otherwise the band will sound terrible. Unity is important in any group. Each person must be working toward the same goal.

What the Bible Says

So we, though many, are one body in Christ, and individually members one of another.

ROMANS 12:5

May the God of endurance and encouragement grant you to live in such harmony with one another, in accord with Christ Jesus, that together you may with one voice glorify the God and Father of our Lord Jesus Christ.

ROMANS 15:5–6

There is one body and one Spirit—just as you were called to the one hope that belongs to your call—one Lord, one faith, one baptism, one God and Father of all, who is over all and through all and in all.

EPHESIANS 4:4–6

"Let's harmonize the world."

Time to Face the Facts

Unity in serving God is important, too. God says that all of his children should have the same goal—serving and loving him. You should be working together with other Christians so that the message of God's love can be spread to all people. There shouldn't be fighting and arguing among God's children. Unity binds you together so that like a good band, you play a beautiful song of God's love together.

Today I Will . . .

Try to be in unity with my family and friends and all other Christians I know. I don't want my arguing or fighting to do anything to stop the message of God's love and care from going out.

What Does the Bible Say about Unselfishness?

An unselfish person does whatever she can to help her friends to succeed. She's happy when they shine, and she helps them win anytime she can. Unselfishness means she shares her time, money, energy, anything she can. What's hers is yours. Unselfishness is a godly trait and shows that Jesus is living in you.

What the Bible Says

So whatever you wish that others would do to you,
do also to them, for this is the Law and the Prophets.

MATTHEW 7:12

Rather, speaking the truth in love, we are to grow up in every way into him who is the head, into Christ, from whom the whole body, joined and held together by every joint with which it is equipped, when each part is working properly, makes the body grow so that it builds itself up in love.

EPHESIANS 4:15–16

As each has received a gift, use it to serve one another,
as good stewards of God's varied grace.

1 PETER 4:10

Time to Face the Facts

There is no room for selfishness in a heart where God lives because God is the role model of unselfishness. He gives to people without stopping every day. He gives so willingly that he gave the life of his only Son—and Jesus came willingly. That's unselfish love. You can pass that unselfishness on to others by willingly sharing whatever you can with others. Unselfishness is love in action.

Today I Will . . .

Stop holding on to my stuff and my time so tightly. Sharing with others is a good way to show that God is living in me. I want to share his love with others by sharing whatever I can.

What Does the Bible Say about Values?

Values are what you believe is important. The things you do show what your values are. That means that your actions should match the words you say. If you spout words about how important honesty is, but you steal candy from the store or sneak peeks at a classmate's test answers, then you might as well save your breath. Your words and actions don't match, and it shows that your values are not very high.

What the Bible Says

For out of the heart come evil thoughts, murder, adultery,
sexual immorality, theft, false witness, slander.

MATTHEW 15:19

But the fruit of the Spirit is love, joy, peace, patience, kindness, goodness,
faithfulness, gentleness, self-control; against such things there is no law.

GALATIANS 5:22–23

He has told you, O man, what is good;
and what does the Lord require of you
but to do justice, and to love kindness,
and to walk humbly with your God?

MICAH 6:8

Time to Face the Facts

Your goal should be for your values to match what God teaches in his Word. If Jesus is in your heart and you desire to live for him, then your values will be the same as his. You can learn his values by reading his Word and learning how to obey him and how to treat other people. Obeying God is not possible if your values do not match his.

Today I Will . . .

Study God's Word. I want to understand God's values and learn to make them mine. I will ask God to help my actions match my words so others will know I love him.

What Does the Bible Say about Vengeance?

Vengeance is all about getting even. When someone hurts or cheats you, you want to make him pay. You want revenge. Vengeance is a natural reaction to when you've been hurt, especially by someone you trust, but it isn't a response God wants you to have.

What the Bible Says

You shall not take vengeance or bear a grudge against the sons of your own people, but you shall love your neighbor as yourself: I am the LORD.

LEVITICUS 19:18

Whoever digs a pit will fall into it,
and a stone will come back on him who starts it rolling.

PROVERBS 26:27

Repay no one evil for evil, but give thought to do what is honorable in the sight of all. If possible, so far as it depends on you, live peaceably with all.

ROMANS 12:17–18

Time to Face the Facts

Getting even for what someone has done may cause that person to get even with you, and then you have to get even with him. See the loop that has been created? There will be no peace for either of you, and your relationship will pretty much be destroyed. God says to turn the other cheek when someone hurts you. In other words, give him the chance to hurt you again. Don't worry about getting even. Leave that up to God. He will take care of you and of those who hurt you. Trust him.

"You just wait till I . . ."

Today I Will . . .

Stop trying to get even. I want revenge so badly, but I will ask God to help me leave it up to him. I will ask him to help me forgive the person who hurt me.

What Does the Bible Say about Violence?

The world you live in seems to grow more violent every day. Murder, bombs, war, robberies—it's a scary thing. Violence is the use of force to get your own way . . . or sometimes there's no reason at all except to be violent. Does God see what is happening in the world and that innocent, good people are often the victims of violence? Does he care?

What the Bible Says

You have heard that it was said, "An eye for an eye and a tooth for a tooth." But I say to you, "Do not resist the one who is evil. But if anyone slaps you on the right cheek, turn to him the other also."

MATTHEW 5:38–39

You have heard that it was said, "You shall love your neighbor and hate your enemy." But I say to you, "Love your enemies and pray for those who persecute you, so that you may be sons of your Father who is in heaven. For he makes his sun rise on the evil and on the good, and sends rain on the just and on the unjust.

MATTHEW 5:43–45

Bless those who persecute you; bless and do not curse them. Rejoice with those who rejoice, weep with those who weep.

ROMANS 12:14–15

Time to Face the Facts

Violence is hard to understand. How can people be so mean to other people? Violence lives in the hearts of people who do not know God. Not all unbelievers are violent, but the point is that believers who seek to serve God and share his love will not treat other people in a violent way. God is peace and love, but he insists on obedience. Even if you disagree with someone, you are not to act in violence to make him agree with you. That's not what God would do, and he doesn't want you to do that.

Today I Will . . .

Pray for victims of violence around the world. Make sure that I am never violent when I disagree with someone.

VULNERABILITY

What Does the Bible Say about Vulnerability?

Are you afraid to let others know who you really are? Do you let them know your deepest feelings? Are you concerned that they would think less of you if they knew your fears, doubts, hurts, or even your dreams? You have to trust the person you allow into your life that deeply. Vulnerability is kind of scary.

What the Bible Says

Let not your hearts be troubled. Believe in God; believe also in me.

JOHN 14:1

Therefore, confess your sins to one another and pray for one another, that you may be healed. The prayer of a righteous person has great power as it is working.

JAMES 5:16

If we confess our sins, he is faithful and just to forgive us our sins and to cleanse us from all unrighteousness. If we say we have not sinned, we make him a liar, and his word is not in us.

1 JOHN 1:9–10

Time to Face the Facts

It is scary to be vulnerable, because you don't always know how other people will respond to you. But it's hard to have a close friendship with someone you can't trust enough to be vulnerable with. God says that close friendships are important. Friends encourage and help each other. Choose your friends wisely. Choose friends who have the same values you have and who love Jesus. Then, be willing to be vulnerable so your friendship can grow closer.

"Who are you really?"

Today I Will . . .

Choose a friend I believe I can trust and be open to and share my feelings with that friend. Hopefully, my friend will share with me, too. Thank you, God, for good friends.

What Does the Bible Say about Waste?

North Americans waste a lot of stuff. Other parts of the world struggle to have enough water to drink. Americans let the water run and run while they brush their teeth. Other parts of the world do not have enough food to eat. Americans throw away tons of food every day. Most Americans do not even think about how much water, food, paper, or energy they waste every day. Is it a sin to be so wasteful?

What the Bible Says

In the beginning, God created the heavens and the earth.

GENESIS 1:1

By faith we understand that the universe was created by the word of God, so that what is seen was not made out of things that are visible.

HEBREWS 11:3

Time to Face the Facts

Yes, it is a sin to be wasteful. A better way to live is to use only what you need to live and be careful not to waste what you don't need to waste. God tells you in his Word to share with others and help others in any way you can. Take care of natural resources so that generations to come have what they need to live. Protect the planet and the things God put on it for people to use. Just think about what you throw away and what you waste. Find ways to use less and save more.

"Got it! Nothing but paw!"

Today I Will . . .

Reuse and recycle. I will be careful about what I throw away: I won't take too much food on my plate and then throw most of it out. I won't let the water run and run. I won't leave the lights on when I'm not in the room. I'll be careful not to waste.

What Does the Bible Say about Wealth?

There is a story in the Bible about a rich man who asked Jesus what he had to do to have eternal life. Jesus told him to give away all his wealth. The man couldn't do it, so he sadly walked away. There is nothing wrong with being wealthy unless it's more important to you than obeying and serving God.

What the Bible Says

All who believed were together and had all things in common.
And they were selling their possessions and belongings
and distributing the proceeds to all, as any had need.

ACTS 2:44–45

If a brother or sister is poorly clothed and lacking in daily food, and one of you says to them, "Go in peace, be warmed and filled," without giving them the things needed for the body, what good is that?

JAMES 2:15–16

But if anyone has the world's goods and sees his brother in need, yet closes his heart against him, how does God's love abide in him?

1 JOHN 3:17

Time to Face the Facts

Wealth—money—is a gift from God. Sure, a person has a job and works to earn the money, but God makes it all possible. The story of the rich man with Jesus shows that the best use of wealth is sharing it with others. So many people in the world do not even have enough food to eat to stay alive. Sharing wealth to help them is God's love in action. Giving to missionaries and others who give their lives to God's work is another good use of wealth. Sharing the wealth God gives you is evidence of a heart that belongs to him.

Today I Will . . .

Start a giving program that will last my whole life. I want to share all that God gives me so that others have enough food and so that God's workers around the world are supported.

What Does the Bible Say about Weather?

There are powerful things in the weather. Tornados, hurricanes, tsunamis, blizzards, and floods can wipe out whole towns and take thousands of lives. Weather goes from bright sunny days to gentle rain to violent storms. Everyone talks about the weather, but no one can do anything about it. Since the weather is so changeable, do you wonder if even God has power over it?

What the Bible Says

He made the storm be still,
and the waves of the sea were hushed.

PSALM 107:29

Then he rose and rebuked the winds and the sea,
and there was a great calm.

MATTHEW 8:26

Time to Face the Facts

God does control the weather. There is plenty of evidence of that in the Bible. One time God made the sun stand still so Joshua and his army could win a battle, and Jesus once told a stormy sea to calm down and it did. God created the weather, so of course he can control it. So, why do such violent things happen that take so many lives? Only God knows the answer to that. What you can know is that God is always present, helping those who call on him. He gives comfort, strength, and perseverance to all who ask for his help.

"Did you remember to turn off the faucet in the kitchen?"

Today I Will . . .

Not worry about the weather. I can't change it. I will trust God to take care of me and my family and give us the strength to face whatever comes.

What Does the Bible Say about Weight?

There are kids who totally wreck their health by starving themselves in order to be very, very skinny. Some kids do even worse things than not eating in order to be thin. The media proclaims the image that super-thin is beautiful. On the flip side are couch potatoes who sit and munch on chips and soda while they watch TV or play video games. These potatoes are overweight and out of shape. Does God have any opinion on either of these weight extremes?

What the Bible Says

Give me understanding, that I may keep your law
and observe it with my whole heart.

PSALM 119:34

Do you not know that your body is a temple of the Holy Spirit within you, whom you have from God? You are not your own.

1 CORINTHIANS 6:19

Time to Face the Facts

Starving yourself in order to be painfully thin is just not smart. It's also not healthy. Your body needs food to use as fuel to keep you going. It needs some fats and some sugars as well as protein, veggies, and fruit. It needs a balanced diet. Chowing down on junk food is not healthy either. Filling up with candy or chips doesn't leave room for the healthy food you need. God does

"Maybe I should have taken my watch off."

care about your weight because he wants you to be healthy and take care of the one body he gave you. Eat healthy and exercise. It's good for you.

Today I Will . . .

Get a healthy attitude about my body. I don't need to be super-thin, and I don't want to be overweight. I'll eat healthy foods and get some exercise each day.

WILLPOWER

What Does the Bible Say about Willpower?

Will and power. Will, as it's used in this word, means your desires, what you want. Power is the strength of your will. So willpower means how strong you are in getting what you want or following through on what you want. The word "willpower" is used a lot by people who are on diets. They talk about having the willpower to stay away from junk food or to not overeat. Willpower is a personal stubbornness.

What the Bible Says

Be strong and courageous. Do not be frightened, and do not be dismayed, for the LORD your God is with you wherever you go.

JOSHUA 1:9

Be watchful, stand firm in the faith, act like men, be strong.

1 CORINTHIANS 16:13

And I am sure of this, that he who began a good work in you will bring it to completion at the day of Jesus Christ.

PHILIPPIANS 1:6

Time to Face the Facts

Everyone has a little willpower. Some people have a lot of it. Willpower is a commitment to stick with something—no matter what. It is not only related to food. It might involve a commitment to spend time with God each day or a commitment to pray for someone. Willpower is what keeps you doing that thing. Can you have willpower without God's help? Yes, but it's a lot easier if God gives you the strength to keep your commitments. Then you're not working on your own, but God is your partner in willpower.

Today I Will . . .

Ask God to give me the strength that will make my willpower stronger. I want to stick with my commitments and honor him by doing that.

What Does the Bible Say about Winning?

Winning is fun. It's cool to work hard on something, such as the skills you need to play a sport. You practice every day, doing the same things over and over so you can get better and better at them. You work with your teammates to play well together. Then you go into the game and play as hard as you can, and you win! Is winning the most important thing?

What the Bible Says

Whoever loves discipline loves knowledge,
but he who hates reproof is stupid.

PROVERBS 12:1

Train yourself for godliness; for while bodily
training is of some value, godliness is of
value in every way, as it holds promise for the
present life and also for the life to come.

1 TIMOTHY 4:7–8

Time to Face the Facts

Winning is fun, but it's not the most important thing. Read through that description above. Practice every day, repeat the same skills, work with teammates to play well together. The process of developing skills that lead to winning is more important than the actual victory. This process helps you learn discipline and hard work, and that is what leads to winning. When you've disciplined your body, mind, and attitude, you have won, regardless of whether you win the game.

"I did it!"

Today I Will . . .

Keep practicing and working hard to make my skills better and better. Then, even if I never win a game, I will have won in life.

What Does the Bible Say about Wisdom?

What do think wisdom is? Solving super-hard math problems? Programming computers? Reading (and understanding) college textbooks? A lot of people spend all their time chasing after wisdom and thinking that the more wisdom they gain, the more successful they will be in life. Is wisdom in things like math and computers the answer to a successful life?

What the Bible Says

For the LORD gives wisdom;
from his mouth come knowledge and understanding.

PROVERBS 2:6

The beginning of wisdom is this: Get wisdom,
and whatever you get, get insight.
Prize her highly, and she will exalt you;
she will honor you if you embrace her.

PROVERBS 4:7–8

If any of you lacks wisdom, let him ask God, who gives generously
to all without reproach, and it will be given him.

JAMES 1:5

Time to Face the Facts

It's okay to study hard in school. In fact, that's a good thing to do. Learn all you can. Gain all the knowledge and wisdom you can. But don't count on that to give you a happy life. God says that knowing and obeying him is the most important thing. After that, relationships with other people are most important. The whole book of Proverbs talks about wisdom and how real wisdom is submitting to God and learning how to obey him. Real wisdom is found only in knowing God.

Today I Will . . .

Establish a regular habit of reading the Bible each day and talking with God. If real wisdom comes from knowing God, then I want that to be part of my life every day.

What Does the Bible Say about Witchcraft?

Witchcraft taps into a spirit world that is dangerous to mess with. Some kids think it's a fun thing to mess around with and that it doesn't do any harm. It's dangerous to take anything to do with evil too lightly. If you can believe that the Holy Spirit is real, then why wouldn't you believe that evil spirits are real, too?

What the Bible Says

And it is my prayer that your love may abound more and more, with knowledge and all discernment, so that you may approve what is excellent, and so be pure and blameless for the day of Christ, filled with the fruit of righteousness that comes through Jesus Christ, to the glory and praise of God.

PHILIPPIANS 1:9–11

Finally, brothers, whatever is true, whatever is honorable, whatever is just, whatever is pure, whatever is lovely, whatever is commendable, if there is any excellence, if there is anything worthy of praise, think about these things.

PHILIPPIANS 4:8

But the wisdom from above is first pure, then peaceable, gentle, open to reason, full of mercy and good fruits, impartial and sincere.

JAMES 3:17

Time to Face the Facts

God tells you to guard your heart. That means you must keep it away from Satan. Don't put yourself in situations where Satan or his demons can creep into your heart. If you give him the chance, he will show you just enough power to pull you in to try more things with him. Exploring witchcraft, even in fun, is a dangerous thing to mess with. Fill your mind and thoughts with pure and healthy things.

"Which witch is which?"

Today I Will . . .

Not mess around with witchcraft stuff, even if my friends want me to. I won't take it lightly, and I will focus my thoughts on God and his Word.

What Does the Bible Say about Witnessing?

Witnessing? You mean talking to other people about God? No way. I'm more the strong, silent type. I'll leave the talking stuff to the minister and to missionaries. I wouldn't know what to say, so it's better if I keep my mouth shut. Guess what? God wants you to know what and why you believe. Then sharing it is no big deal.

What the Bible Says

Go therefore and make disciples of all nations, baptizing them in the name of the Father and of the Son and of the Holy Spirit, teaching them to observe all that I have commanded you. And behold, I am with you always, to the end of the age.

MATTHEW 28:19–20

For Christ did not send me to baptize but to preach the gospel, and not with words of eloquent wisdom, lest the cross of Christ be emptied of its power.

1 CORINTHIANS 1:17

In your hearts honor Christ the Lord as holy, always being prepared to make a defense to anyone who asks you for a reason for the hope that is in you. . . .

1 PETER 3:15

Time to Face the Facts

You've got the best news in the world: God loves mankind. Why not tell someone? Sharing your faith helps cement it in your mind. If you understand it well enough to share it, then you understand it enough to live it.

Today I Will . . .

Write down why I believe and what I believe. Think it through so I know it's clear.

"I've got something to tell you."

What Does the Bible Say about Word of God?

Well, it's the same thing. Duh. The Word of God is another name for the Bible. Why is it called that? Because the Bible is God's Word. He wrote it. Well, he told the writers what to write. It is the message God wants you to have.

What the Bible Says

Your word is a lamp to my feet
and a light to my path.

PSALM 119:105

I have stored up your word in my heart,
that I might not sin against you.

PSALM 119:11

All Scripture is breathed out by God and
profitable for teaching, for reproof,
for correction, and for training
in righteousness.

2 TIMOTHY 3:16

Time to Face the Facts

The Bible is made up of sixty-six different books written by more than forty men. God told each of them what to write. Some of the things in the Word of God are stories of how God worked in people's lives. You read about his power, strength, and patience with his people. Some of the Word of God is instruction on how to live for God. It teaches how to obey him and trust him. Reading God's Word will help you learn to trust him and love him.

Today I Will . . .

Read God's Word. I want to know him better, and I must read his message to me to get to know him.

What Does the Bible Say about Work?

Work is . . . work. Your work each day may be just to go to school and keep your grades up. You may have some chores to do at home, too. How do you feel about your work? Does it really matter whether you do well in school or whether you have a good attitude about it?

What the Bible Says

And whatever you do, in word or deed, do everything in the name of the Lord Jesus, giving thanks to God the Father through him.

COLOSSIANS 3:17

Whatever you do, work heartily, as for the Lord and not for men.

COLOSSIANS 3:23

For you yourselves know how you ought to imitate us, because we were not idle when we were with you, nor did we eat anyone's bread without paying for it, but with toil and labor we worked night and day, that we might not be a burden to any of you.

2 THESSALONIANS 3:7–8

Time to Face the Facts

God cares about your daily work and even about your attitude toward it. He says that you should always do your best and work hard at the job you have. Working hard and doing it with a good attitude honors God. When people know you are a Christian, your work ethic reflects in a positive way on God. Do your best. Work hard. Give God the glory for all you accomplish.

Today I Will . . .

Make sure my attitude is good toward the work I do each day. I'll do my best and make God proud of me!

"Hey, Kitty, how do you spell excellent?"

WORLD HUNGER

What Does the Bible Say about World Hunger?

Thousands of people around the world go to bed hungry at night . . . in fact, night after night. Some people even die from starvation. That may be hard to get your mind around if you always have more than enough to eat. Does God care that people are hungry? In fact, he instructs his children to do something about world hunger.

What the Bible Says

But if anyone has the world's goods and sees his brother in need, yet closes his heart against him, how does God's love abide in him?

1 JOHN 3:17

So whatever you wish that others would do to you, do also to them, for this is the Law and the Prophets.

MATTHEW 7:12

For I was hungry and you gave me food, I was thirsty and you gave me drink, I was a stranger and you welcomed me.

MATTHEW 25:35

Time to Face the Facts

A person who lives in obedience to God cares about the needs of others around the world. God instructs his children to see others' problems and to help them in any way they can.

Today I Will . . .

See what I can do to help others . . . here in my town and around the world. It may mean giving my time and my money, but I will do it.

"Yeah—this is not just a place to get rid of brussels sprouts."

What Does the Bible Say about World Missions?

Look around your town as you're driving to the mall. How many churches can you count? Look around your house. How many Bibles, Christian books, and Christian CDs are there? You probably have many, many opportunities to learn about God and his love for you. Is that true around the whole world? Are there people who have never heard about God? Should you care about that?

What the Bible Says

Go therefore and make disciples of all nations, baptizing them in the name of the Father and of the Son and of the Holy Spirit, teaching them to observe all that I have commanded you. And behold, I am with you always, to the end of the age.

MATTHEW 28:19–20

Go into all the world and proclaim the gospel to the whole creation. Whoever believes and is baptized will be saved, but whoever does not believe will be condemned.

MARK 16:15–16

But you will receive power when the Holy Spirit has come upon you, and you will be my witnesses in Jerusalem and in all Judea and Samaria, and to the end of the earth.

ACTS 1:8

Time to Face the Facts

Did you know there are people who have never heard about God? Did you know there are people in the world who do not have the Bible available in their language? That's amazing, isn't it? Yes, you should care about this because Jesus instructed his followers to go into the whole world and teach about him—the whole world. Not just North America or South America but remote villages in Africa and the outback of Australia. God loves the whole world, every person. He wants every person to have the opportunity to follow him.

Today I Will . . .

Pray for missionaries our church supports. I will pray for them as they share God's love in difficult places. It must be hard work to get people to understand. I will pray for their strength and encouragement.

What Does the Bible Say about Worry?

That nagging fear that occupies your thoughts; the frantic planning to "fix" things; the knot in the pit of your stomach. Does God care at all about what worry does to you? If you're asking that, you haven't learned that God wants to take care of all your worries. He wants you to trust him.

What the Bible Says

God is our refuge and strength,
a very present help in trouble.

PSALM 46:1

Trust in the LORD with all your heart,
and do not lean on your own understanding.
In all your ways acknowledge him,
and he will make straight your paths.

PROVERBS 3:5–6

You keep him in perfect peace
whose mind is stayed on you,
because he trusts in you.

ISAIAH 26:3

Time to Face the Facts

It's a scientific fact that two separate pieces of matter cannot occupy the same space at the same time. The same is true of worry and trust in your heart. If you say you love God, then shouldn't you trust him to take care of things? In that case worry should not be your favorite pastime.

"Does 'D' stand for 'dynamite'?"

Today I Will . . .

Come clean with God. Tell him you need help in learning to trust, and let him show you how.

What Does the Bible Say about Worship?

Worship is a word that is most often used when talking about God or spiritual things. But if you look at how people feel about other things, you will see that some people worship money. Some worship sports. Some worship fashion. Anything that you give lots of attention to and make very important in your life is something you worship.

What the Bible Says

You shall have no other gods before me.

EXODUS 20:3

For great is the LORD, and greatly to be praised;
he is to be feared above all gods.

PSALM 96:4

God is spirit, and those who worship him must worship in spirit and truth.

JOHN 4:24

Time to Face the Facts

God says that he is a jealous God. He will not accept second place to anything else. God wants your worship. He is the only Person worthy of your worship. He is the Creator of everything. He loves you so much that he sent Jesus to die for you. He has a place in heaven for you for eternity. Only God is worthy of your worship. Other things and other people may be important to you but should never be more important than God.

"O great and powerful . . . cell phone."

Today I Will . . .

Make sure nothing is more important to me than God. I will worship him. That means I adore him; I love and respect him. He is worthy of my worship.